Intrametropolitan Industrial Location

Intrametropolitan Industrial Location

The Pattern and Process of Change

Raymond J. Struyk
Franklin J. James
The Urban Institute

Lexington Books
D. C. Heath and Company
Lexington, Massachusetts
Toronto   London

Library of Congress Cataloging in Publication Data

Struyk, Raymond J
    Intrametropolitan industrial location.

    Includes index.
    1. Industries, Location of—United States.
2. Metropolitan areas—United States. I. James, Franklin J., joint
author. II. Title.
HC110.D5S85   338'.0973   75-6278
ISBN 0-669-99895-8

Published simultaneously in Canada

Printed in the United States of America

International Standard Book Number: 0-669-99895-8

Library of Congress Catalog Card Number: 75-6278

Contents

List of Figures

List of Tables

Preface

This study of intrametropolitan industrial location was initiated in 1968, while both authors were at the National Bureau of Economic Research, and was largely completed by early 1972. It is the first of the series of studies on urban industry location supported by the National Bureau to be published.[a]

The common goal of this study series has been the documentation of job location patterns within urban areas, and the description and analysis of overall change in these patterns and the behavior of individual manufacturing establishments that produce these changes. We and others at the National Bureau believe this type of analysis is required to attain useful insight into the determinants of many dimensions of urban growth.

This volume examines patterns of industry location in Boston, Phoenix, Cleveland, and Minneapolis-St. Paul for the three-year period ending in 1968. We have not attempted formal theoretical or empirical models of the location decisions of manufacturing establishments in these metropolitan areas. We hope our work will provide useful guidance in future attempts to develop such models.

The work has greatly profited from personal and institutional assistance. John R. Meyer and John F. Kain of the National Bureau suggested this project and organized the study series as a whole. The National Bureau of Economic Research sponsored the work, although it has no responsibility for the contents of this volume. The entire effort was made possible by the assembly of essential data by the Dun and Bradstreet Corporation and their provision of these data to the National Bureau. Since the data has been substantially altered in the research process, Dun and Bradstreet are not responsible for the tables and inferences presented here. While both authors are currently at The Urban Institute, this institution has had no involvement with this work.

John R. Meyer and John F. Kain were instrumental in the accomplishment of our work. Royce Ginn, James Brown, Robert Leone, and Emanuel Tobier reviewed the manuscript at various stages and provided extremely useful comments. We are also grateful to Ester Moskowitz for editing the manuscript competently, and to Irving Forman for preparing the maps and charts. We wish to thank Christine Bishop for making available to us the Massachusetts Census data that she had prepared for

[a] Although this research was done under the auspices of the National Bureau of Economic Research, the findings reported herein have not yet undergone the full critical review accorded the National Bureau's studies, including review by the Board of Directors, and therefore the NBER bears no responsibility for the findings of this analysis.

machine use. We have profited additionally from the discussion and analysis of her senior honor's thesis, "An Analysis of the Response of Population Change to Employment Change in an Urban Area," Radcliffe College, March 1968. We also wish to thank Minton Moore of the Valley National Bank of Phoenix for providing a map and other materials on the historical development of the Phoenix manufacturing sector. Finally, the *Review of Regional Studies* has been good enough to allow us to use some material that appeared earlier there (vol. III, no. 1).

1

Introduction

Purpose and Outline of Study

The importance of the location of manufacturing activity within metropolitan areas scarcely needs to be emphasized. Hardly a week passes without some public figure advocating various programs to revitalize the major cities in the United States by making them more attractive to industry and households of all income and social strata. A fact that frequently strikes thoughtful students of the city is the limited understanding of the processes and functions of cities upon which these policy statements and programs for the cities have been forced to rely. Clearly, the careful delineation of the patterns and ultimately the causes of the location choices of households and employers is required for a rational urban policy.

The work reported in this book is concerned with the changing pattern of the location of manufacturing employment in four metropolitan areas over a three-year period ending in 1968. Its purpose is to quantify certain changes in the intrametropolitan distribution of manufacturing employment and to examine in detail the processes that together have produced these changes. It does not explain the changes in terms of economic and other factors entering into a firm's decision-making process. It does, however, provide much of the background for approaching a study of the determinants of industry location within a consistent and comprehensive framework.

The importance of workplace as a determinant of household choice of residence has been thoroughly documented,[1] and its significance is reflected in the structuring of the land use-transportation models produced by various cities.[2] These studies have made clear that in some sense the location of manufacturing employment producing for regional and national markets can be thought of as the prime factor in the shaping of metropolitan areas. It is clear, of course, that the interrelationships among workplaces, residences, infrastructure investment, public services, and other factors is simultaneous and not unidirectional, but the strength of workplace as a determinant of aggregated urban locational decisions is among the most important. Thus, the attainment of an understanding of the process of industrial location is a major step toward comprehending the growth pattern of cities.

The largely descriptive and exploratory work contained in this volume results from an effort to examine, on a geographically and industrially disaggregated basis, the change in the locational pattern of industries in the Cleveland, Boston, Minneapolis-St. Paul, and Phoenix metropolitan areas over the period 1965-68. The main data used in this work, the Dun and Bradstreet establishment-level Duns Market Indentifiers manufacturing file, contain actual street address information; so it is possible to go beyond the distinctions between the central city and the rest of the Standard Metropolitan Statistical Area (SMSA) that have been widely employed in studies of metropolitan industrial location. This permits the quantification of the site competitiveness of different areas within the central cities and similarly of different types of areas on the periphery as reflected in the change in the level of employment present over the observation period. In addition to examining the net change in employment in these various areas, it is likewise possible to probe the manner in which these changes have been effected. Change in manufacturing employment in an area can be accomplished by several different processes: (1) changes in the employment levels of establishments in existence at the start of the period; (2) establishment relocation; and (3) firms going into business or out of existence. The principal advantage of the present study is that by using a common body of data for the same period, assembled and analyzed in the same manner, it is possible to determine the extent to which observed patterns are consistent across metropolitan areas. The search for regularities in the initial location and changing pattern of manufacturing industries is the central focus of this study.

Separating net employment level changes into the basic components producing them is important for several reasons. First, because the processes of establishment relocation and birth involve entrepreneurial decisions specifically concerned with the proper location of the establishment, analysis of the resulting locational pattern can add greatly to the understanding of the locational determinants of the establishments involved. The second reason concerns the usefulness of the findings of this study for land use-transportation models. The projection devices employed in these models have typically been regression models correlating some simple measure of an area's attractiveness to industrial activity with selected characteristics of the area. Some of these models may be quite good predictive devices, but none has proved to be of much analytical value. At best these models are probably reduced-form proxies for more complete models of a wide range of entrepreneurial decisions with quite different determinants. Separate analysis of the spatial patterns and locational regularities of moving, new, defunct, and stationary establishment growth and decline certainly offers promise of substantial analytical progress in the understanding of the determinants of industry location. If this promise proves to be true, it is highly possible that analytical progress can eventually be translated into much improved techniques for projecting employment location patterns.

Additionally, the lack of understanding of the determinants of industry-location decisions has hampered attempts to create effective and efficient policy to channel industry-location changes in socially desirable directions. It might be, for instance, that the locational determinants of new establishments are quite different from those of moving establishments. This might suggest that it would be relatively easy to channel new establishments into central-city locations where certain essential services are available. Yet, without real knowledge of the current locational patterns of both new and relocating establishments, such thoughts remain unverified hypotheses.

Context of the Present Work

The scale of previous research has not been commensurate with the importance of intrametropolitan industrial location. Much of the progress that has been made rests in unpublished papers that have not been widely circulated. The following discussion provides a summary of previous research that helped to structure our own effort and that comprises the research context within which the results of our work can be interpreted and applied. This discussion also delineates the role and rationale of our work in this overall effort. Reference is made throughout to the findings of a number of these related research efforts. This section provides a general overview, a task that is somewhat overdue.

The bulk of previous empirical research has aimed at measuring and describing change in overall job location patterns, attempting to determine the pattern and scale of job decentralization within urban areas. This research has typically been limited to information provided from national censuses of economic activities, and so it has been very difficult to ascertain differences in the location patterns of individual industries. Likewise, geographic detail has been minimal, often relying on crude comparisons of job growth in central cities versus the rest of the metropolitan areas.[a]

---

[a] For examples of this literature, see John F. Kain, "The Distribution and Movement of Jobs and Industry," in James Q. Wilson, ed., *The Metropolitan Enigma,* Washington, D.C., Chamber of Commerce of the United States, 1967; and Daniel Creamer assisted by Walter B. Brown, *Manufacturing Employment by Type of Location,* New York, National Industrial Conference Board, 1969. Creamer employs a more complex geographic taxonomy than do most researchers in this area, dividing metropolitan and nonmetropolitan areas into a number of types of locations. Types of locations are defined largely on the basis of the sizes of city populations. Bennett Harrison

These studies have aroused much of the current interest in the determinants of job location, but their severe constraints of geographic and industrial detail have hobbled their usefulness for analysis of the causes of job decentralization within urban areas.[3]

Theories developed to account for the distribution of jobs have been similarly pauce. Some attempts have been made to adapt formal models of land rent and land allocation among competing users structured along the lines established by Heinrich Johann von Thunen to the analysis of the location of employers and jobs within urban areas.[b] These models result in a chiaroscuro representation of urban land use, with various types of land users rigorously confined by their assumed production requirements and location needs into concentric rings emanating from the city center. These models often produce a commercial and interregional transportation center at the heart of the city, enclosed by a second ring of manufacturing activity, which in turn is imbedded in a zone devoted to residential activity. In more complex versions of these models, some land uses, such as intraregional transportation facilities, and perhaps retail-type activities, intrude into several of these rings. Land rents decline more or less continuously with distance from the city center. Land rents, as well as the conditions under which land is transferred from one use to another are the primary characteristics of the city explained by these models.[4]

These models achieve definitive and manageable conclusions at great costs. Their overall depiction of the geography of the city is not to be taken seriously as a description of the contemporary urban area, and oftentimes, the models are built on assumptions that, taken literally, deny the possibility of urban areas. Agglomerative economies, urbanization economies, and economies of scale in production are often assumed not to exist, and without these forces, there is little reason for cities.[c]

More useful theories of job location have grown from observation of characteristics of actual urban economies. Job decentralization has commonly been attributed to a number of relative disadvantages of core areas

---

provides a summary of more recent evidence in his *Urban Economic Development: Suburbanization, Minority Opportunity, and the Condition of the Central City,* Washington, D.C., The Urban Institute, 1974.

[b] Heinrich Johann von Thunen, *Von Thunen's Isolated State, trans.* Carla M. Wartenberg, ed. Peter Hall, Edinburgh, Pergamon Press, 1966. Von Thunen's model has been the basis of theories of household location discussed above.

[c] This is discussed in some length in Edwin S. Mills, *Studies in the Structure of the Urban Economy,* Baltimore, Resources for the Future, 1972, chap. 1. Mills does allow economies of scale in some sectors in his model. For a recent attempt to model location choices of industrial establishments incorporating interdependence among industries, see G. S. Goldstein and L. N. Moses, "Interdependence and the Location of Economic Activities," *Journal of Urban Economics,* January 1975, pp. 63-84.

—traffic congestion, obsolescence of facilities, environmental deficiencies, high land and tax costs, and crime.[d] Some of these factors have been organized into more or less cogent models, the most elegant of which is that designed by Leon Moses and Harold Williamson for the analysis of location choices of manufacturers insensitive to intraurban market locations.[5] It suggests that the location choice of an establishment relative to the metropolitan core is determined by a land price gradient, which declines monotonically with distance from the core, and an input (comprising the cost of labor, materials, communications, etc.) price gradient, which increases monotonically as distance from the core increases. Force toward decentralization is produced in their model by either (1) movement of the land price gradient upward, or (2) movement of the input price gradient downward. They suggest that the introduction of the motor truck and automobile spurred decentralization by reducing the input price gradient relative to the land price gradient. Both automotive innovations decreased the cost of moving away from centrally located transportation facilities and from core area concentrations of labor. John Kain supplemented this model with considerations of more recent changes in manufacturing technology.[6] One of these is the growing use of single-story production lines, a phenomenon that significantly reduces production costs. Another is the growing use of private automobiles, necessitating increased parking facilities. Both of these changes tend, of course, to make manufacturing establishments more land-intensive, thus, tending to raise the land-price gradient, and consequently moving equilibrium locations away from the core. Finally, as Edgar M. Hoover and Raymond Vernon pointed out some time ago, the increasing reliance by manufacturers on highway transportation may do more than reduce the degree of intraregional variation in transportation costs. It may also encourage a suburban location choice since such a move would bypass the core area impediments to both loading and unloading and truck movement.[7] The foregoing models have not been empirically tested in any satisfactory way.[8] However, in one form or another, they have played important roles in urban planning programs and policy prescription.

Because of the overriding importance of job location in shaping urban land use, a number of attempts have been made to develop quantitative models of job location useful as planning tools. Models adopted for predicting and planning the location of employment have been deficient in several respects. Typically, these models embody no aspects of the be-

---

[d] Andrew Hamer provides explicit measures of production and space cost differences in the Boston metropolitan area. See Andrew M. Hamer, *Industrial Exodus from the Central City: Public Policy and the Comparative Cost of Locations,* Lexington, Massachusetts, Lexington Books, D. C. Heath and Co., 1973.

havior of establishments. The design of many of these models were so constrained by data limitations that the information they do produce can be assumed to be biased and inaccurate. The utilization of such unsatisfactory models, at times, tended to compromise the value of enormously expensive quantitative regional models.

The general structure of these employment allocation models either rests on ad hoc relationships between the level of activity in an area and its characteristics, or between the growth of activity in an area and the features of the area. The zonal characteristics considered include such attributes as population density, land availability, and land price; access to markets for output, and to inputs, including labor; zoning constraints; and public service and tax levels.[e] The results of the first type of model are biased toward replicating the initial distribution of employment. This model is based on the assumption that concentration of economic activity in a zone implies attractiveness of the zone. Because the distribution of activity is the result of decisions made over a substantial length of time, and under a wide range of conditions, this assumption need not be true.[9] The second type of model is probably a more accurate predictive device.[f] For short periods, it amounts to the shift-share predictive technique.[10] If only small changes occur in the characteristics of zones, then the relative rate of growth of activity of a zone is projected substantially unchanged through time. In essence, models of the second type project into the future the trends in activity occurring during the study period. Thus, analysis of industry location has tended to be unsatisfactory. Neither planning nor theoretical models offer greatly useful insight or even point clearly in directions where progress can be made.

Although progress has been hampered by the inadequacy of most extant data, the major stumbling block has been the theoretical shortcomings of

---

[e] For examples of the first model type, see: (1) the models employed by the Delaware Valley Regional Planning Commission to allocate nonmanufacturing employment presented in *1985 Regional Projection for the Delaware Valley*, DVRPC Plan Report No. 1, 1967; (2) the models employed in the Bay Area Transportation Study, as reported in *BATSC Locational Model System*, August 1969. For two examples of the second type, see: (1) the models employed by the Delaware Valley Regional Planning Commission to allocate manufacturing employment, which are also presented in *1985 Regional Projections for the Delaware Valley;* (2) the models employed in the Detroit Traffic and Land Use Study reported in *An Urban-Regional Model of Small Area Change for Southeastern Michigan*, Consad Research Corporation, July 1969.

[f] The Detroit TALUS employment projections seem highly questionable. See Franklin J. James and Raymond Struyk, "Recent Trends in Industrial Composition and Location," in *The NBER Urban Simulation Model*, Vol. II, ed. J. F. Kain, New York, National Bureau of Economic Research, 1971. Problems were perhaps produced by exogenous constraints imposed on the operation of the model, expressly to increase the inertia of the distribution of employment.

the models themselves. These models, and their more completely articulated offshoots, are designed to replicate long-run equilibria of a sort never to be attained or observed. Job growth is obviously an incremental process. For instance, without any doubt the most powerful force influencing the location of manufacturing activity is the stock of manufacturing structures. These facilities have extremely long, useful lives, and over this entire period their use will influence current location choices to conform to the obsolescent forms of the past.[g]

Recent research appears to have adopted two basic premises: First, it has become increasingly clear that both planning and analytical models of industry location must focus on incremental change. Understanding of the determinants of industry location is too limited to generate reliably distributions of employment de novo. The considerations important in the location decision of an individual establishment in a specified environment are more clear, and their importance is subject to measurement. Second, research has begun to focus intensively on current location decisions by individual establishments or groups of establishments. The level of employment and production in an area is determined by a complex process of establishment relocation, birth, death, and expansion and contraction. It has become increasingly evident that the determinants of the incidence of these individual processes may be substantially different. As a result, lumping them all together in analyses of overall employment growth may offer little insight into actual behavior, and the determinants of the behavior.

The analysis of the establishment behavior that produces change in employment location patterns offers four clear advantages over previous research. First, the location choices of both new and relocating establishments can be assumed to reflect entrepreneurial decisions regarding the optimal location of the operation. These location choices offer immediate insight into considerations currently of importance in determining business location needs. Second, establishment location can be presumed to be only

---

[g] See James B. Kenyon, *Industrial Localization and Metropolitan Growth: The Paterson Passaic District,* Chicago, Illinois, The University of Chicago Press, 1960, for a dramatic example of this sort of influence. The Millrace section of Paterson, originally designed in the early nineteenth century by Alexander Hamilton's Society for Establishing Useful Manufacturers, was still in partial use in 1960. Rebuilding following the Great Fire of Chicago presents a unique opportunity for urban research because such a great portion of the standing stock of industrial facilities was destroyed. For an analysis of industrial location following the fire, see Raymond L. Fales and Leon N. Moses, "Thunen, Weber and the Spatial Structure of the Nineteenth Century City," in Mark Perlman, Charles Leven, and Benjamin Chinitz, eds., *Spatial, Regional and Population Economics: Essays in Honor of Edgar M. Hoover,* New York, Gordon and Breach, 1972, reprinted in Franklin J. James, ed., *Models of Employment and Residence Location,* New Brunswick, N.J., Center for Urban Policy Research, 1974.

one of many determinants of the expansion or decline of stationary establishments, or the demise of businesses. Gauging the importance of these latter two processes in effecting change in the intrametropolitan distribution of jobs offers suggestive evidence on the importance of location needs per se in effecting location change. The greater the significance of these latter two processes, the less likely it is that change in the distribution of jobs can be attributed to locational disequilibrium per se. Third, the relative importance of these four processes (relocation, birth, death, and expansion or contraction) offer key guidance into research priorities useful for allocating research resources. It appears reasonable to focus effort at least initially on the establishment behavior that bulks largest in producing change in the distribution of jobs, unless it can be demonstrated that interactions among the four processes are so important as to require their analysis as an explicit simultaneous system. Fourth, examination of the location choices of new and relocating establishments offers potential insight into the economic function of types of areas within the metropolis. It has been suggested that the central industrial district in the metropolitan core may act as an incubator for new business ventures. The concentrated availability of business services and suppliers and of rental production space in these areas has been suggested to release new establishments from considerable capital requirements, and thus to enhance their chances for viability and growth.[h] Traditional manufacturing locations within suburban areas may also perform this incubation function. This type of functional differentiation can be examined only using actual description of the behavior and change of individual establishments.

The bulk of research on establishment behavior producing patterns of job growth has been attitudinal surveys of relocating businesses, with the aim of determining businessmen's perceptions of the reasons for relocation and the rationale of their location choice. Businessmen are often very aware of considerations widely considered to be proper and relevant to location decisions. As a result, the findings of these surveys are to a degree interpretable as descriptions of what the businessmen believe they ought to have considered according to texts in business management, rather than their true considerations. In addition, relatively often, businessmen appear to mix policy advocacy with objective reporting of the relative importance of taxing and other government programs on their location choices, so that the significance of these programs on establishment location decisions are exaggerated in attitudinal research reports. As a result of these considera-

---

[h] This hypothesis was originally suggested by Edgar M. Hoover and Raymond Vernon, *Anatomy of a Metropolis*, Garden City, New York, Doubleday and Co., Inc., 1962, on the basis of their analysis of job growth in the New York metropolitan area.

tions, the results of attitudinal surveys must be viewed with a healthy skepticism.[11]

Statistical analyses aimed at inferring the relative importance of factors affecting location decisions from the characteristics of actual location choices have and will continue to prove more valuable. Moses and Williamson examined the location choices of a sample of relocating manufacturing establishments in the Chicago area in order to test some of the implications of their model of employment location described above.[12] They measured spatial variation in the propensity of establishments to relocate, and attempted to explain choices of new locations using a group of explanatory variables of clear and widely acknowledged importance. Thus, their analysis presents an excellent test of the likely success of analysis of the location behavior of individual establishments, and their results are very encouraging. First, they established (and other studies have confirmed) that there is little systematic spatial variation in the probability that an establishment will relocate. Establishment size was suggested to be much more important than location in affecting this probability. Second, they found that the choices by smaller establishments among new locations tend to be more confined than those of larger establishments, and that they tend to move shorter distances. They argued that this resulted from the greater market power of larger establishments, and their greater ability to maintain established relations with suppliers and markets, or to establish new relations if necessary,[i] and that the tendency of establishments to move short distances creates a degree of inertia in the spatial distribution of economic activity. Finally and most importantly, they determined that relocations were predominantly in the direction of the urban periphery, and that choices by these mobile establishments among small analysis areas were related to transportation facilities, land uses, and location in reasonable and sensible ways. This appears to verify the usefulness of a focus on samples of similar types of entrepreneurial decisions, rather than on aggregate change in activity levels and the advantages of statistical inference over attitudinal surveys.

These encouraging results were instrumental in creating high levels of professional interest in undertaking more explicitly behavioral analyses of the determinants of the location of jobs in cities. The type of analysis pioneered by Moses and Williamson has been followed up by others, with valuable results.[13]

---

[i] It seems just as reasonable to argue that larger establishments move greater distances because they move less often, making greater adjustments in their location with each move. The tendency of smaller establishments to move smaller distances need not imply that their costs of relocation are greater; just the opposite may be true.

Some notion of the relative importance of the various processes altering overall patterns of employment location is necessary in order to design an effective research program focusing on the establishment behavior producing employment change in an area. Three analyses have attempted more general descriptions of patterns of job growth within urban areas, and the relative importance of various types of establishment behavior in producing overall job redistributions within cities. The questions addressed in these studies were quite similar to those addressed in the present volume, so a detailed summary of their findings is useful.

The most important of these three descriptive analyses is an examination of job growth within the New York metropolitan area during the period 1967 to 1969.[14] This study highlighted the value of both establishment behavior and microgeographic detail for understanding urban job location. For instance, it was found that within the New York region, establishment function (headquarters, branch manufacturing plant, etc.) was of tantamount importance with the establishment's industry in understanding location choices. It was also found that the process of job growth differed substantially within the region. The Manhattan central business district (CBD) experienced rapid growth in overall manufacturing job levels between 1967 and 1969, produced largely by job growth in existing establishments in the area together with a high rate of formation of new establishments, in spite of the fact that the CBD experienced net out-migration of employers. The rest of Manhattan north of Central Park South experienced substantial job loss largely due to employment declines in immobile establishments, in spite of the fact that this area of the city experienced net in-migration.

This analysis portrays surprising patterns of overall job growth within the New York region, with very rapid job growth in the central business district, and job loss in the New York suburban counties of the SMSA. A major force producing job growth in the central business district was the fact that over one-half of employment in new manufacturing establishments was concentrated in the CBD. Thus strong evidence was found for the power of the incubator function of the urban core both to attract large numbers of new establishments and to maintain high levels of production activity in the urban core. Unfortunately, because this analysis focuses on only a single area, and perhaps a unique area as well, these findings cannot be generalized and thus do not offer reliable guides for future research.

A second analysis focused on location choices of manufacturing establishments in the Clydeside region in west central Scotland between 1958 and 1968.[15] This study examined the location choices of relocating and new establishments, and geographic patterns of establishment demise. Three initial conclusions emerged: (1) As Moses and Williamson found, establishment relocation worked to reduce activity levels in the urban core of the region and enhance activity in urban subcenters and developing portions of the region; (2) contrary to the observations of the New York study, establishment birth rates increased with distance from the urban core; and (3) spatial variation in death rates was small. The central finding of the study was that the location choices of new establishments tended to "replicate the pattern of their parent industry with regard to access to the center." [16] This was interpreted as evidence for the existence of significant agglomerative forces that mold the locational advantages for manufacturing activity.

A third description of the process of change in the location of manufacturing activity has been provided by Franklin J. James and James W. Hughes.[17] This analysis focused on job growth in New Jersey during 1967 and 1968. James and Hughes document a high degree of locational mobility of manufacturing establishments. Their analysis was limited to establishments employing 20 or more persons; yet, it was found that during 1967 and 1968, relocating, new, and defunct establishments amounted to 12 per cent of the total establishments in the state in 1967. They concluded that this high degree of mobility suggests substantial ability on the part of manufacturers to adjust their location and facilities when necessary.

They also found that establishment relocation, birth, and death are by no means the most important determinants of change in the level of employment within a small area. Rather, employment expansion or contraction by immobile establishments was far larger in magnitude, and indicated consistently the overall direction of employment growth in an area. This finding emphasizes the hazards of attempting to explain directly geographic patterns of employment growth and decline without information on the establishment behavior producing change. Employment growth and decline of immobile establishments may be only tenuously attributable to characteristics of their location. They conclude that such factors as the industry and the size or age of the establishment may be much more important.

Finally, they demonstrate the potential complexity of the behavior of individual establishments. They found a substantial level of cross-migration of relocating establishments. Relocations were not all directed toward the urban periphery; suburban establishments occasionally relocate to the urban core. In addition, the location choices of new establishments were found to be puzzling in some respects. For instance, large new establishments were found often to choose locations in the urban core, while small establishments, which might have been expected to be attracted by the rental production space and other supportive services of the core, were widely dispersed.

Structure of This Study

Previous analysis has been fertile as a source of hypotheses. Clear empirical findings have been reported, but because data sources and time periods are diverse and because each previous study examined job growth in only a single region, the results of these previous studies cannot be generalized. The most pressing priority for research into urban job location is analysis of the patterns and process of job location change in several disparate areas, using comparable data and definitions. Our work is designed to meet this pressing need. In this volume no attempt is made to present a formal model of industrial location, nor do we resolve in any final sense all the policy and research issues and problems that motivated our undertaking. As noted, the investigation is primarily descriptive, but within this limitation several aspects of intrametropolitan location have been addressed. In Part I each of the four metropolitan areas is examined separately. The industrial composition of manufacturing employment in 1965 and the spatial distribution of the major industries within the SMSA are first set out. Each metropolitan area, including the central cities, is divided into and analyzed using relatively small geographic areas (analysis zones). Next the pattern of net change in the location of manufacturing employment in recent years is discussed, with emphasis on the 1965-68 period. Special attention is given to shifts within the central cities. The composition of net change in employment is then examined both in terms of its components (employment associated with moving, new and dying, and stationary establishments) and of the industry mix in the area. The final chapter of Part I contains a general summary of the regularities described in the four preceding chapters.

Part II consists of four short chapters, each of which contains a test or the development of a hypothesis based on the findings of the first part. In Chapter 7 we examine the hypothesis that some industries consistently tend to be located in highly centralized locations and that these concentrated industries are growing more rapidly at these locations. In Chapter 8 we test the so-called incubator hypothesis, advanced mainly on the basis of findings for the New York area, that new manufacturing establishments are attracted to centralized locations that offer services essential to their operation but that they are unable to provide because of their small size or limited resources. In Chapter 9 we analyze the industrial composition, average wage rates, and labor intensities of manufacturing establishments located in urban poverty areas to determine if these industries as a group can be characterized as low-wage industries. In the final chapter we test the hypothesis that the spatial concentrations of individual manufacturing industries, documented in Part I, are continuing to influence the locational behavior of establishments in the same industries.

Summary of Findings

1. The most striking result is the uniformly high degree of mobility of manufacturing employment over the relatively short period 1965-68. In the four areas, the total employment associated with moving, new, and defunct establishments represented 17 per cent of the 1965 base employment. Likewise, the number of establishments involved in relocations and new or defunct businesses was equivalent to 37 per cent of the establishments tallied at the beginning of the observation period. This high degree of mobility accomplished an unexpected degree of change in the geographic distribution of manufacturing employment within these metropolitan areas.

These enormous mobility rates alone may imply that industry location may be much more amenable to direction and change through public policy than has heretofore been thought. This in turn adds a great deal of impetus to the need for understanding the determinants of industry-location preference so that public policies can be designed efficiently and intelligently to accomplish social goals in this area. On a purely technical level these mobility rates imply that statistical problems of sample size are much less severe than might have been anticipated in a study of the components of locational change.

2. The general pattern in the shift of the location of manufacturing employment was one of increased decentralization. At the same time, though the central cities of the metropolitan areas lost manufacturing employment in the aggregate, there were areas within every one of the central cities in which the share of total manufacturing employment was increasing.

3. The composition of the net change of employment associated with relocating and stationary establishments and establishments beginning or ceasing operations varied sharply among the SMSAs and the areas within them. Still, several patterns emerge. The single most important component of change was in the level of employment of establishments stationary throughout the observation period. This component was not so dominant, however, that its direction of change could be relied upon consistently to indicate the direction of total net change in an analysis zone or larger area such as the central city. In general the pattern of change produced by the combination of establishments beginning business and going out of business (natural increase) greatly favored the areas outside of the central cities; and, indeed, net natural increase was substantially more important in producing the overall outward shift in manufacturing employment than was net migration. The locational patterns produced by the process of natural increase and by net migration tend to be reinforcing, however, as there is a rough positive correlation between the destinations of the em-

ployment of moving establishments and the initial location of new establishments. Little systematic variance in the spatial incidence of establishments going out of business was found, and no evidence was uncovered that establishments located in core areas have a consistently higher propensity to die.

4. The incubator hypothesis, which states that new manufacturing establishments are attracted to centralized locations because of essential services provided there (e.g., rentable production space), was tested for several types of locations in each of the SMSAs. The hypothesis was not supported for either establishments or employment in central industrial districts,[j] in central cities in general, or in areas that had been traditional centers of manufacturing activity. The lack of support seems to be explained by the availability of sites with sufficient external economies for new establishments at decentralized locations.

5. Areas in Boston, Cleveland, and Minneapolis-St. Paul that had been defined as *poverty areas* by the Census Bureau on the basis of 1960 data were generally losing manufacturing employment in large amounts over the observation period. Except for two waterfront zones in Boston, there was only one analysis zone (South Boston) in these three SMSAs that had been classified as poverty areas and in which there was an increase in the number of manufacturing jobs present over the period.[k] The results were further reinforced when employment change was standardized for the SMSA-wide growth rates of the industries present in each zone in the base year. However, it was found that some industries were relatively concentrated in these poverty areas. Also, several industries located in these areas had grown over the study period. Census of Manufactures SMSA-average payroll and value added data for each industry was used to determine if those industries relatively more frequently located or growing in poverty areas could be classified as low-wage or labor-intensive compared with the average of all industries. The industries in all four of the SMSAs fell into two groups: industries paying below-average wages and nuisance industries such as chemicals, petroleum, and primary metals. It seems clear that the low-wage industries are being attracted to areas where large pools of low-skilled workers reside. An interesting question, which, however, is not taken up in this study, is whether poverty-area residents are being employed by the relatively high-wage nuisance industries located in the poverty areas.

---

[j] A central industrial district is an area encompassing and substantially greater than the central business district in each central city.

[k] The extremely high growth rate of manufacturing employment and the suburban location of the poverty areas in Phoenix makes it a special case. See Chapters 5 and 9 for a full discussion.

6. The spatial distribution of employment of the major industries [1] in each SMSA in 1965 were such that every industry was found to be significantly concentrated in one or more geographic areas within each metropolitan area. For each industry, employment equivalent to at least twice that which would have been present in an analysis zone if the industry's employment were evenly distributed across the area was found in some analysis zones. The universality of this finding—for all major industries, "new" and "old," in each SMSA—strongly suggests the importance of external economies in the locational decision of manufacturing enterprises. Each of the industries also exhibited a distinctive locational pattern of its own. However, examination of the locational patterns of the same industries across the four metropolitan areas showed that in several industries there was a consistent preference for centralized locations and that the industries grew more rapidly at these locations than elsewhere.

7. The implicit hypothesis that the net change in employment in the analysis zones was being significantly influenced by the industry mix in the zone was tested using shift-share measures developed for a similar purpose in studies of regional growth. The overall relationship between the growth of employment in a zone relative to SMSA average growth and the weighted average of the growth of its industries relative to the SMSA average was found to be quite weak. For two-thirds of the analysis zones the direction of the net change in employment and the industry-mix measure were the same. This high correspondence, however, occurred mainly because the shift measure, also, was in the same direction. In general, the magnitude of the shift component was substantially greater than the share component of net change.

8. Our data support the hypothesis that the spatial clustering of establishments and the employment characteristics of an industry continue to influence the locational behavior of firms in that industry. The test is essentially a comparison of the locational behavior of industries that were and were not concentrated within the same analysis zone. In this way many of the characteristics of the zones were held constant. Locational behavior was measured by the net employment growth rates and the propensities to move, to begin business, and to cease business of the two types of industry (concentrated and nonconcentrated). The raw data showed the concentrated industries were on average growing more slowly than the others and that there was significantly less locational activity where firms of a given industry clustered. Regression analysis of the growth and locational activity of concentrated and nonconcentrated industries showed that the growth and change of employment of concentrated industries was

---

[1] A major industry is one that accounts for at least 5 percent of total SMSA manufacturing employment.

significantly more systematically related to several economic factors than were the nonconcentrated industries. These differential responses may be caused by differences in the kinds of firms dominant at the two types of locations, with those producing for local markets being less concerned with external production economies available at the concentrated locations. These findings suggest that making projections of the locations of manufacturing activity in urban areas might be simplified by using the dichotomous behavior of the same industry at the two types of location.

9. A final summary point is in essence a qualification of the previous eight. The study period 1965-68 was characterized by a highly expansionary national economy. Such circumstances no doubt affect the degree, type, and distribution of industrial locational activity in metropolitan areas. We have no real basis for asserting how the above findings would be altered if a more representative observation period were chosen, but the reader should bear this basic qualification in mind in assessing the findings of this study.

The Sample and the Data

The Sample SMSAs

In selecting the metropolitan areas, as much divergence as possible in the limited sample was desired in order to enrich the results.[m] It was also thought, however, that to be able to make the comparisons among the areas clear it would be helpful to have some factors in common among at least part of the sample. The choice of areas was subject to only two constraints: (1) for economy of data processing, each metropolitan area had to lie entirely within a single state; and (2) the area had to be of sufficient size to guarantee reasonably large samples of marginal establishments. The selected areas—Cleveland, Boston, Minneapolis-St. Paul, and Phoenix—represent an extremely varied sample in terms of age of area, form of spatial development, and industrial composition. Of these areas only Boston developed any significant amount of industry in the era in

---

[m] Note that no real attempt was made to assemble a sample of representative metropolitan areas. "Representativeness" of SMSAs is clearly a multidimensional phenomenon that would include at a minimum such factors as size (of population and area), importance of the central city (economically and spatially), age, economic base, topography, and region. Even if one were to determine some type of average for these various characteristics for all SMSAs, it is not clear that they would be meaningful. Thus, our sample might best be viewed as essentially random, subject to the very broad constraints outlined in the text and a minimum establishment sample size.

which water was the primary source of power, and the position of small outlying on-stream locations has remained to influence the present-day locational patterns. Phoenix, at the other end of the spectrum, has only begun its industrial development in the past 30 years. Both Boston's and Cleveland's growth have been constrained by their location beside a major body of water. In both cases this has caused development to spread along the shore initially and back away from the water's edge later. Minneapolis-St. Paul and Phoenix are both landlocked cities, although the abundant

Table 1-1

Fraction of Employment in Major [a] Industries in the Sample Metropolitan Areas, 1963

		Fraction of Total Manufacturing Workers Employed			
SIC	Industry Description	Boston [c]	Cleveland	Minneapolis-St. Paul	Phoenix
20	Food products	0.091	b	0.133	0.127
23	Apparel	0.078	b	b	b
27	Printing and publishing	0.086	b	0.115	0.069
31	Leather products	0.067	b	b	b
33	Primary metals	b	0.143	b	b
34	Fabricated metals	0.065	0.126	0.069	b
35	Nonelectrical machinery	0.099	0.156	0.189	0.137
36	Electrical machinery	0.175	0.086	0.108	0.222
37	Transportation equipment	0.060	0.176	b	0.138
All other industries		0.279	0.313	0.386	0.306

Source: Census of Manufactures, 1963, vol. III. Central Administrative and Auxilliary employment is not included in industry or area employment figures.
[a] A major industry accounts for 5 per cent or more of the total manufacturing jobs in the SMSA.
[b] Not a major industry in this SMSA.
[c] Two major industries in Boston are not listed in the table. These are rubber products (SIC 30) and instruments (SIC 38).

lakes and the Mississippi River in the Twin Cities have had tangible effects.

The industrial structure of these areas, while diverse, has some strong common elements. Table 1-1 contains the distribution of manufacturing employment on a two-digit Standard Industrial Classification (SIC) basis. Shown are the largest industries in the areas and the fraction of manufacturing jobs that each industry provides. The machinery (SIC 35) and electrical machinery (SIC 36) industries are overall the two most dominant. In Boston and Phoenix the electrical machinery industry is the most important manufacturing employer; it ranks fourth in the Twin Cities and fifth in the Cleveland area. For three of the areas the nonelectrical machinery industry is the second largest employer, and it is first in the

Minneapolis-St. Paul area. In the nation as a whole SIC groups 35 and 36 rank fourth and third, respectively, in total manufacturing employment. The relative importance of these two industries differs sharply, however, among the four areas. In Phoenix the two machinery categories account for almost 36 per cent of manufacturing jobs. Adding those employed in the production of transportation equipment (SIC 37) and food products (SIC 20), almost two-thirds of the industrial employment in the area is accounted for. The only other major employer is the printing and publishing industry.

Surprisingly, the other sample SMSA most like Phoenix in industrial structure is Boston. As mentioned above, SICs 36 and 35 rank first and second in job importance in both areas, although in Boston they account for only slightly more than one-fourth of manufacturing employment. Food processing and printing and publishing are also dominant industries in Boston, employing about 18 per cent of the industrial work force. The Boston industrial base is, however, the broadest of the four SMSAs with seven major manufacturing industries responsible for only about two-thirds of all industrial jobs. All together, at the two-digit classification level 10 industries individually account for more than 5 per cent of the manufacturing workers in the area.

Fewer major industries exist in Minneapolis-St. Paul than in Boston. The two machinery industries combined account for a slightly greater fraction of jobs than do the same industries in the Boston area (27 per cent versus 29 per cent). As expected, the food-processing industry (SIC 20) is of more importance to the Twin Cities than any of the other sample SMSAs. The only other large-share employers are the printing and publishing industry (SIC 27) and the fabricated metals industry (SIC 34). Combined, these five industries employ well over 60 percent of all the industrial workers in the area.

The Data

The data on which this study is based are taken from the DMI (Duns Market Identifiers) file of manufacturing establishment data collected by the Dun and Bradstreet Corporation. The DMI file represents an attempt by the Dun and Bradstreet Corporation to compile an exhaustive sample of manufacturing establishments operating in the United States. These data are reported on an establishment level, with each establishment report including one primary and up to five secondary four-digit SIC codes of the products of the establishment, the total employment of the establishment and that of the firm to which it may belong, the net worth and sales of the firm, the physical location and zip code of the establishment, and the year in which the firm began operations.[n]

In addition, each establishment in the file is assigned a unique nine-digit integer identification number. This assignment is permanent; the "DUNS" (**D**uns **U**niversal **N**umbering **S**ystem) number, once issued, is never reissued to any other establishment. Use of this number allows relatively easy machine matching of establishments in separate annual files, so that any establishment or group of establishments can be followed through time. All together, four geographic codes are available for each establishment. Separate codes are included for the state, county, city,[o] and zip code of the establishment.

The DMI sample was first compiled in 1965. Through the generosity of the Dun & Bradstreet Corporation, the National Bureau of Economic Research obtained copies of the files as they existed at several points in time. This report is based on the files current in October 1965 and June 1968. For each of the four metropolitan areas studied in this report, cross-sectional establishment lists were drawn from the national DMI files for each of the two years. In order to identify establishments that moved, died, or left the areas, or were born or migrated into the areas, establishments in the 1965 and 1968 cross sections were matched in each of the four areas, using each establishment's DUNS number.

Since the DMI files were not constructed with studies of locational behavior in mind, it was not surprising to find that the files required substantial editing and checking before the establishments could be finally classified as relocators, births, etc. A detailed description of the process used to create and check our files is presented in Appendix A. The entries in Table 1-2 show the results of the process. A full description and partial evaluation of these data has been provided elsewhere.[18]

While there are no other data available to test the accuracy of the moving, dead, and new-establishment files, the sample totals can be compared

---

[n] The DMI data also provide codes on the functions of the establishment: headquarters; branch headquarters; no manufacturing done on the premises; etc. Full analysis of how the different functions have affected the locations of these establishments has not been conducted. Preliminary analysis indicated that the number of establishments having the specialized functions was relatively small, and it was decided that the information from this additional dimension of the problem would not be likely to justify the increase in cost it would entail. Robert Leone, in his work on the New York metropolitan area, found the codes to be an extremely useful classifying variable. However, headquarters and other specialized operations are substantially more important in New York than in the sample cities of this study; so the omission of this aspect of the locational pattern would not appear to be significant for our work.

[o] The city code, however, follows postal areas, not incorporated city boundaries.

Table 1-2

Final Classification of Establishments in the Four Sample Metropolitan Areas, 1965 and 1968

Metropolitan Areas	Number of Establishments				
	1965	1968	Relocated	New	Defunct
Boston	5,813	5,696	567	354	779
Cleveland	4,656	4,678	644	464	655
Minneapolis-St. Paul	3,044	3,227	485	374	548
Phoenix	1,190	1,287	106	290	240

with several other data sources. It should be clear from the outset, though, that other comprehensive data sets on employment are in general subject to the same kind of error as the DMI set and for this reason discrepancies among sources cannot be attributed completely to the DMI file. Thus, in the following discussion of the quality of the DMI sample, consistent differences in broad directions of change between the DMI sample and other data sets will be emphasized.

The DMI file was assembled primarily as a guide for marketing and promotion of goods and services. Listed establishments and estimates of their employment were intended to be useful for estimating the magnitude of the potential market for various products. In some cases headquarters establishments that undertake no manufacturing activity are included in the file. However, the bulk of central administrative and auxiliary employment is excluded from the lists. Whenever possible, this sector of manufacturing activity will be deleted from census or other data files used to supplement or assess the value of the basic DMI data.

Establishments. Two auxiliary sources of data on the number of establishments in metropolitan areas are available in County Business Patterns (CBP), prepared by the Census Bureau in cooperation with the Social Security Administration, and in the Census of Manufactures. For our purposes there are advantages and limitations to both sources. While the CBP is available for the same years as the DMI files (1965 and 1968), its definition for the Boston SMSA differs sharply from ours, making meaningful comparisons impossible. The census, on the other hand, employs geographic definitions similar to ours but was conducted for 1963 and 1967. Because we wanted to compare general trends, we used the census data to make the detailed industry comparisons for the four SMSAs. These are reported in Appendix Table B-2. Less detailed data from the DMI files, the CBP, and the census are presented in Table 1-3. Both tables show that, in general, the DMI establishment counts exceed

Table 1-3

Comparison of Establishment Counts of Duns Market Identifier (DMI), County Business Patterns, 1965-68, and Census of Manufactures, 1963-67 [b] **(Number of Establishments)**

	Boston	Cleveland	Minneapolis-St. Paul	Phoenix
DMI				
1965 level	5,813	4,656	3,044	1,190
Net change, 1965-68	−117	22	183	97
County Business Patterns				
1965 level	a	3,853	2,459	885
Net change, 1965-68	a	37	−27	103
Census				
1963 level	5,358	4,046	2,596	965
Net change, 1963-67	−273	−4	10	80

[a] Definition of the SMSA differs substantially from that used by the other sources.
[b] Central Administrative and Auxiliary establishments are deleted from all figures.

those of the other data sources. This is attributable to the fact that DMI data files include establishments with zero full time employment, while CBP and census files do not.[19] The industry distribution of establishments in the DMI and census files are quite comparable (Table B-2). In terms of the measures of change in numbers of establishments over the period, the differences between the CBP and the census estimates (Table 1-3) are often greater than those between the DMI and the CBP or census counts, with no particular pattern evident. For the individual industries, the change shown over the period by the DMI and census data is in most cases in the same direction; but there are sizable differences in the magnitude of the variation between the two files (Table B-2).

Employment. Additional data on employment for the sample SMSAs is available for 1965-68 from the Bureau of Labor Statistics (BLS) and from the Annual Survey of Manufactures (ASM). Table 1-4 contains the average annual rates of change in total SMSA manufacturing employment indicated by these five data sets. These figures show wide variation between the DMI employment data and the employment data from the other sources. For Boston and Phoenix both the levels of total manufacturing employment (shown in Table 1-4) and the average annual rates of change seem to be consistent among sources. Even in these SMSAs, however, for particular industries there is substantial variation between the DMI and census sample, especially in growth rates (Table B-1). In Phoenix, for example, for five of the 12 2-digit industries for which census data were

Table 1-4
Levels and Change in Manufacturing Employment in Sample SMSAs, Various Data Sources

	Boston SMSA		Cleveland SMSA		Minneapolis-St. Paul SMSA		Phoenix SMSA	
	Initial Employment Level	Average Annual Per Cent Change	Initial Employment Level	Average Annual Per Cent Change	Initial Employment Level	Average Annual Per Cent Change	Initial Employment Level	Average Annual Per Cent Level
Duns Market Identifier, 1965-68	298,118	1.3	297,992	-1.6	150,591	-1.7	52,816	9.0
County Business Patterns, 1965-68	a	a	277,667 [b]	1.7 [b]	149,128 [b]	7.9 [b]	45,514 [b]	12.8 [b]
Bureau of Labor Statistics, 1965-68	284,100	1.7	296,000	1.9	172,800	7.5	49,900	11.8
Census of Manufacturers, 1963-67	271,704 [b]	2.1 [b]	258,461 [b]	2.9 [b]	149,604 [b]	5.2 [b]	40,970 [b]	11.2 [b]
Annual Survey of Manufacturers, 1965-68	293,082 (272,660) [b]	1.8	285,761 (268,489) [b]	3.0	169,383 (152,136) [b]	7.7	44,741 (43,996) [b]	15.5

[a] Definition of the SMSA differs substantially from that used by other sources.
[b] Central administrative and auxiliary employment excluded from figures.

available, the signs of the growth rates differed between the two samples.

The DMI samples for Cleveland and the Twin Cities appear to be less reliable; for both the DMI sample shows a decline in manufacturing jobs over the period, while all the other sources show an increase. The problem is especially serious in the Twin Cities DMI data. The problems are, of course, evident also in the comparisons of individual industries, which are presented in Table B-1. At the same time initial employment levels are quite consistent among the several data sources, which implies that the DMI files were basically sound for the two areas.

The central question is how the differences in the samples affect the analyses pursued in this study. First, note that two likely sources for the apparent downward bias in the 1968 DMI employment counts for Cleveland and the Twin Cities. As Dun and Bradstreet is more concerned with the fact of existence of an establishment rather than with the vicissitudes of its employment, it is to be expected that expansions or contractions in employment of establishments not changing either location or financial status (e.g., through merger) will not be closely monitored. During a period of rapid national economic expansion this can clearly be a formidable problem.[p]

The second source seems to be in the treatment of national firms with multiple local branches. Because of special financial relationships, some of these branches are not recorded as separate establishments and their employment is included only in the national total, not in the local figures. In spite of the strenuous efforts made to assure accurate establishment counts (recorded in Appendix A and verified by the comparisons made in the previous section), we have been unable to correct the discrepancies in a completely satisfactory way.

The final test of the reliability of these files, especially for Minneapolis-St. Paul, is the discrepancy between their spatial and industrial patterns and those found for the other SMSAs. In the process of testing hypotheses and summarizing observations, the patterns observed in each of the four SMSAs were compared: the patterns for the Twin Cities were not deviant. And it is the high degree of consistency in the results of the analysis that provides the necessary measure of confidence in the DMI data as a *sample* of the changes in intrametropolitan industrial location.

---

[p] The DMI data are assembled to provide interested parties with an accurate indication of the "normal" market for various products. Consequently, the employment figure reported should generally not be affected by cyclical considerations. In a recession the Dun's data should, therefore, tend to be biased upward; during an expansion, such as during 1965-68, the data may be biased downward. To the extent, though, that expansions in employment are believed by the company to be permanent (and thus that the market for various products has expanded permanently, the employment figures are adjusted upward in the DMI file.

A Reader's Guide

Although the general scope and organization of the study has already been sketched, an additional word to the reader is in order. The next four chapters contain a fairly detailed discussion of the industrial location pattern in each sample metropolitan area. Each chapter contains a large amount of data, which unfortunately may not be easily digested by those who do not have a real interest in a particular area. This suggests, therefore, that some readers initially may wish to concentrate their attention on just one of these chapters and on the summary remarks on all four chapters that appear in Chapter 6. This should be sufficient to provide a basis for understanding the more general issues pursued in Part II. Finally, note that many of the operational definitions are set out in Chapter 2, in which the locational patterns in Cleveland are described. In the other chapters references are made to the definitions in the Cleveland chapter; thus, the reader will find the most self-contained discussion in Chapter 2.

**Part I
Trend and Composition of the Spatial
Distribution of Manufacturing Employment
in Four Metropolitan Areas**

2 Cleveland

Cleveland began taking on economic importance after the opening of the Ohio Canal in 1832. During the mid-nineteenth century the city became a major transhipment point for the complex of waterways that were the main arteries of commerce in that era. Cleveland's strategic geographic position in the area of the junctions of the Great Lakes, Erie Canal, and Mississippi and Ohio rivers provided impetus to commercial activity. The industrial beginnings of Cleveland were fed by the strong economic demands of the Civil War and after that by the demands of the railroads for their rapid westward expansions. However, the heavy-industry character of the city dates from the opening of the Marquette range in 1884 and its development over the next decade by the city's iron industry. Rapid industrial and population growth continued in Cleveland from the Civil War to the 1930s. After that time its growth rate fell to about that of the rest of the country.

In the following discussion the *Cleveland metropolitan area* is defined as comprising Cuyahoga and Lake counties. This contrasts with the four-county definition adopted by the 1963 Census of Manufactures, which also includes Geauga and Medina counties. The former definition was adopted because over 94 per cent of the industrial employment of the four counties in 1963 was in Cuyahoga and Lake counties and because it was felt that the examination of the two-county area would provide adequate insight into the patterns of industrial location with which this study is concerned.

Industrial Composition

Cleveland has traditionally been characterized as a heavy-industry town. Indeed, in 1960, after some reduction in recent years, 40 per cent of all nonagricultural jobs were in the manufacturing sector, and of these about 65 per cent were concentrated in five industries producing durable goods. The relative importance of these five dominant industries over the last two decades is depicted in Table 2-1. The table presents both the level and share of total manufacturing employment in each of these dominant industries for several years from 1947 to 1968. The employment history of these industries in Cleveland mirrors national industrial trends. Employ-

Table 2-1

Employment in Selected Manufacturing Industries, Cleveland Metropolitan Area, 1947-68

Industry	1947 [a]	1958 [a]	1963 [a]	1965 [b]	1968 [b]
Employment as Fraction of Total SMSA Manufacturing Employment					
Transportation equipment	0.132	0.182	0.176	0.157	0.144
Machinery	.205	.145	.156	.181	.192
Primary metals	.160	.139	.143	.140	.128
Fabricated metals	.121	.120	.126	.135	.146
Electrical machinery	.085	.085	.086	.087	.088
Fraction of total	0.703	0.673	0.687	0.700	0.698
Number of Manufacturing Employees					
Transportation equipment	35,491	46,149	45,493	46,698	41,097
Machinery	55,060	36,927	40,321	54,037	54,554
Primary metals	43,126	35,198	37,064	41,684	36,398
Fabricated metals	32,527	30,484	32,496	40,327	41,454
Electrical machinery	22,789	21,496	22,132	25,835	25,124
Total itemized	188,993	170,254	177,506	208,581	198,627

[a] *Census of Manufactures*, vol. III.
[b] Based on tabulations of Dun and Bradstreet data.

ment fell by 10 percent from high levels in the immediate postwar period to a nadir in the recession of 1958, then grew slowly in response to the beginnings of economic recovery in the early sixties, accelerating through at least 1965. The year 1958 divides the postwar economic history of Cleveland, separating the industrial somnolence of the fifties from the rapid growth of the sixties.[1]

Employment levels in the nonelectrical machinery industry dominate these trends. Job levels in this industry fell by 18,000 jobs during the fifties. As a result of rapid growth during the sixties, the industry had reattained its postwar dominance by 1968. The employment history of the primary metals industry is quite similar. Together, these two industries account for about one-third of manufacturing jobs in Cleveland. Employment change in the fabricated metals and electrical machinery industries, on the other hand, underwent a somewhat different history. Activity in these industries held constant over the period 1947 to 1963, then grew rapidly in the sixties. The transportation equipment industry was the only dynamic element of the industrial base of Cleveland during the fifties. In both 1958 and 1963, this was the single largest industrial employer in the area. But its growth was spent by the end of the fifties, and its position was eclipsed by the recovery of nonelectrical machinery industry during the sixties.

The performance of other industries in the area has generally been weak. Only the paper and allied products and the printing and publishing industries showed sizable gains over the entire period. The textile, lumber, and petroleum and coal products industries all suffered absolute declines in jobs. Though the apparel and chemical industries remained about even in terms of number of employees, they declined slightly in their importance to the industrial sector. The chemical industry was the only industry besides the five major ones in the area to employ more than 5 per cent of manufacturing workers in 1947. By 1963 none besides the major five industries had this distinction.

Analysis of the awakening of the major industries in the Cleveland area during the study period after their slumber of the fifties and early sixties should aid in the study of industrial locational activity. This type of expansion may have occurred through modernization of existing facilities and movement to new plants, especially since much of the capacity could have become technologically obsolete over the stagnant period. At the same time, it is possible that the number of firms going out of business and their spatial distribution are not representative of the pattern present under more "normal" circumstances.

Spatial Distribution of Major Industries in 1965

There are two reasons for examining the location of the major industries within the Standard Metropolitan Statistical Area (SMSA) before studying the pattern of aggregate change in the location of manufacturing employment during the observation period 1965-68: Knowledge of the growth and initial location of these industries doubtlessly provides, first, some immediate insights into the causes for the growth or decline of various areas and, second, an information base for forming and testing hypotheses regarding the spatial concentration of individual industries. Assessment of the current importance of agglomerative patterns and of the importance of the industrial structure of small areas in determining their growth potential is of great importance in understanding patterns of intrametropolitan job growth. These tasks require knowledge of the spatial distribution of major industries, and of the degree of their geographic concentration within urban areas. If the analyses in these early chapters indicate that there are significant geographic concentrations of some industries, two questions can be considered in the following chapters. First, is the relative importance of these spatial concentrations of industrial activity being maintained? If so, what marginal elements are accounting for this? And second, do these concentrations and their associated external economies continue to exert a significant influence on the current locational behavior of firms?

Clearly, it is necessary to describe the basis on which the metropolitan areas have been spatially disaggregated and to define what is meant by a "concentration" of a given industry. Investigation of the spatial distribution of employment is facilitated by finely disaggregated data, but the resulting detail must not be so fine as to be overwhelming. In addition, it is desirable for the boundaries of analysis zones to be consistent with those of other major data sources, such as the various censuses. The Dun and Bradstreet (D&B) files make employment data available at the zip code level for most areas, which offers a high level of disaggregation. There are, however, two problems for location analysis inherent to the D&B system. The major problem is that in the DMI (Duns Market Identifier) files cities are not defined on the basis of their legal limits, but rather on the basis of boundaries of post office jurisdictions. For instance, all zip codes that come under the jurisdiction of the Cleveland post office, that is, all 441 zip codes, are coded by D&B to be in the city of Cleveland. The second and complementary problem is that the municipal or town boundaries are not coterminus with the zip code boundaries. This introduces some noncomparability with other data sources.[a]

Several additional factors needed to be taken into account in defining the "analysis zones" within the metropolitan area. Given employment on a zip code basis, the *analysis zones* were defined by aggregating zip code areas on the basis of the following criteria:

1. Limiting the fraction of total manufacturing employment in a zone to 15 per cent, and, more frequently, to about 10 per cent, regardless of the employment density
2. Limiting the land area in each zone from becoming so large that the zone loses identity as a community or industrial area
3. Matching zip codes and legal boundaries to the greatest extent possible
4. Taking various natural demarcations such as lakes and ocean inlets into account
5. Grouping zip code areas having the same broad economic, social, and industrial characteristics

Obviously this procedure relies heavily on the weighting of various factors and on judgment and opinion. In Cleveland this procedure resulted in the establishment of 18 analysis zones. The exact definitions of these zones appear in appendix Table C-1. Figure 2-1 is a map of the area showing the boundaries of the analysis zones.

---

[a] This geographic coding system does, however, have at least one important advantage, namely, all of the United States can be unambiguously coded. Legally unincorporated areas cause some difficulty when legal city boundaries are used for city definitions, but these areas are accounted for under the zip code system.

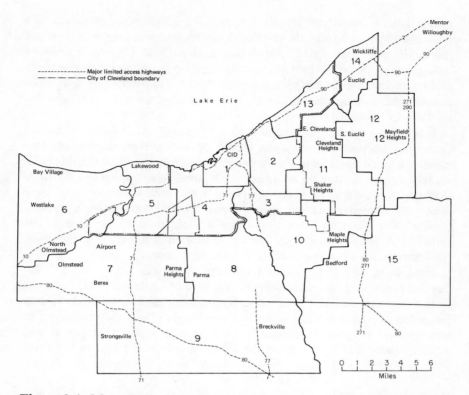

Figure 2-1. Map of Analysis Zones in the Cleveland Metropolitan Area

A comparison of Figure 2-1 with a jurisdictional map of Cleveland demonstrates two things: First, our definitions result in analysis zones that in some cases cut through political jurisdictions. Obvious examples of this are Parma (zones 7 and 8) and Cleveland Heights (zones 11 and 12). For reasons already stated these problems could not be easily overcome. Second, outside of the city of Cleveland itself there are large areas that are not incorporated into particular communities. For both of these reasons, one should keep in mind the approximate nature of the identifying labels attached to the analysis zones.

The division of the metropolitan area into 18 analysis zones still confronts the reader with a formidable amount of detail. In an attempt to provide a simplifying classification scheme, the position of each zone with respect to the central-most point of the area, the central industrial district (CID), is given. All zones in ring I are adjacent to the CID, all those in ring II are separated from the CID by one other zone, and so forth. It should be stressed that this system is essentially arbitrary and is employed primarily as a simplifying device. For most of the cities the included area does not have a circular shape. Consequently, the outlying areas do not fall neatly into a final ring. For example, ring IV in Cleveland contains only the area far to the east along Lake Erie, since the areas to the south and west located the same distance from the CID as the eastern fringe are not included in the metropolitan area. In the tables the rings are identified by Roman numerals.

It remains to define the "spatial concentration" of an industry. In approaching this problem we tacitly accept the null hypothesis that employment of a given industry is evenly distributed across the area. On this basis we take employment in an analysis zone equivalent to approximately twice that which would have been present if total SMSA employment were evenly distributed across the metropolitan area as constituting a concentration.[b] For Cleveland this means that if more than 11 per cent of the total SMSA employment of an industry is located in a given analysis zone, the industry is said to be concentrated in that zone.

If numbers of establishments rather than jobs were used to define industrial concentrations, the results would be quite different. This is shown in the summary figures presented in Table 2-2, which are based on data presented in Appendix H. The criterion outlined in the previous paragraph was applied to major industries in each SMSA, using employment and establishments as the classifying variables. In only about half of the cases

Table 2-2
Number of Zones Containing Concentrations of a Major Industry

	Classified by Level of Employment	Classified by Number of Establishments	Classified by Both Employment and Establishments
Cleveland	17	17	8
Boston	22	19	11
Minneapolis-St. Paul	17	17	9
Phoenix	12	9	5

[b] It is realized that defining concentrations in this way is a potential source of problems since the land area of the zones is not the same, nor has the number of employees included in a zone been standardized by the size of the zone. Given the zip code boundaries of the zones, there was no measure of their land area available from secondary sources, and original, accurate measurement was impractical. The guidelines used in defining the zones provide some safeguards against finding concentrations in a zone because it has a great number of employees and/or is very large in area, because both the fraction of total manufacturing employment present and the size of the zone were bounded by implicit maxima and minima, subject to the other criteria used in the defining process and outlined above. It is felt that the procedures adopted are sufficient to prevent fallacious results.

would an industry have been classified as concentrated in the same zones using both employment and establishments as criteria.

In most cases, when an industry was classified as concentrated in a zone on the basis of employment, it was found that a relatively large number of firms in that industry were located there.[c] Since the focus of this study is on the location of manufacturing jobs within the sample cities, more immediate results for our purposes could be obtained using employment as the classifying variable.

Table 2-3 shows the distribution of employment in each of the five major industries in the Cleveland area. In terms of the criterion just defined, all five industries are judged to be concentrated within the Cleveland area. In fact, the primary metals and transportation equipment industries show more than twice the required minimum of concentration in some zones. Concentrations of some industries appear to have had significant effects on the locations of other related industries. For instance, the several concentrations of the fabricated metals group might be partially explained by the bipolar concentration of primary metals in zones 3 and 4 and in Euclid. Over 50 per cent of primary metals employment is located in these zones. Given this situation one might expect to find fabricated metals spaced between these two poles. This is borne out to a large extent by the finding that about 50 percent of fabricated metals employment is located in zones 2, 3, 4, and 13.[d]

The most spatially dispersed industry is clearly the electrical machinery group. There are no fewer than eight zones with more than 7 percent of its employment, and four with over 11 per cent. Although the bulk of these jobs are in the CID and the two zones to the east along the coast, there are sizable concentrations to the south (ring II) where the importance of other industries is quite limited. The producers of transportation equipment have clustered their employment at two locations at opposite ends of the area. Almost 30 per cent of the jobs are located in the Berea area, undoubtedly owing to the location there of the area's major airport and of rail facilities. The second concentration, comprising only

---

[c] Employment concentrations produced by the locations of only a few massive establishments were found in the electrical machinery and transportation equipment industries in Phoenix.

[d] The location of heavy industries at relatively centralized locations has been found in other studies. Warren Seyfried, in his study of the location of all types of employment in Spokane Washington, for 1969 found that of all manufacturing industry primary and fabricated metals industries were more highly centralized than any others. In Chapter 7 other industries are found to be consistently more centralized than the metals groups in our sample SMSAs, but Seyfried's findings support the type of locational pattern that is being observed for Cleveland. For further details, see his article, "Location and the Centrality of Land Values," *Land Economics,* August 1970, pp. 329-33.

Table 2-3

Geographic Distribution of Employment in Major Industries, Cleveland Metropolitan Area, 1965
(Per Cent of Total SMSA Manufacturing Employment in the Industry)

Number	Analysis Zone Description	Primary Metals	Fabri- cated Metals	Ma- chinery	Electrical Ma- chinery	Transpor- tation Equip- ment
	Cleveland City					
1	CID	8.87	7.97	8.64	12.65	8.13
2	Hough(I)	8.38	13.47	12.53	16.04	15.52
3	Southeast of CID(I)	29.47	15.12	8.70	2.09	6.76
4	Southwest of CID(I)	12.84	11.99	6.22	6.94	4.43
5	West of CID(I)	4.54	6.59	5.99	7.77	5.49
13	Northeast of CID(II)	5.57	10.63	12.83	16.29	6.73
	Rest of Area					
6	Bay Village-Westlake(II)	0.02	0.92	0.62	1.63	0.03
7	Berea-N. Olmstead(II)	6.01	1.47	1 68	0.27	23.90
8	Parma-Independence(II)	——	2.53	1.08	0.30	0.26
10	Maple Heights- Garfield Heights(II)	2.01	4.29	3.21	14.73	1.15
11	East Cleveland- Shaker Heights(II)	0.03	3.29	2.52	9.04	7.92
9	Brecksville- Strongsville(III)	——	0.12	0.08	——	0.01
12	South Euclid(III)	0.17	0.35	0.27	0.07	——
14	Euclid(III)	19.43	4.00	26.68	6.97	14.19
15	Bedford-Solon- Chagrin Falls(III)	2.06	11.94	4.15	2.95	5.00
16	Wickliffe-Willoughby- Mentor(IV)	0.41	4.61	3.62	1.15	0.29
17	Painsville-Grand River- Fairport Harbor(IV)	0.11	0.36	0.90	——	0.08
18	Madison-Perry- Bainbridge(IV)	——	0.27	0.18	1.04	——

Note: Roman numerals identify "rings"; see section "Spatial Distribution of Major Industries in 1965" in this chapter for explanation.
Source: Tabulations of Dun and Bradstreet data.

16 per cent of jobs in the industry, is in Euclid, where both rail facilities and the presence of heavy steel works have resulted in the establishment there of a boxcar construction industry. The rest of the jobs in this industry are generally distributed about the area.

Net Change in the Spatial Distribution of Total Manufacturing Employment

The distribution of employment within the Cleveland area over the period 1947-68 is presented in Table 2-4. Because of the lack of disaggregated

Table 2-4

Spatial Distribution of Manufacturing Employment, Cleveland Metropolitan Area, 1947-68

(Fractions of Total SMSA Manufacturing Employment)

Number	Analysis Zone Description	1947 [a]	1958 [a]	1963 [a]	1965 [b]	1968 [b]
1-5,13 [c]	Cleveland	0.831	0.690	0.620	0.628	0.594
6	Bay Village-Westlake(II)	——	——	——	.005	.006
7 [d]	Berea-Olmstead Falls-N. Olmstead(II)	.002	.002	——	.057	.077
8	Parma-Independence(II)	——	.025	.033	.008	.013
10	Maple Heights-Garfield Heights(II)	.003	.012	.013	.035	.038
11	East Cleveland-Shaker Heights-Cleveland Heights(II)	.017	.020	.022	.039	.038
9	Brecksville-Strongsville(III)	——	——	——	.002	.002
12	South Euclid(III)	——	.002	.002	.004	.004
14 [d]	Euclid(III)	.068	.087	.077	.111	.114
15	Bedford-Solon-Chagrin Falls(III)	——	.012	.023	.049	.054
16	Wickliffe-Willoughby-Mentor(IV)	——	.028	.034	.030	.038
17	Painsville-Grand River-Fairport Harbor(IV)	.012	.008	.009	.030	.021
18	Madison-Perry-Bainbridge(IV)	——	——	——	0.002	0.002
	Not accounted for	0.068	0.114	0.167	——	——

Note: Roman numerals identify "rings"; see section "Spatial Distribution of Major Industries in 1965" in this chapter for explanation.
[a] *Census of Manufactures*, vol. III.
[b] Based on tabulations of Dun and Bradstreet data.
[c] Traditional manufacturing area; poverty area.
[d] Traditional manufacturing area.

data before 1965 for the city of Cleveland, changes within the city are discussed separately. Zones identified as "traditional" centers of manufacturing activity are noted in the table [e] as are zones identified by the census as being residential areas for persons with poverty-level incomes.[f]

---

[e] A central-city zone was considered to be a traditional center if the zone contained 5 per cent or more of the total SMSA manufacturing employment in 1965 and/or had been indicated by knowledgeable persons as having once been an important industrial center. A noncentral-city zone had to contain 5 percent or more of total SMSA manufacturing employment in 1947 in order to be considered a traditional manufacturing center.

[f] Using 1960 census tract data, the Bureau of the Census compiled a composite index of poverty based on general household characteristics including income, the skill status of adults, housing conditions, and the percentage of children not living with both parents. Using the index, census tracts were classified as being poverty areas or

Table 2-4 is based on two distinct bodies of data: the Census of Manufactures and the Dun & Bradstreet files. Because the employment reported in the census for a given community is only that within its jurisdictional boundaries and the D&B data cover all of that within an area, large discrepancies are to be expected. It was hoped that in spite of these definitional inconsistencies, historical trends would be evident; this hope in large part has been justified.[g] In general each zone's share of total manufacturing employment in the SMSA, rather than the absolute number of persons employed, is used in this chapter to describe the spatial or geographic distribution of employment. This has been done in order to abstract from changes in level that are due to the business cycle and to differing data sources.

As shown in the table, the city of Cleveland, like most major cities, has been losing significant portions of manufacturing employment to its suburbs since the Second World War. The share of Euclid, the other major employment center, has grown substantially over the period. In 1947 the main employment concentration ran northeast, following the coastline from the heart of the central city to Euclid, with some inland concentration in East Cleveland and Cleveland Heights. The only other major concentration was in Painsville, which lies past Euclid on the coast of Lake Erie. By 1968 the pattern had changed markedly. All of the original employment centers, save the city of Cleveland, had grown in relative importance. New concentrations occurred in two areas: One was in Lake County in Wickliffe, Mentor, and Willoughby (ring IV), which is between Euclid and Painsville, thus creating a nearly continuous belt of industrialization following the coast of Lake Erie eastward.

The second thrust seems to have taken place in the southeastern and

---

not. This simple binary decision obviously cannot be very discriminating, and, in general, large areas of each SMSA are defined as poverty areas even though within these areas there is presumably a great deal of variation in the extent and severity of poverty. The boundaries of the analysis zones used in this study are not perfectly comparable to the boundaries defined by census poverty areas. It has been possible, however, to approximate these areas of poverty by grouping the analysis zones. For further description, see Bureau of the Census, *Maps of Major Concentrations of Poverty in Standard Metropolitan Statistical Areas of 250,000 or More Population,* Washington, D.C., 1966, vol. 1 (Boston and Cleveland) and vol. 2 (Minneapolis-St. Paul and Phoenix).

[g] It is, of course, also true that the Census of Manufactures does not provide data for every city, but rather only for those with populations over 10,000. Thus, some growth in the proportion of employment in each of the analysis zones is due simply to the increase in the number of cities reported by the census. Observation of the employment trends of individual cities within each zone is not really an adequate substitute for complete census figures but has been used in ambiguous situations. In forming our conclusions we also placed a great deal of weight on trends appearing in the Dun and Bradstreet data between 1965 and 1968.

southern suburbs, in rings II and III (analysis zones 10, 11, and 15). East Cleveland-Cleveland Heights (zone 11) appears to have grown substantially, with most of this growth occurring in East Cleveland as did the Maple Heights-Garfield (zone 10) and the Bedford-Solon areas (zone 15). This general area has developed into an important industrial center since 1960. However, the most rapidly growing area is in rings II and III, south and southwest of the CID. Between 1965 and 1968 zones 7, 8, and 9 increased their share of SMSA manufacturing employment from 6.7 per cent to 9.2 per cent, with the Berea area absorbing the bulk of this employment increase.[h]

The major highway construction programs in the Cleveland area were initiated in the latter part of the 1950s. A major new route was the Lakeland Freeway (State Route 2 and Interstate 90), which follows the coast of Lake Erie east to Euclid and beyond. The second major link, most of which was opened by 1965, was the Outer Belt East (Interstate 271), cutting south from Interstate 90 just east of South Euclid through Bedford. These transportation facilities have no doubt acted as a strong attraction to industry. Although the complete highway plan calls for major east-west links both along Lake Erie and as an outer belt, these have not yet been completed. The only new major highway in the western part of the city is the Medina Freeway (Interstate 71), where the first segment was completed in 1965 and the opening of other sections continued until 1969. The Medina Highway enters from the south at Strongsville and proceeds north through the Berea area and then cuts toward the CID. This combined with the presence of the area's major airport may account for the surge in industrial activity in the Berea area.

The city of Cleveland has been divided into six zones for this analysis, and the changes in the distribution of employment within the city from 1965 to 1968 are presented in Table 2-5. The distribution of 1965 employment corresponds closely to the directions described in the previous paragraphs: The heaviest concentration is from the central industrial district (CID) northeasterly along the coast and then fanning inland with the concentration diminishing with distance from the CID.[i] The CID together with the zones immediately adjacent to it to the east in rings I and II (zones 2, 3, and 13) contained almost one-half of regional manufacturing jobs in 1965. The changes over the period are less straightforward. In spite of the long-term relative decline of employment in the central city, the share of employment in the CID actually increased during the study

---

[h] The series for each of these areas is extremely discontinuous because in our classification the city of Parma falls partly into zone 7 and partly into zone 8.

[i] The CID can most appropriately be thought of as a greatly augmented central business district as defined by the Census of Business.

Table 2-5

Fraction of Total Cleveland SMSA Manufacturing Employment Located in Central-city Analysis Zones, 1965 and 1968

Number	Analysis Zone Description	1965	1968
1 [a]	CID	0.148	0.153
2 [a]	Hough(I)	.130	.108
3 [b]	Southeast of CID(I)	.114	.114
4 [a]	Southwest of CID(I)	.104	.090
5	West of CID(I)	.055	.049
13 [b]	Northeast of CID(II)	0.076	0.080

Note: Roman numerals identify "rings"; see section "Spatial Distribution of Major Industries in 1965" in this chapter for explanation.
[a] Traditional manufacturing area; poverty area.
[b] Traditional manufacturing area.

period, as did the employment shares of zone 3 to the southeast of the central industrial district, and zone 13 at the eastern edge of Cleveland on Lake Erie. As will be seen below, a major component of employment growth in each of these three zones was the expansion of stationary establishments. Though long-term growth trends within Cleveland are unknown, it appears likely that the economic renascence of heavy manufacturing industries in Cleveland may be responsible for the relatively strong growth performance of these traditional manufacturing zones.[j]

Manufacturing activity declined rapidly in both the Hough area (zone 2) and the analysis zone to the southwest of the CID (zone 4), in spite of the importance of heavy manufacturing activity in both zones, and in spite of highway construction activity enhancing transportation services to employers in these areas. Large-scale poverty exists in both of these zones, and race rioting rocked the Hough area during the study period. The social problems of these areas may be in part responsible for their industrial decline. Industrial activity is quite limited in zone 5 to the west of the central industrial district. The relative decline of employment in this area of the city reflects the general shift of manufacturing activity to eastern and southern portions of the region.

The Process of Change

In this section we describe two aspects of the process that has produced the pattern of net change of manufacturing employment. First are the lo-

---

[j] Together, in 1965 analysis zones 1, 3 and 13 contained 44 per cent of region employment in the primary metals industry, 34 per cent of jobs in the fabricated metals industry, and 37 per cent of employment involved in the manufacture of nonelectrical machinery. See Table 2-3 for additional information on the industrial structure of manufacturing activity in these zones.

cational elements producing the aggregate patterns, that is, relocating firms, births, deaths, and changes in the level of employment in establishments not changing their physical location. Second is the importance of the industrial composition of a zone in determining the net change in employment in the zone. This aspect ties together much of the material presented in the first three sections of the chapter.

The Composition of Net Change

There are two important facts to appreciate about the process of net change ongoing in Cleveland and the other sample cities. First, there is a great deal of locational activity, and, second, there are very substantial changes in nonrelocating establishments that affect the spatial distribution of employment. Table 2-6 gives an idea of the magnitude of overall relocational activity. The amount of movement is indeed great. On an annual basis over 12 per cent of all establishments and 5 per cent of all employment are included in one of these three categories. This finding combined with the large net changes in the distribution of employment discussed above runs counter to the general view that the location of manufacturing activity in a metropolitan area shifts very slowly over time. The magnitude of change in Cleveland suggests that the overall pattern could be changed dramatically in a relatively short period, given appropriate public policies. The activity rates based on numbers of establishments are greater than those based on employment simply because small firms have a greater propensity to move, start up, and fail than do large ones.[k]

Table 2-6

Numbers of Relocating, New, and Defunct Establishments and Employment in Cleveland, 1965-68

	Relocations		New		Defunct	
	Number	Percentage of 1965 Base	Number	Percentage of 1965 Base	Number	Percentage of 1965 Base
Establishments	644	13.83	464	9.97	655	14.07
Employment	17,199 [a]	5.77	7,708	2.59	23,092	7.75

[a] This is the employment of relocating establishments at their original location.

---

[k] Leone in his similar study has examined the size distribution of establishments in each of these classes. See Robert Leone, "The Location of Manufacturing Activity in the New York Metropolitan Area," Ph.D. diss., Yale University, 1971. This finding was verified by Franklin J. James and James W. Hughes, "The Process of Employment Location Change: An Empirical Analysis," *Land Economics*, November 1973, pp. 404-13, reprinted in Franklin J. James, *Models of Employment and*

Of the three locational elements shown in the table, defunct establishments comprise by far the largest group; and the combination of births and deaths, if dominantly at reinforcing locations, will easily be more important for net change than the relocation of establishments.

Table 2-7 contains data detailing the composition of the net change in employment in each Cleveland-area analysis zone. Shown are the number of employees in establishments moving into and out of each zone, the number employed by establishments beginning business (births), the number employed by establishments ending operations (deaths), and the change in the number employed by establishments remaining in the zone over the entire period (change in stationary establishments). Several general points can be made: First, with a few very minor exceptions, the number of employees in defunct establishments is greater than the number in new establishments. Second, net immigration of employees varies greatly among zones. Finally, the migration flows and the "natural increase" (births minus deaths) in each zone, are nearly always smaller individually than the change in employment in stationary establishments.

In terms of absolute change, all the central-city zones except that to the northeast adjacent to Euclid (zone 13) lost substantial numbers of jobs. The poverty-area zones faired the worst, on balance, but received sizable immigration. For example, firms with over 1,700 employees moved into Hough, which had lost over 8,000 jobs. This suggests that not all enterprises are finding these locations unprofitable. (This is pursued in detail in Chapter 9.) The poverty-area zones (except the CID) suffered very large declines, the largest in the SMSA, in employment in existing establishments, which may harbinger further increases in establishment deaths and/or emigration. Although both poverty areas within the central city suffered large losses from the birth-death process, the losses in Hough were particularly severe. When these changes are standardized by their 1965 employment, however, Hough does relatively better. The CID and the zone to its southeast (zone 3) were able to keep their losses modest primarily through the expansion of employment in stationary establishments. The CID also received large amounts of employment from both new and relocating establishments.

The experience of the rapidly growing zones was substantially different. The Berea, Parma, and Wickliffe zones (7, 8, and 16) experienced the largest absolute increases over the period. All benefited from net immigration of relocating establishments and, except in the Parma zone, immigration was substantial. In contrast to the central city these growing zones

Residence Location, New Brunswick, N.J., Center for Urban Policy Research, 1974; and Gordon C. Cameron, "Intraurban Location and the New Plant," *Papers of the Regional Science Association,* 1973, pp. 125-43.

Table 2-7

Composition of Net Change in Manufacturing Employment, Cleveland Metropolitan Area Analysis Zones, 1965 vs. 1968 (Number of Employees)

	1965 Base	Net Change	Moyers		Births	Deaths	Change in Stationary Establishments
			Origin	Destination			
City of Cleveland							
1 a CID	44,319	−981	3,581	2,714	2,262	3,368	992
2 a Hough(I)	38,798	−8,286	2,793	1,767	296	3,608	−3,948
3 b Southeast of CID(I)	33,845	−1,420	2,089	1,097	418	1,915	1,069
4 a Southwest of CID(I)	31,107	−5,530	1,825	888	962	2,092	−3,463
5 West of CID(I)	16,568	−2,668	2,626	1,834	310	2,209	23
13 b Northeast of CID(II)	22,553	239	510	683	836	3,036	2,266
Cleveland Total	187,190	−18,646	13,424	8,983	5,084	16,228	−3,061
Rest of area							
6 Bay Village-Westlake(II)	1,506	305	24	339	106	418	302
7 b Berea-N. Olmstead(II)	17,069	4,857	390	2,368	350	514	3,043
8 Parma-Independence(II)	2,275	1,144	401	443	64	60	1,098
10 Maple and Garfield Heights(II)	10,566	329	593	1,391	246	780	65
11 E. Cleveland-Shaker Heights(II)	11,613	−939	240	415	437	1,083	−468
9 Brecksville-Strongsville(III)	422	214	110	232	76	19	35
12 South Euclid(III)	1,129	−60	61	50	10	118	59
14 b Euclid(III)	33,210	−855	763	590	609	1,464	173
15 Bedford-Solon(III)	14,648	558	648	1,235	379	1,821	1,413
16 Wickliffe-Willoughby(IV)	8,821	1,995	379	1,035	318	529	1,550
17 Painsville-Grand River(IV)	8,854	−2,787	164	159	24	58	−2,748
18 Madison-Perry(IV)	689	−134	2	2	5	0	−139
Total	297,992	−14,019	17,199	17,242	7,708	23,092	1,322

Note: Roman numerals identify "rings"; see section "Spatial Distribution of Major Industries in 1965" in this chapter for explanation.
a Traditional manufacturing center; poverty area.
b Traditional manufacturing center.

suffered very small losses from the birth-death process. The Berea area even had a positive natural increase. Again, however, it is the expansion of stationary establishments that accounts for much of the change.

One other area of interest includes Euclid and the central-city zone adjacent to it. Both have been classed as traditional sites for manufacturing activity. Both showed little net change, but they demonstrate the importance of disaggregating net change into its components, for the amount of activity leading to their similar outcomes differed greatly. In Euclid deaths contributed heavily to its modest decline. In the central-city area adjacent to Euclid (zone 13), on the other hand, there was a great deal of locational activity resulting in a net change of about 1 per cent of 1965 employment, which is similar to the change in Euclid. It actually gained employment through relocations and lost about the same number through natural increase that it gained from the prosperity of stationary establishments. Both employment growth in stationary establishments and the difference in the aggregate employment of new and defunct establishments amounted to about 10 per cent of total 1965 employment. In short, examination of the net change in the location of employment can be extremely misleading about the amount of locational activity and of growth and decline occurring in the area.

The geographic distribution of the components of the net change in employment over the period are summarized in Figure 2-2. For clarity, employment associated with births and deaths has been aggregated in a "natural increase" category, and the employment associated with moving establishments has been aggregated in a "net migration" category. The graph shows how the components of net change have varied as the distance from the CID increases. Several points stand out: The CID did better in every component than did the central-city area around it. In addition, the CID had a larger natural increase than any other general area (i.e., ring) except the peripheral ring. The graph also makes it clear that the net migration and change in stationary establishments greatly favored the outlying areas, especially the areas encompassed by rings II and III.

Importance of the Industry Mix

It is clear that in analyzing the growth or decline of manufacturing employment in a given analysis zone, it would be extremely useful to be able to isolate the effects that result from the mix of industries located in the zone. Shift-share analysis, a simple method of accounting for industry effects, has been developed by Victor Fuchs and others studying the changes in regional employment patterns over time. Because this type of

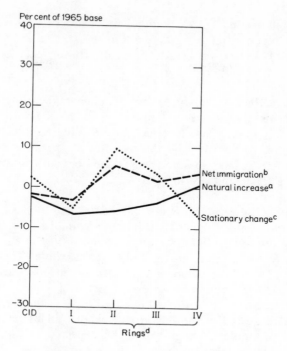

Per cent of 1965 base

Net immigration[b]
Natural increase[a]
Stationary change[c]

Rings[d]

[a] Equals employment of new establishments minus employment of establishments going out of business.
[b] Equals employment of in-migrating establishments minus employment of out-migrating establishments.
[c] Equals the change in employment of establishments that did not change their location over the period.
[d] Rings indicate distance from the CID; for explanation, see the section "Spatial Distribution of Major Industries in 1965" in this chapter. The zones included in each ring are identified in Table 2-3.

Figure 2-2. Components of Change in the Spatial Distribution of Employment, Cleveland Metropolitan Area, 1965-68

analysis has been so widely used, it is not extensively described in this book. Instead, the three shift-share measures that are used in the study are listed and discussed below and defined algebraically in Appendix D. Throughout, the description and notation are those used by Fuchs.[2] The list below gives the title by which the measure will be referred to in the text and tables. All measures are expressed as percentages of the overall level of employment in the zone.

1. Growth Relative to SMSA. Actual gain or loss of total manufacturing employment in zone i relative to growth in the same zone if employment grew at the SMSA average rate for all manufacturing industries combined over the period.

2. Competitive Change. Gain or loss of all manufacturing employment in zone i adjusted for industry mix in the zone. This measure of "competitive change" is approximately equal to the difference between actual "growth relative to SMSA" and the measure of "comparative industrial structure." (This reflects in some senses the competitive position of the zone as a site for manufacturing activity).

3. Comparative Industrial Structure. Expected gain or loss of all manufacturing employment in zone i attributable to industrial mix, calculated by weighting the relative importance of each industry in the zone by the growth rate of the industry in the SMSA as a whole. This measure of comparative industrial structure is equivalent to the measure of "growth relative to SMSA," which would be expected if employment in each individual industry in the zone had changed at the same rate at which it increased or decreased in the region as a whole. (This reflects the relative rapidity of employment growth to be expected in the zone on the basis of its industrial mix).

The use of these measures can be demonstrated for the Cleveland CID as shown in Table 2-8. The relative growth figure (column 1) is 2.49 per cent, which indicates that 1968 manufacturing employment in the CID was 2.49 per cent more than it would have been if employment levels in the CID had grown at the same rate as the SMSA between 1965 and 1968.

The shift-share component termed "comparative industrial structure" and presented in column (3) is 3.32 per cent for the central industrial district. This implies that if employment in each individual industry in the CID had grown at the same rate in the CID as in the SMSA, then total 1968 employment levels in the CID would have been 3.32 per cent higher than if total employment in the zone had grown at the same rate as did total employment in the region; that is, relatively rapidly growing industries comprised a larger than average share of industrial activity in the central industrial district.

The measure of comparative industrial structure exceeds the actual growth relative to the SMSA of the CID. This implies that, on average, employment in individual industries grew less rapidly in the CID than the SMSA as a whole. This slower growth of individual industries implies some type of competitive disadvantage limited their employment growth in the CID. This lack of competitiveness is measured by the shift com-

Table 2-8

Shift-Share Analysis of Job Growth, Cleveland Metropolitan Area, 1965 to 1968 (Per Cent)

Number	Analysis Zone Description	Growth Relative to SMSA (1)	Competitive Advantage (2)	Comparative Industrial Structure (3)
	City of Cleveland			
1 [a]	CID	2.49	−0.85	3.32
2 [a]	Hough(I)	−17.47	−17.87	0.48
3 [b]	Southeast of CID(I)	0.54	2.94	−2.42
4 [a]	Southwest of CID(I)	−13.71	−15.22	1.75
5	West of CID(I)	−11.96	−12.19	0.26
13 [b]	Northeast of CID(II)	5.71	4.23	1.54
	Rest of area			
6	Bay Village-Westlake(II)	20.76	20.36	0.41
7	Berea-N. Olmstead(II)	25.82	30.39	−6.16
10	Maple and Garfield Heights(II)	7.59	6.79	0.85
11	E. Cleveland-Shaker Heights(II)	−3.54	−0.90	−2.67
8	Parma-Independence(III)	36.59	33.19	5.09
9	Brecksville-Strongsville(III)	36.77	36.33	0.69
12	South Euclid(III)	−0.63	5.57	−6.17
14 [b]	Euclid(III)	2.19	2.59	−0.41
15	Bedford-Solon(III)	8.21	6.66	1.66
16	Wickliffe-Willoughby(IV)	22.29	17.17	6.18
17	Painsville-Grand River(IV)	−28.09	−16.85	−13.52
18	Madison-Perry(IV)	−15.47	−14.57	−1.04

Note: Roman numerals identify "rings"; see section "Spatial Distribution of Major Industries in 1965" in this chapter for explanation.
[a] Traditional manufacturing center; poverty area.
[b] Traditional manufacturing center.

ponent labeled competitive advantage, which is presented in column (2). This measure is negative for the CID, indicating relatively slow employment growth in the CID after taking the industrial structure of the zone into account. The measure of the competitive advantage of the central industrial district is (−0.85) per cent, which in this and all other cases is approximately equal to the difference between comparative industrial structure and growth relative to SMSA.[1]

---

[1] It should be noted that columns 2 and 3 are not so defined as to equal the relative growth figure in column 1. This arises solely from an index problem: This non-identity is introduced because the changes over the period are expressed as the average of the two bases. The last two columns will approximately equal the first. The important point, however, is that on a scale from −100 to +100 per cent each measure reflects the growth of manufacturing employment in the zone relative to that of the SMSA. In each instance if the zone were identical to the SMSA, the measure would equal zero.

Examining the other entries in the first two columns it is seen that more rapid than average rates of employment growth occurred in three central-city zones, as indicated by shift measure 1. In this regard it is interesting to examine the decline of the two non-CID poverty areas, zones 2 and 4. At the beginning of the period both zones contained industrial structures that should have provided them with above-average rates of growth, as indicated by shift measure 3. Yet, with the exception of Painsville, which had by far the worst industry mix, these zones were the least competitive after accounting for industry mix (column 2). This pattern of little correlation between industry mix and growth is borne out in the rapidly growing zones southwest of the central city—zones 6, 7, 8, and 9. Parma-Independence contained the best industry mix of any zone, but its general attractiveness far outweighed this factor. The unfavorable industry mix in the Berea area probably reflects its longer importance as an industrial center, but it grew very rapidly in relative terms in spite of this. On balance, then, the industry mix in a zone seems to be a poor predictor of the rate of growth of a zone's manufacturing employment over the period.

3 Minneapolis-St. Paul

The Twin Cities received their growth impetus with the westward expansion in the 1850s and especially with the coming of the railroad after the Civil War. The cities' two most important industries were founded and grew rapidly in those early years. Grain milling for several of the northern plain states, a large livestock market, and meatpacking facilities and other food-processing activities begun in these years gave the city its economic image. The production of machinery, especially farm machinery, was important from the start. During World War II the industrial structure in the area was changed markedly by the establishment there of large electrical machinery works and metal fabrication facilities.

Our definition of the *Minneapolis-St. Paul metropolitan area* comprises Anoka, Dakota, Hennepin (Minneapolis City), and Ramsey (St. Paul City) counties. The census definition includes an additional area, Washington County. The scale of manufacturing activity in this county is very small, and its inclusion was unnecessary for this analysis. In 1960 Hennepin held over half of the area's population and Ramsey about one-fourth, the remainder being about evenly divided between Anoka and Dakota counties. Since 1963, however, the smaller counties have been growing at rates twice those of the more populated counties.

Industrial Composition

Data on the relative importance of the five industries employing the greatest number of workers in the Twin Cities are contained in Table 3-1. Interestingly, two of these are nondurables producers, food and food products (SIC 20), and printing and publishing (SIC 27). The Boston area is the only other sample Standard Metropolitan Statistical Area (SMSA) that has a comparable concentration of employment in the nondurables sector. The concentration in this sector should serve to make the area much less sensitive to national economic cycles.[1]

Two aspects of the statistics presented in the table are of immediate interest. First, the food-processing and nonelectrical machinery industries have remained dominant. By 1968 they employed 40 per cent of the area's industrial workers. The second is the amazing growth of the machinery

47

Table 3-1

Employment in Selected Manufacturing Industries, Minneapolis-St. Paul Metropolitan Area, 1947-68

Industry	1947 [a]	1958 [a]	1963 [a]	1965 [b]	1968 [b]
Employment as Fraction of Total SMSA Manufacturing Employment					
Machinery	0.169	0.160	0.189	0.205	0.247
Food products	.175	.164	.133	.156	.160
Publishing	.125	.122	.115	.099	.088
Electrical machinery	.116	.053	.108	.096	.072
Fabricated metals	.074	.071	.069	.086	.082
Fraction of total	0.660	0.571	0.615	0.642	0.648
Number of Manufacturing Employees					
Machinery	20,039	21,571	28,331	30,893	35,300
Food products	20,853	22,272	19,955	23,474	22,851
Publishing	14,852	16,546	17,221	14,896	12,535
Electrical machinery	13,803	7,186	16,207	14,460	10,343
Fabricated metals	8,842	9,619	10,289	12,900	11,750
Total itemized	78,389	77,194	92,003	96,623	92,779

[a] *Census of Manufactures*, vol. III.
[b] Based on tabulations of Dun and Bradstreet data.

industry. With the exception of a slight dip in response to the 1958 recession the importance of the industry has risen steadily over the 20-year period shown. Among the major firms of this industry in the area are Farmhand, Inc., and Minneapolis-Moline—both large producers of farm machinery and implements—and Napco Industries, producers of trucks for the federal government and various support vehicles for the United States Air Force. It seems probable that much of the upswing in the importance of machinery production to the area's economy can be attributed to the demands of the Vietnam War.

In the decade following World War II the electrical machinery industry (SIC 36) suffered a substantial decline, losing some 6,600 jobs between 1947 and 1958 of an original 13,800. From that point onward, however, growth was sustained at a high rate until 1963. In only five years about 9,000 new jobs were created. During the five-year period 1963-68 the number of jobs plummeted in the electrical machinery industry. The 1968 level of employment in the industry indicated by our data is less than the 1947 employment level reported by the census. Among the major firms in the area (employing more than 500 persons) are Control Data, Electric Machinery Manufacturing, Honeywell, Magnetic Controls, Northern Ordnance, and Thermo King. The electrical machinery industry is quite significant in the regional economy, and in this respect the Twin Cities resemble the Boston and Phoenix areas.

Employment in the other industries in the area has grown at a rate faster than the national average. However, their fraction of total area employment has remained roughly constant. The petroleum and products and motor vehicles industries have grown consistently. Only the apparel and textile industries have declined absolutely and relatively.

The manufacturing sector is considerably less important in Minneapolis-St. Paul than in Cleveland. Its importance has diminished somewhat over the period, falling from 30 per cent to around 27 per cent of total non-agricultural employment. The sector with the largest gain was the service industry (12 to 16 per cent of the total) as has been generally the case nationally, although the Twin Cities growth in this area far exceeded the national average.[a] Other sectors growing in importance at the expense of the construction trade and transportation sectors were the financial and government sectors. Overall, the growth of employment has been about twice that of other major cities over the 1950-65 period, with every sector except transportation growing at greater than national rates.[b]

Spatial Distribution of Major Industries in 1965

Following the guidelines set out in the previous chapter, 25 analysis zones have been delineated for the Twin Cities area: 7 in the city of Minneapolis, 5 in the city of St. Paul, and 13 in the surrounding area. Figure 3-1 is a map showing the analysis zones; definitions of the zones are provided in Table C-1. Table 3-2 presents the percentage distribution of manufacturing employment of the five major industries in the SMSA. Again, the location of each zone among concentric rings surrounding the central industrial district is indicated by Roman numerals following each zonal title. For the Twin Cities, two sets of rings are defined, with the rings moving outward from each central city—Minneapolis to the west and St. Paul to the east. Since there are 25 analysis zones, at least 8 per cent of an industry's manufacturing employment must be in the analysis zone for the industry to be defined as "concentrated" in that zone.[c] The single most

---

[a] Data on the performance of 28 sectors, including 14 manufacturing ones, for our sample cities of Boston, Cleveland, and Minneapolis-St. Paul relative to the performance of these sectors nationally were prepared by the Federal Reserve Bank of Cleveland and were published in the bank's *Economic Review,* January 1968.

[b] The Minneapolis-St. Paul performance was compared with the aggregate performance of a 13-city group comprising Baltimore, Boston, Buffalo, Chicago, Cincinnati, Cleveland, Detroit, Kansas City, Milwaukee, Minneapolis-St. Paul, Philadelphia, Pittsburgh, and St. Louis.

[c] The criteria used to define the analysis zones and the definition of an employment concentration are given in Chapter 2, "Spatial Distribution of Major Industries in 1965." The use of "rings" to indicate distance from the CID is also discussed there.

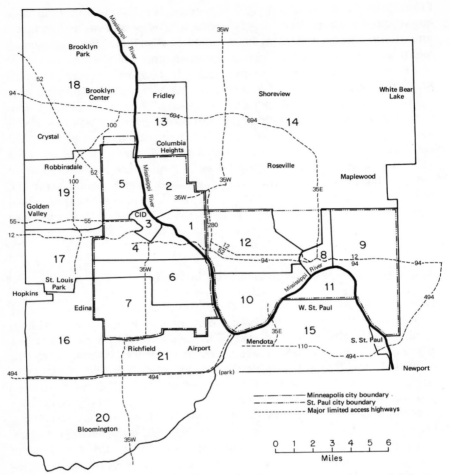

Figure 3-1. Map of Analysis Zones in the Minneapolis-St. Paul Metropolitan Area

striking aspect of the distributions is that there are only two concentrations outside of the central cities—one in Newport-St. Paul and one in Bloomington.

Consider first the two nondurables industries, food processing (SIC 20) and publishing (SIC 27). The former is substantially spread out, with its four concentrations occurring in the two central industrial districts (CIDs) (zones 3 and 8), the Minneapolis zone north and across the Mississippi from the Minneapolis CID (zone 2), and an extreme concentration in the Newport-St. Paul Park area in the southeast corner of the SMSA

Table 3-2

Geographic Distribution of Employment in Major Manufacturing Industries, Minneapolis-St. Paul Metropolitan Area, 1965
(Per Cent of Total SMSA Manufacturing Employment in the Industry)

Number	Analysis Zone Description	Food Products	Printing and Publishing	Fabricated Metals	Machinery	Electrical Machinery
	City of Minneapolis					
1	East of Miss. R., S. (I)	4.60	2.01	8.85	4.09	3.11
2	East of Miss. R., N. (I)	8.42	0.78	11.68	8.83	16.56
3	CID	16.79	38.52	4.30	6.49	5.22
4	Southwest of CID (I)	4.81	6.17	5.66	4.45	0.58
5	Northwest of CID (I)	3.52	1.05	3.49	2.62	2.95
6	Southeast of CID (II)	2.78	2.07	15.28	7.99	4.86
7	South of CID (II)	——	0.19	0.43	0.63	0.36
	City of St. Paul					
8	CID	9.35	10.55	1.82	3.82	5.53
9	East of CID (I)	0.04	0.02	0.01	5.66	10.43
10	Southwest of CID (I)	3.83	12.48	0.41	5.15	0.10
11	South of CID (I)	0.62	0.09	1.19	5.59	——
12	Northwest of CID (I)	5.22	15.47	17.67	5.51	23.56
13	Columbia Heights-Findley (M-II)	1.01	0.11	1.34	1.01	0.11
16	Edina (M-II)	——	2.71	1.23	2.49	1.49
17	St. Louis Park (M-II)	4.91	1.14	2.21	3.77	5.93
19	Golden Valley-Robbinsdale (M-II)	3.10	1.48	6.02	2.27	4.88
25	Hopkins-Mound (M-III)	1.36	0.95	4.40	6.66	3.13
18	Crystal-Brooklyn Park (M-III)	0.03	0.58	2.01	2.02	2.43
21	Richfield-Intl. Airport (M-III)	0.13	0.34	0.76	1.24	——
20	Bloomington (M-IV)	0.88	0.36	1.91	9.06	3.01
22	Anoka-Hugo (M-IV)	0.17	0.32	1.12	1.81	2.04
14	North & West St. Paul suburbs (S-II)	0.76	1.98	5.58	7.95	3.40
15	Mendota, W. St. Paul (S-II)	0.06	0.02	0.76	0.50	0.26
24	Newport-St. Paul Park (S-III)	27.25	0.27	1.64	0.14	——
23	Mahtomedi-Bayport (S-IV)	0.29	0.30	0.22	0.22	0.04

Note: Roman numerals indicate distance from CID. Thus, M-III is in third ring from Minneapolis CID, S-III is in third ring from St. Paul, etc; for explanation, see Chapter 2 "Spatial Distribution of Major Industries in 1965."

(zone 24). The concentrations in the Minneapolis CID and St. Paul Park zones account for over 25 per cent of the total number of jobs, and the four concentrations for nearly 60 per cent. The publishing industry, on the other hand, is extremely compact, with the four concentrations occurring in the two CIDs and the zones between them. Nearly 40 per cent of all publishing jobs are in the Minneapolis CID, and the four concentrations account for more than three out of every four jobs in the industry.

The least concentrated industry is the very important nonelectrical machinery group (SIC 35). There were only two zones that met the minimum criteria—one in Minneapolis ring I east of the Mississippi River and the other in Bloomington in Minneapolis ring IV. However, there are four more zones with over 6 per cent of total employment and another six with more than 4 per cent, including four of the five zones in St. Paul City. Part of the reason for this extremely even distribution rests in the composition of the industry itself, which in the SIC system includes computer equipment. The locational pattern of the electrical machinery group suggests which zones contain the greatest amount of this computer production. All three zones in which the electrical machinery industry is concentrated also contain significant amounts of employment in the nonelectrical machinery industry.[d]

Net Change in the Spatial Distribution of Total Manufacturing Employment

The distribution of employment in the Twin Cities metropolitan area over the period 1947-68 is presented in Table 3-3. In defining traditional manufacturing sites, the same criteria were applied to this area as to Cleveland, and none were defined outside the central cities. Likewise, all poverty areas are in the central cities. A cursory reading of the table indicates that there is a distinct difference in the amount of employment shown in some analysis zones by our two data sources. The most striking difference is in the case of the city of St. Paul. The rapid downward trend indicated by the Census of Manufactures data is sharply reversed according to the Dun and Bradstreet (D&B) figures. This problem may result from inexact matching of boundaries. The St. Paul and Hopkins statistics may also represent a combination of coverage differences and actual changes. It is

---

[d] Although the D&B data give one primary and up to four secondary four-digit SIC codes, they provide only a single employment figure. Normally the establishments producing computer hardware were producing a variety of other equipment, some classified as electrical and some not. Since there was no way to divide the employment among these different product lines the two-digit primary code was used throughout.

Table 3-3

Spatial Distribution of Manufacturing Employment, Minneapolis-St. Paul Metropolitan Area, 1947-68
(Fraction of Total SMSA Manufacturing Employment)

Number	Analysis Zone Description	1947 [a]	1958 [a]	1963 [a]	1965 [b]	1968 [b]
1-7	City of Minneapolis	0.521	0.432	0.409	0.385	0.315
8-12	City of St. Paul	.341	.309	.255	.292	.298
13	Columbia Heights-Findley (M-II)	——	.007	.003	.011	.015
16	Edina (M-II)	——	.001	.002	.014	.025
17	St. Louis Park (M-II)	——	.012	.017	.039	.041
19	Golden Valley-Robbinsdale (M-II)	——	.013	.019	.046	.051
25	Hopkins-Mound (M-III)	——	——	.026	.051	.040
18	Crystal-Brooklyn Park (M-III)	——	.001	.002	.010	.016
21	Richfield-Intl. Airport (M-III)	——	.002	.002	.005	.007
20	Bloomington (M-IV)	——	.009	.028	.028	.035
22	Anoka-Hugo (M-IV)	——	.007	.011	.014	.015
14	North & West St. Paul suburbs (S-II)	——	——	——	.042	.048
15	Mendota, W. St. Paul (S-II)	——	——	——	.007	.007
24	Newport-St. Paul Park (S-III)	——	——	——	.060	.071
23	Mahtomedi-Bayport (S-IV)	——	——	——	0.012	0.013
	SMSA employment not reported by city	0.138	0.207	0.226	——	——

Note: Roman numerals show distance from CID. Thus, M-III is in third ring from Minneapolis CID, etc.; for explanation, see Chapter 2, "Spatial Distribution of Major Industries in 1965."
[a] *Census of Manufactures*, vol. III.
[b] Based on tabulations of Dun and Bradstreet data.

encouraging that employment growth trends are in general comparable between the two series. This means in most cases that the changing pattern of locations that are examined should be representative of those occurring over a longer period. On the basis of evidence presented below, the actual reversal of the decline in St. Paul's share of manufacturing employment appears to be substantiated.

The general pattern of the change in industrial employment locations over the period has been one of movement out of both central cities. Manufacturing growth was concentrated around the periphery of Minneapolis and southeast of St. Paul. The share of manufacturing jobs in the city of Minneapolis has fallen from over half to about 30 per cent. That of St. Paul has declined slightly over the entire period. There has been one other major employment node in the area throughout the period, the combined Hopkins and St. Louis Park-Golden Valley area. In many respects this is simply a continuation of Minneapolis; but it is probably better viewed as a line anchored on either end by Hopkins and the Minneapolis central city, much like the Cleveland-Euclid situation but on a smaller scale.

While the entire western crescent around Minneapolis has grown, those south and southwest of the city have grown most rapidly. In particular, the area composed of the Edina, Richfield, and Bloomington analysis zones (spanning three rings) has increased its share of employment by a full 2 per cent between 1965 and 1968. The real concentration is in Richfield and Bloomington; Edina is better characterized as an upper middle income residential suburb, although some industry is present. The slightly larger zones to the west of the city have grown somewhat less rapidly.

The area around St. Paul is largely made up of quiet residential suburbs. One exception to this is the Newport-St. Paul Park area, which has become an important employment center in the sixties increasing its share of area employment by 1.1 per cent over the study period. Other suburbs have increased growth substantially in recent years, but the pattern remains quite diffused.

The relationship between completed major highways and the movement of manufacturing establishments is not as clear in the Twin Cities zone as for other of the sample SMSAs. By 1965 three major interstate elements of the highway system in the area had been largely completed: (1) the section of the Interstate 494-94-694 beltway from the regional airport west and then north, turning east again just west of Brooklyn Park, and ending beyond its junction with Interstate 35 in New Brighton; (2) Interstate 35, running south to north through the heart of Minneapolis, coming out through Bloomington and Richfield; (3) Interstate 94, connecting the two central cities and tying into interstates 35W and 35E at either end. Surprisingly, none of these roads serviced the rapid development of the area along the line from the Minneapolis CID to Hopkins, nor are major roads planned in this area. This may partially explain the recent slowing of the area's growth. The massive growth of the Richfield-Edina-Bloomington area can be partially attributed to its position at the junction of the beltway and 35W, the former providing superior access to the blue-collar residential areas. Likewise, the emergence of the Crystal-Brooklyn Park area as an industrial center might be explained to some extent by its location on the beltway. Probably as important, however, is the planned Interstate 95 link to the heart of Minneapolis and the extension of the same highway northward.

The changes in the spatial distribution of employment within the central cities (shown in Table 3-4) are extremely interesting. The two central cities have been divided into a total of 12 zones for this analysis. The grouping of the zip codes was done primarily to attain homogeneity of the industrial development within the zones.

Table 3-4

Distribution of Manufacturing Employment, Minneapolis-St. Paul, 1965 and 1968

(Fraction of SMSA Employment)

Number	Analysis Zone Description	1965	1968
	Minneapolis		
1	East of Miss. River, South (I)	0.042	0.039
2 [a]	East of Miss. River, North (I)	.087	.071
3 [b]	Central industrial district	.111	.094
4 [b]	Southwest of CID (I)	.059	.039
5	Northwest of CID (I)	.030	.025
6	Southeast of CID (II)	.051	.042
7	South of CID (II)	.005	.005
	Total	0.385	0.315
	St. Paul		
8 [b]	Central industrial district	0.084	0.061
9	East of CID (I)	.024	.026
10	Southwest of CID (I)	.044	.098
11 [c]	South of CID (I)	.020	.011
12 [a]	Northwest of CID (I)	.120	.102
	Total	0.292	0.298

Note: Roman numerals indicate distance from CID; for explanation see Chapter 2, "Spatial Distribution of Major Industries in 1965."
[a] Traditional manufacturing center.
[b] Traditional manufacturing center; poverty area.
[c] Poverty area.

In Minneapolis none of the seven analysis zones had a larger portion of total manufacturing employment in 1968 than in 1965. Actually only two of the zones, both adjacent to the CID, lost less than 0.6 per cent of their share of total employment; and the share of the least industrially important zone (7) remained unchanged. The central industrial district and the zone adjacent to it to the southwest both lost over 20 per cent of their base year industrial jobs. The latter loss is particularly surprising since the adjacent zone is close to the St. Louis Park-Golden Valley area, although it is effectively separated from these by a chain of lakes. Overall, the city of Minneapolis seems to be declining as a viable location for manufacturing activity.

The position of St. Paul contrasts in aggregate with that of Minneapolis, but a closer examination reveals similarities. While the city as a whole has been able to maintain its share of industrial employment, the CID and zones adjacent to it to the south and west (11 and 12, respectively) have all suffered substantial reductions in employment. In total the three zones have lost 8,850 jobs over the study period. It has only been the 5 per cent increase in the area share of zone 10, all in the electrical machinery industry, which has countered the losses in other parts of the city.

The role of the highway system in aiding the competitiveness of central cities is not clear for the Twin Cities proper. The presence of highways or major interchanges appears to have had little effect for most zones. The performance of the areas south of the Minneapolis CID and the St. Paul CID itself seem to bear this out. One reason for this may simply be that the expressway system in the area has been so extensively developed that the effect of any one highway or interchange is not as pervasive as it might be in other circumstances. Witness, for example, the pattern of Cleveland. This underscores the problems of attempting to forecast too much from the positioning of highways in metropolitan areas when others are already present; expressways and the access they provide are frequently likely to be near substitutes for each other in the locational decisions.

The patterns for traditional manufacturing areas and poverty areas are not at all clear for the Twin Cities. The general decline in the central cities makes it difficult to discern whether these areas have any distinct pattern. One point is evident, however. The two zones in St. Paul that increased their share of total manufacturing employment were neither traditional manufacturing nor poverty areas.

The Process of Change

The Composition of Net Change

As shown in Table 3-5, the rate of locational activity in the Twin Cities was quite high. In total about 25 per cent of the base-year employment was involved in these three classes of activity. This is considerably higher than the similar figures for Boston and Cleveland (17 and 16 per cent)

Table 3-5

Numbers of Relocating, New, and Defunct Establishments and Employment in Minneapolis-St. Paul, 1965-68

	Relocations		New		Defunct	
	Number	Percentage of 1965 Base	Number	Percentage of 1965 Base	Number	Percentage of 1965 Base
Establishments	485	15.93	374	12.29	548	18.00
Employment	12,462 [a]	8.28	9,297	6.17	16,943	11.25

[a] This is the employment of relocating establishments at their original locations.

and about the same as for Phoenix. All three rates for both establishments and employment are higher than for Boston and Cleveland.[e]

The processes of change in the two central cities provide an interesting contrast, as shown by the data in Table 3-6. In the city of Minneapolis every zone without exception experienced a net out-migration of manufacturing employment, and provided the bulk of the over 2,000 jobs relocating out of both central cities. It should be noted, though, that most of the zones did receive a large number of in-migrating employees. Every zone in Minneapolis also lost employment through the birth-death process. The surprising thing, however, is the small number of employees in new establishments in several of the zones. In most of the areas adjacent to the CID and one central-city area further out (zones 1, 2, 4, 6) new employment was 20 per cent or less than that in dying firms. For three zones the importance of the change in employment of stationary establishments is much less than it was in Cleveland. The situation in St. Paul is much different. With the exception of CID, net migrations were either unimportant or net in-migrations occurred. While in most zones the imbalance between births and deaths remained, the zone southwest of the CID showed a natural increase of nearly 5,000 jobs resulting from the opening of a single very large branch plant. For these zones the importance of employment change in stationary establishments again exerts itself.

The pattern in the composition of net change is quite diverse in the area outside of the central cities. Among the zones showing strong growth over the period,[f] almost all showed large net in-migrations of employment. Only in the Crystal-Brooklyn Park area (ring M-III to the north) were a significant number of jobs lost in this way. New firms definitely acted as a much stronger impetus in these zones than in those in the central cities, and there is a rough positive correlation between the destination of relocating establishments and new establishments. This is similar to the pattern in the outlying areas in Cleveland. One pattern that differs from that of Cleveland is the importance of changes in employment in sta-

---

[e] Actually, the death rate among establishments and the employment data for them struck us as being inflated. The description of the data and the manner in which they were verified, given in Appendix A, make it clear that such an inflation might have occurred in several ways and that it may have been that some of the "false" deaths were not caught. This problem was not unique, of course, to the Twin Cities; but it appeared stronger in this case. Careful qualitative and quantitative analysis of the pattern of employment in defunct establishments in the other three sample SMSAs produced very little evidence of systematic spatial variation. This provides a measure of additional confidence in the patterns observed for the Twin Cities. Overall, though, it appears that the death rate is inflated and that the aggregate net change over the period is accordingly deflated. The magnitude of the potential error is extremely difficult to judge, but 20 per cent would seem to be the maximum.

[f] Zones 14, 16, 18, 20, and 24.

Table 3-6

Composition of Net Change in Manufacturing Employment, Minneapolis-St. Paul Metropolitan Area Analysis Zones, 1965 vs. 1968 (Number of Employees)

Number	Analysis Zone Description	1965 Base	Net Change	Movers Origins	Movers Destinations	Births	Deaths	Change in Stationary Establishments
	City of Minneapolis							
1	East of Miss. River, South (I)	6,388	−808	737	479	73	470	−153
2 [a]	East of Miss. River, North (I)	13,204	−3,088	557	483	81	2,573	−522
3 [b]	Central industrial district	16,720	−3,229	1,256	830	374	1,600	−1,577
4 [b]	Southwest of CID (I)	8,985	−3,448	1,191	811	116	2,208	−976
5	Northwest of CID (I)	4,511	−934	975	176	325	747	287
6	Southeast of CID (II)	7,736	−1,740	1,074	526	220	1,069	−343
7	South of CID (II)	718	13	34	34	16	39	36
	Minneapolis total	58,262	−13,234	5,824	3,339	1,205	8,706	−3,248
	City of St. Paul							
8 [b]	Central industrial district	12,781	−3,982	2,086	1,419	134	1,191	−2,258
9	East of CID (I)	3,600	134		60	18	154	210
10	Southwest of CID (I)	6,692	7,348	269	257	5,040	42	2,362
11 [c]	South of CID (I)	2,962	−1,377	245	186	75	275	−1,118
12 [a]	Northwest of CID (I)	18,038	−3,488	961	1,360	250	2,554	−1,583
	St. Paul total	44,073	−1,365	3,561	3,282	5,517	4,216	−2,387
	Rest of Area							
13	Columbia Heights-Findley (M-II)	1,745	404	120	322	67	481	192
16	Edina (M-II)	2,216	1,421	256	703	278	46	742
17	St. Louis Park (M-II)	5,912	−35	1,046	972	167	641	513
19	Golden Valley-Robbinsdale (M-II)	7,066	267	199	952	172	386	−272
25	Hopkins-Mound (M-III)	5,407	313	137	613	548	367	−344
18	Crystal-Brooklyn Park (M-III)	1,443	890	682	182	301	7	1,096
21	Richfield-Intl. Airport (M-III)	760	308	45	105	66	37	219
20	Bloomington (M-IV)	4,276	715	323	959	165	450	364
22	Anoka-Hugo (M-IV)	2,081	−31	51	84	91	613	524
14	North & West St. Paul suburbs (S-II)	6,331	614	28	692	294	358	14
15	Mendota, W. St. Paul (S-II)	1,026	31	85	276	34	116	−78
24	Newport-St. Paul Park (S-III)	9,167	1,134	50	41	352	121	912
23	Mahtomedi-Bayport (S-IV)	1,826	−24 [d]	55	45	40	398	344
	Total	151,591	−8,592 [d]	12,462	12,567	9,297	16,943	−1,417

Note: Roman numerals indicate distance from CID; for explanation, see Chapter 2, "Spatial Distribution of Major Industries in 1965."

[a] Traditional manufacturing area.

[b] Traditional manufacturing area; poverty area.

[c] Poverty area.

[d] See note d in this chapter for a discussion of the size of this figure.

tionary firms on net changes in employment. For example, the Golden Valley-Robbinsdale and Hopkins-Mound areas registered absolute increases in employment in spite of sizable declines in employment in stationary establishments. In Cleveland in not a single instance did the number of jobs in a zone increase unless there was an increase in employment in the stationary firms.

The spatial distribution of the components of net change are summarized in Figure 3-2. A separate graph is provided for each of the two central cities and for the areas on their peripheries not accounted for by the other. In other words, the Minneapolis periphery basically includes the area to the west, and that of St. Paul the area to the east. A quick glance at the two graphs shows that the distribution of the components of change varied significantly between the two cities. In Minneapolis the CID

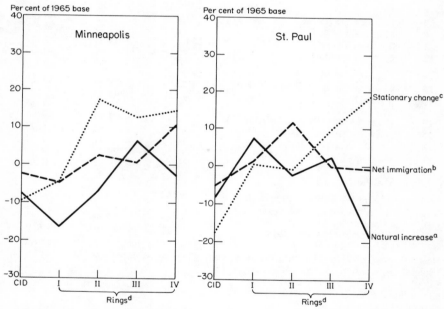

[a] Equals employment of new establishments minus employment of establishments going out of business.
[b] Equals employment of in-migrating establishments minus employment of out-migrating establishments.
[c] Equals the change in employment of establishments that did not change their location over the period.
[d] Rings indicate distance from the CID; for explanation, see the section "Spatial Distribution of Major Industries in 1965" in this chapter. The zones included in each ring are identified in Table 3-2.

Figure 3-2. Components of Change in Spatial Distribution of Employment, Minneapolis-St. Paul Metropolitan Area, 1965-68

Table 3-7

Shift-Share Measures for Minneapolis-St. Paul SMSA, 1968 Relative to 1965 (Per Cent)

Number	Analysis Zone Description	Growth Relative to SMSA	Competitive Advantage	Comparative Industrial Structure
	City of Minneapolis			
1	East of Miss. R., S. (I)	−8.07	−11.18	3.39
2 [a]	East of Miss. R., N. (I)	−19.37	−18.93	−0.53
3 [b]	CID	−15.08	−9.10	−6.55
4 [b]	Southwest of CID (I)	−35.15	−26.51	−11.72
5	Northwest of CID (I)	−16.55	−16.24	−0.34
6	Southeast of CID (II)	−18.43	−19.34	1.12
7	South of CID (II)	6.67	4.98	1.69
	City of St. Paul			
8 [b]	CID	−27.55	−23.87	−4.81
9	East of CID (I)	8.39	9.27	−0.96
10	Southwest of CID (I)	54.71	51.29	6.93
11 [c]	South of CID (I)	−43.68	−45.83	3.87
12 [a]	Northwest of CID (I)	−15.11	−9.63	−6.06
	Rest of Area			
13	Columbia Heights-Findley (M-II)	22.84	17.54	6.42
16	Edina (M-II)	42.11	40.40	2.70
17	St. Louis Park (M-II)	4.41	4.94	−0.56
19	Golden Valley-Robbinsdale (M-II)	8.44	1.95	6.61
25	Hopkins-Mound (M-III)	10.18	6.15	4.23
18	Crystal-Brooklyn Park (M-III)	41.23	38.71	4.06
21	Richfield-Intl. Airport (M-III)	32.38	24.78	10.10
20	Bloomington (M-IV)	18.59	9.31	10.23
22	Anoka-Hugo (M-IV)	8.03	6.97	1.12
14	N. and W. St. Paul suburbs (S-II)	13.38	6.67	7.18
15	Mendota-W. St. Paul (S-II)	7.77	−1.00	8.68
24	Newport-St. Paul Park (S-III)	15.44	12.88	2.94
23	Mahtomedi-Bayport (S-IV)	3.71	10.06	−6.59

Note: Roman numerals indicate distance from CID; for explanation, see Chapter 2, "Spatial Distribution of Major Industries in 1965."
[a] Traditional manufacturing area.
[b] Traditional manufacturing area; poverty area.
[c] Poverty area.

had higher rates of in-migration and natural increase compared to the area adjacent to it. In St. Paul the CID rates were lower than in the other areas in all categories. (The large changes in the St. Paul ring IV should be discounted, as the base employment was only 1,800.) The decentralizing pattern of out-migrations is pervasive in both cities, as are the effects of the employment expansion of stationary establishments. Overall, the pattern exhibited by Minneapolis, with the general upward slope to the right, is substantially like that of Cleveland, whereas the low rates in the St. Paul CID sharply distinguish it from the others.

Importance of Industry Mix

The same type of shift-share analysis is used here as in the previous chapter, but with significantly different results.[g] Table 3-7 contains the three shift-share measures for each analysis zone. A general point can be made immediately: The comparative industrial structure provides a generally reliable indication of the *direction* of change in the relative growth of total manufacturing employment in these zones. For 19 of the 25 zones the direction of change corresponds with the sign of the comparative industrial measure. At the same time it does not provide any meaningful information on the magnitude of change.

Minneapolis central city with the exception of a single peripheral zone is shown to be unattractive to industry after correcting for the industry mix in each zone. Both of the growing zones in St. Paul are attractive, as one would expect, but the St. Paul CID and the zone south of it are shown to be two of the three most uncompetitive zones in the SMSA. In the rest of the area all the zones save two have a favorable industrial mix. St. Louis Park, which was losing employment through net out-migration, had a negligible handicap. In the Mahtomedi-Newport zone, on the other hand, there were a substantial number of jobs in the lumber industry, in which the number of establishments declined about 25 per cent throughout the SMSA over the observation period. The Bloomington and Richfield zones had the most favorable industry mix of all zones, both being dominated by the nonelectrical machinery industry.

---

[g] See Chapter 2, "The Process of Change," for a description of the shift-share measures and a discussion of their use in this context.

4 Boston

It is important in Boston to draw a clear distinction between Boston's traditional commerce and that which has revitalized the metropolitan area since the end of World War II. From the earliest times Boston depended upon its fishing fleet, and still remains one of the largest fishing ports in the United States. Until the end of the eighteenth century, the city remained a pleasant, uncrowded seaport. During the nineteenth century, with the coming of the industrial revolution, the city took the lead in the manufacture of textiles and paper and in the printing and publishing field. It also became the center of the shoe and leather industry and of the wholesale wool trade of the country. With the turn of the century manufacturing activity began to suffer a steady decline, which was to persist until the Second World War. The decline was brought about largely by the movement of the textile processors to the South and by the shift of leather goods manufactures to the Midwest. The erosion of the economy was not arrested by the revival of these traditional industries but by a major change in the industrial structure of the area's economy as a result of the emergence of the electronics industry.

The city of Boston offers the only example among the sample cities of this study of the dimensions of the problems that confront the older cities in the northeastern section of the United States.[1] There were two reasons for the inclusion of Boston in particular among the sample cities: First, the importance of the electrical machinery industry gives it an industrial structure similar in some respects to those of Phoenix and Minneapolis-St. Paul. Second, it is a much older city and one that is in some senses representative of the cities in the northeastern part of the country. It should be noted from the outset that the definition of the Boston metropolitan area employed in the Dun and Bradstreet (D&B) tabulations differs slightly from that employed by the census.[a]

Industrial Composition

Not surprisingly, the importance of the manufacturing sector in providing nonagricultural employment has declined markedly in Boston since the

---

[a] Towns included by the census but excluded in the present definition were Hamilton, Beverly, Manchester, Middletown, Ashland, Shuborn, Millis, Norfolk, and Marshfield. Additions to the census coverage were Foxborough, Stoughton, Avon, and Brockton.

late 1940s. In fact, it has gone from providing about one out of three jobs in the area in 1947 to providing one of four in 1965. The transportation and trade sectors have also declined but at lower rates. The greatest growth has been in the service sector. Services provided 21 per cent of all jobs in 1965 versus only 15 per cent in 1947, with the number of jobs increasing by over 100,000. The government and construction sectors have both remained roughly constant in relative terms.

On balance, the growth in employment in the Boston area has been well below the national average during the two decades ending in 1968. The number of manufacturing jobs in the region was no greater in 1963 than in 1947.

The hallmark of industrial development in the Boston area since the end of World War II has been the growth of the electronics industry, which has offset the declines in the other major industries. This point is clearly made in Table 4-1. At the end of the Second World War one out of every nine industrial jobs was in the electronics (electrical machinery) industry. Since then, the importance of the industry has increased steadily. By 1968 it employed 24,000 more people than the next largest manufacturing industry. The development of this industry in the Boston area is frequently attributed to the presence of the massive advanced educational facilities in the area. The existence of a large amount of available space for embryonic firms of the industry is thought to have been important as well. The growth of the same industry in Minneapolis-St. Paul and Phoenix has also been impressive. The industry in the Boston area appears to be research-oriented; in Phoenix, it is production-oriented; and in the Twin Cities, there is a mix of both activities.

Table 4-1 also demonstrates the extreme diversity of the area's industrial structure. The seven industries employing the greatest number of persons in 1963 are listed in the table, but there were actually three others —transportation equipment (SIC 37), scientific instruments (SIC 38), and rubber products (SIC 30)—which accounted for more than 5 per cent of manufacturing jobs in 1963. This diversity has been caused by the grafting of several emerging industries onto the existing, traditional industrial structure. Those industries that characterized the Boston manufacturing sector throughout the first third of the present century were food products, apparel, printing and publishing, and the leather and shoe industry. Each of these industries has declined in absolute and relative importance in terms of jobs provided to the area's economy over the last two decades. The declines are the continuation of a pattern begun at the end of the last century.

The situation in fabricated metals and nonelectrical machinery is somewhat less clear. Both of them declined somewhat in importance in the decade ending in 1958, although the actual number of persons employed

Table 4-1

Employment in Selected Manufacturing Industries, Boston Metropolitan Area, 1947-68

Industry	1947 [a]	1958 [a]	1963 [a]	1965 [b]	1968 [b]
Employment as Fraction of Total SMSA Manufacturing Employment					
Electrical machinery	0.111	0.149	0.175	0.191	0.178
Machinery	.095	.090	.099	.095	.096
Food products	.109	.107	.091	.085	.074
Publishing	.086	.079	.086	.073	.068
Apparel	.090	.090	.078	.073	.065
Leather products	.104	.081	.067	.075	.068
Fabricated metals	.063	.061	.065	.087	.086
Fraction of total	0.657	0.658	0.661	0.679	0.630
Number of Manufacturing Employees					
Electrical machinery	30,089	42,679	47,522	57,211	54,784
Machinery	25,697	25,770	26,832	28,249	29,544
Food products	29,604	30,517	24,813	25,198	22,950
Publishing	23,206	22,584	23,472	22,019	20,751
Apparel	24,301	25,681	21,069	21,599	19,899
Leather products	28,245	23,176	18,294	22,211	20,603
Fabricated metals	17,099	17,500	17,603	25,664	26,539
Total itemized	178,241	187,907	179,605	202,151	195,070

[a] *Census of Manufactures*, 1963, vol. III.
[b] Based on tabulations of Dun and Bradstreet data.

remained almost constant from 1947 through 1963. The Boston economy has responded massively to each war in this century, perhaps because of the considerable excess capacity that has been available in the area.[b] It seems probable that the recent surge in the fabricated metals and non-electrical machinery industries can be explained in large measure by the demands of the Vietnam War and the national economic expansion that accompanied it.

Spatial Distribution of Major Industries in 1965

On the basis of the criteria set out in Chapter 2 the *Boston metropolitan area* has been divided into 20 analysis zones; seven of these are within the city of Boston.[c] Figure 4-1 shows the boundaries of the zones, and

---

[b] See Table 4-3, below, for the trend in employment at five-year intervals from 1920-65.

[c] The criteria used to define the analysis zones are given in Chapter 2, "Spatial Distribution of Major Industries in 1965." The use of "rings" to indicate distance from the CID is also discussed there.

Table C-3 gives their formal definitions. The need to reduce the spatial detail to a manageable level has resulted in a degree of heterogeneity within some of the zones. This should be kept in mind when the analysis zones are referred to in the discussion. Since there are 20 zones, 10 per cent of the employment of a given industry is required to be in a single zone in order for the industry to be considered "concentrated" in that zone.[d]

0 1 2 3 4 5 6
Miles

—·—·—·—City of Boston boundary
No highways shown due to large scale of map.
Labels in zones are descriptive; other towns may be in zones.

Figure 4-1. Map of Major Analysis Zones in the Boston Metropolitan Area

[d] Our definition of industrial concentration and its justification is also set out in "Spatial Distribution of Major Industries in 1965" in Chapter 2.

Table 4-2 displays the 1965 distribution of the seven largest industries within the metropolitan area. As in the other areas analysis zones were grouped into concentric rings surrounding the CID (central industrial district). The Roman numerals once again refer to these geographic rings. The first four industries listed in the table have declined since the end of World War II. In general these industries show major concentrations in the cities of Boston and Cambridge and in the Peabody-Lynn-Salem and Somerville-Everett analysis zones. The analysis zones within the city are interesting in that all contain more than 10 per cent of the area's total employment in one or more of these declining industries, including the concentration of the printing and publishing industry in Roxbury. To obtain a better idea of the great importance in the city of Boston proper of the food-processing, apparel, and publishing industries note the following: For food processing two of the four zones with employment concentrations of over 8 per cent are in Boston; for publishing six of eight concentrations of over 7 per cent are in Boston. It can easily be hypothesized that the past and continued massing of these industries in the central city no doubt accounts for a good part of the continuing decline of its industrial importance. In the case of the leather and shoe industry, Boston is relatively unimportant. Peabody-Lynn-Salem and Brockton at the opposite ends of ring IV together accounted for 60 per cent of 1965 employment in this industry.

The distribution of the fabricated metals and nonelectrical machinery industries represents a situation somewhere between that of the industries just reviewed and the electrical machinery industry, the "youngest" industry. For both fabricated metals and nonelectrical machinery, there is at least one concentration of over 10 per cent in the city and in Cambridge (ring II) or Peabody-Salem (ring IV to the north), but there are also concentrations in the Waltham-Newton analysis zone (ring II). For the electrical machinery industry nearly 50 per cent of all employment is in the Waltham-Newton (ring II) and Woburn-Burlington (ring III) analysis zones. The city of Boston had no major concentrations of this dynamic industry. The Peabody-Salem-Lynn zone best reflects the industrial heritage of the region. It contains major concentrations of employment in declining industries (leather products), stable industries (nonelectrical machinery) and of the electronics industry as well.

Net Change in the Spatial Distribution of Total Manufacturing Employment

Boston is unusual among major cities in general and our four sample cities in particular in that data are available describing the location of

Table 4-2

Geographic Distribution of Employment in Major Manufacturing Industries, Boston Metropolitan Area, 1965

(Per Cent of Total SMSA Manufacturing Employment in the Industry)

Number	Analysis Zone Description	Food Products	Apparel	Printing and Publishing	Leather Products	Fabricated Metals	Machinery	Electrical Machinery
	City of Boston							
1	CID	6.21	11.19	11.01	0.05	5.56	14.04	0.12
2	South Boston (I)	2.08	3.69	14.36	1.51	12.65	6.19	1.64
3	Charlestown-E. Boston (I)	25.40	3.35	0.18	0.09	24.30	0.57	1.31
4	Adjacent to CID (I)	8.77	32.96	10.69	14.01	0.59	0.62	0.13
6	CID Waterfront (I)	1.93	4.68	8.46	1.73	0.21	0.26	0.13
5	Roxbury (II)	4.89	6.10	10.75	0.89	4.56	0.96	1.15
7	W. Boston-Dorchester (II)	8.44	17.48	7.47	1.56	5.07	6.15	4.73
	Rest of Area							
10	Somerville-Everett (II)	8.52	2.54	6.38	3.92	9.67	5.56	2.05
11	Cambridge (II)	12.20	3.55	7.97	5.83	10.24	9.77	5.36
13	Waltham-Newton (II)	3.16	2.11	4.15	1.02	8.34	12.50	24.63
9	Wakefield-Reading (III)	0.52	0.42	1.76	2.63	0.06	0.50	3.65
12	Woburn-Burlington (III)	3.34	0.08	0.30	0.86	3.47	4.41	23.76
14	Sudbury-Lexington (III)	0.02	0.00	0.20	—	0.07	0.41	12.05
16	Needham-Walpole (III)	0.26	0.22	5.07	0.02	0.24	2.02	1.64
17	Quincy-Braintree (III)	2.58	0.02	1.97	0.76	3.18	5.14	0.39
18	Norwood-Milton (III)	1.51	1.57	4.44	1.85	4.72	3.31	4.24
8	Peabody-Salem-Lynn (IV)	3.25	4.14	2.58	41.44	4.58	22.90	10.86
15	Framingham-Natick (IV)	5.98	1.67	0.48	0.51	1.50	3.39	0.97
19	Hingham-Norwell (IV)		0.02	0.07	2.47	0.12	0.67	0.42
20	Brockton (IV)	0.93	4.20	1.69	18.82	0.88	0.59	0.76

Note: Roman numerals indicate distance from CID; for explanation see Chapter 2, "Spatial Distribution of Major Industries in 1965."

manufacturing employment on a spatially highly disaggregated basis and covering a long time span. The Massachusetts State Bureau of Labor and Industries has conducted a yearly survey of manufacturing since 1907, with data currently available for most towns on an annual basis since 1920. The yearly figures are averages of data taken on a monthly basis by the Statistics Division. One remarkable feature of these data are their consistency: Definitions have not changed since the survey was begun. In some cases this has proved to be a problem, especially in the classification of products which were not produced at the time the survey was initiated.

The historic developments of the manufacturing sector of the city of Boston and the noncentral-city analysis zones are presented in Table 4-3 for the period 1920-68. The longer time series data have also been used to define the traditional locations of manufacturing activity. For zones outside of Boston, the general criterion was that the zone had to contain 5 per cent or more of the area's total manufacturing employment in 1920. Such zones are specially noted in the tables.

Two further general notes on Table 4-3: The fraction of total employment at each point in time has been used in order to abstract from the very large cyclical changes that took place over this period, as alluded to in the first section of this chapter. Finally, there is a substantial difference between the figures for 1965 employment based on the Massachusetts census and computations based on the Dun and Bradstreet data, mainly it seems, because the Massachusetts data are restricted to firms having four or more employees while the D&B data have no such restriction. One would expect areas with large numbers of small firms, such as the city of Boston, Cambridge, and Peabody-Salem-Lynn to be underrepresented in the state data. It is probable that other differences in coverage also distort this relatively simple adjustment. Fortunately, the employment trends in the Massachusetts data are generally preserved over the 1965-68 period, so we do not have to confront the problem of determining whether the source of a difference in trend is due to a real change or simply arises from definitional differences.

During most of the 45-year period covered by the Massachusetts census, regional manufacturing employment declined. However, manufacturing activity in Boston grew strongly during both major wars of this century. In both cases, though, this growth proved evanescent. The levels of employment in 1930 and 1960 were approximately the same; both considerably below wartime highs. The period 1965 to 1968 included the Vietnam buildup and high levels of demand; again, as in previous war periods, manufacturing employment grew rapidly.

A major portion of the job loss over the period 1920-65, amounting to 40 per cent of the total, has been concentrated in the city of Boston. Boston's share of total employment in the area declined by 3 per cent be-

Table 4-3

Spatial Distribution of Manufacturing Employment, Boston Metropolitan Area, 1920-68
(Fraction of Total SMSA Manufacturing Employment)

Analysis Zone Number	Description	1920[a]	1925[a]	1930[a]	1935[a]	1940[a]	1945[a]	1950[a]	1955[a]	1960[a]	1965[a]	1965[b]	1968[b]
1-7	City of Boston	0.361	0.361	0.356	0.328	0.348	0.338	0.340	0.316	0.301	0.275	0.311	0.289
10[c]	Somerville-Everett (II)[d]	.096	.107	.111	.116	.111	.089	.110	.105	.095	.086	.076	.080
		.093	.102	.102	.103	.098	.073	.091	.089	.081	.081	.093	.087
11[c]	Cambridge (II)	.079	.073	.071	.073	.078	.084	.090	.117	.120	.112	.119	.105
13[c]	Waltham-Newton (II)	.016	.019	.016	.015	.015	.016	.020	.024	.035	.029	.016	.017
9	Wakefield-Reading (III)	.012	.015	.012	.013	.011	.009	.012	.017	.025	.033	.064	.058
12	Woburn-Burlington (III)	.001	.001	.001	.001	.001	.001	.001	.001	.004	.006	.027	.028
14	Sudbury-Lexington (III)	.007	.018	.017	.020	.021	.008	.020	.033	.034	.042	.031	.035
16	Needham-Walpole (III)	.040	.031	.038	.045	.055	.079	.048	.045	.062	.063	.029	.049
17[c]	Quincy-Braintree (III)	.029	.028	.030	.037	.036	.038	.036	.036	.041	.049	.049	.054
18	Norwood-Milton (III)	.030	.029	.030	.034	.033	.036	.035	.033	.031	.030	.029	.028
8[c]	Peabody-Salem-Lynn (IV)	.155	.145	.151	.151	.151	.178	.153	.144	.126	.134	.122	.132
15	Framingham-Natick (IV)	.027	.024	.020	.022	.024	.016	.028	.029	.029	.043	.031	.031
19	Hingham-Norwell (IV)	.018	.017	.013	.013	.009	.031	.010	.012	.012	.013	.006	.006
20	Brockton (IV)	.067	.061	.061	.061	.041	.036	.038	.030	.032	.033	.028	.028
	Total Employment	251,025	218,625	195,301	165,044	184,204	239,474	215,091	216,647	198,741	187,410	298,118	309,335

[a] Source: Unpublished data provided by the Massachusetts State Bureau of Labor and Industries. For description of data see Christene Bishop, "An Analysis of the Response of Population Change to Employment Change in an Urban Area," (Senior Thesis, Radcliffe College, 1968).

[b] Source: Dun and Bradstreet data.

[c] Traditional manufacturing area.

[d] Roman numerals show distance from CID; for explanation, see Chapter 2, "Spatial Distribution of Major Industries in 1965."

tween 1920 and 1935. This relative decline has continued to the present with a loss of over 20,000 jobs (over three-fourths of regional job loss) in the 15 years ending in 1965.

In 1965 there were five analysis zones outside the city of Boston that contained more than 5 per cent of all manufacturing jobs (based on D&B data). Of these the Peabody-Salem-Lynn (ring IV), the Somerville-Everett (ring II), and the Cambridge (ring II) zones have all maintained about the same fraction of manufacturing employment since 1920. These three zones formed a relatively continuous peninsula of industrial activity similar to the Cleveland City-Euclid pattern. The Woburn-Burlington (III) and Waltham-Newton (II) zones, on the other hand, have had their surge in manufacturing employment during the sixties. Three other analysis zones have experienced substantial amounts of manufacturing employment growth over recent years: The Sudbury-Lexington zone (ring III) has attracted manufacturing jobs only recently, while Quincy-Braintree (III) and Norwood-Milton (IV) are attaining levels not seen since the end of the World War II boom. Looking at the overall pattern that emerges one observes that Boston City is being ringed to the west and south with developing areas much like the areas west and south of Minneapolis. There is, however, a distinct difference in this case. In addition to these areas, which are practically adjacent to the central city, developments more removed are also occurring. Witness the experience of Woburn-Burlington (zone 12) and the developments of Norwood-Milton (zone 18) that have centered in Norwood, Randolph, and Stoughton.

It is possible that this dispersed pattern of growth may be partially explained by the age of the metropolitan area. The initial distribution of industry in the Boston area came during the period in which water provided the primary source of power. Thus, areas like Framingham-Natick, which were relatively far from the economic center of the area, became small industrial centers. Although this period passed with the introduction of steam power, it left a considerable capital stock of buildings and an industrial tradition. These factors have made the areas attractive locations for new, small firms and for other firms seeking locations with less congestion and lower site rents. Combined, these various elements have served to preserve, and sometimes greatly increase, the manufacturing activities in these areas.

Patterns of industrial succession in the regional economy also appear to have exerted an important impact on spatial patterns of growth. The renewed growth of the Waltham-Newton area, and recent industrial development in the Sudbury-Lexington and Woburn-Burlington areas represent clear departures from historic growth patterns in the region. This growth was produced in large part by the growth of the electronics industry near the famous circumferential Route 128. As was shown in the previous section, these three zones received over 60 per cent of the employment in this new industry. The dynamism of this industry pushed development into new areas and apparently has remade the traditional economy of the Waltham area.

Another factor of considerable importance is the spatial development of major highways. One can observe effects of the opening of Route 128 from Wakefield (in zone 9) to Needham (in zone 16) in 1951 on the analysis zones along its route by examining the change in the fraction of manufacturing employment in each of these zones over the 1950-55 period (Table 4-3). Needham-Walpole, Waltham-Newton, and Woburn-Burlington to a lesser extent, all show substantial increases. These gains were at the expense of the more traditional manufacturing zones, which lay along a line from Boston to Peabody. The linking of major highways to Route 128 from the south in the later half of the fifties no doubt has stimulated growth in the Quincy-Braintree area. Less clear are the effects on nearby analysis zones of the opening, north of the Boston Standard Metropolitan Statistical Area (SMSA), of Interstate 495 in the early sixties. Christine Bishop indicates in her study that the *employment potential* of the Wakefield-Reading and Woburn-Burlington zones increased markedly over the period 1959-64 while that of the analysis zones to the east of these zones generally declined.[2]

Unfortunately, the data on the distribution of manufacturing employment within the city of Boston is available only from the DMI (Duns Market Identifier) file. The city has been divided into seven analysis zones, which are shown in Figure 3-1 and listed in Table 4-4. The table presents the fraction of total SMSA manufacturing employment present in each zone in both years. Three of the zones, all in ring I, represent areas with significant commercial waterfront facilities: Charlestown-East Boston (zone 3) includes the northern side of the main harbor; on the southern side of the harbor is South Boston (zone 2); to the east and to the west is the CID Waterfront (zone 6), composed of a single zip code containing only dockside and wharf facilities. The West Boston-Dorchester area in ring II is really best thought of as a "rest of the city" category. Each of the other six analysis zones within the city contains high concentrations of industrial employment. The West Boston-Dorchester zone has a number of jobs spread quite evenly over a relatively large area. Historically, manufacturing activity was concentrated in the harbor area and then spread back from the waterfront in South Boston and along the Charles River shore.

The city as a whole lost approximately 2,000 manufacturing jobs between 1965 and 1968. As a result it experienced a major decline in its share of SMSA manufacturing employment. The experience of individual zones within the city has been surprisingly uneven. The CID accounted for

Table 4-4

Distribution of Manufacturing Employment, Boston, 1965 and 1968 (Fraction of SMSA Employment)

Number	Analysis Zone Description	1965	1968
1 [a]	Central industrial district	0.046	0.025
2 [a]	South Boston (I)	.045	.060
3 [a]	Charlestown-E. Boston (I)	.053	.054
4 [b]	Adjacent to CID (I)	.058	.051
6 [c]	CID Waterfront (I)	.017	.016
5 [c]	Roxbury (II)	.030	.022
7 [b]	W. Boston-Dorchester (II)	.062	.061
	City total	0.311	0.289

Note: Roman numerals indicate distance from CID; see Chapter 2, "Spatial Distribution of Major Industries in 1965," for explanation.
[a] Traditional manufacturing area; poverty area.
[b] Traditional manufacturing area.
[c] Poverty area.

two-thirds of the total number of job losses in the city. Likewise, the area to the south and adjacent to the CID suffered major losses of employment. The Roxbury area lost the second largest share of employment. The census definition of Roxbury and the CID itself as poverty areas ought to be noted.

Interestingly, both the South Boston and Charlestown-East Boston analysis zones showed gains and the CID waterfront zone remained practically unchanged. This may reflect a resurgent demand for waterfront locations by production-supporting activities, although potential savings on transportation costs associated with the moving of supplies from the wharf district may attract production operations to these areas. Both the CID waterfront and the Charlestown-East Boston areas are relatively sparsely populated, so their being defined as poverty areas should not connote an image of the urban ghetto.

The Process of Change

The Composition of Net Change

As indicated in Table 4-5, the rate of overall locational activity in the Boston area was relatively modest. It had the lowest rate of relocation of employment within the area and the second lowest rate of employment of new firms of the four sample SMSAs. The employment in relocating,

Table 4-5

Numbers of Relocating, New, and Defunct Establishments and Employment in Boston, 1965-68

	Relocations		New		Defunct	
	Number	Percentage of 1965 Base	Number	Percentage of 1965 Base	Number	Percentage of 1965 Base
Establishments	567	9.8	354	6.1	779	13.4
Employment	13,998 [a]	4.7	3,884	1.3	23,849	8.0

[a] This is the employment of relocating establishments at their origin location.

new, and defunct establishments, though, is still over 5 per cent of the 1965 base on an annual basis.

The basic data on the composition of the net change in employment in each of the Boston area analysis zones is presented in Table 4-6. Because of the relatively diffused pattern of traditional manufacturing centers and the traditions of similar activity in some zones at the periphery of the metropolitan area, we might anticipate finding much more heterogeneous patterns and processes of employment change in Boston than in the other sample regions. The pattern of growing and declining areas confirms this to some extent. Six zones lost employment over the period, three in Boston. Besides Roxbury only one of these, Woburn-Burlington, is not a traditional manufacturing site. There is general consistency among these zones in the composition of their losses: Five of six experienced net out-migration of employment, usually large, and the same five were the only zones in the SMSA to lose employment from the contraction of stationary establishments. The exception in both cases was Cambridge, which included growing establishments (almost 3,000 jobs) and had a net in-migration of nearly 900 jobs, many of which came from Boston. A very large death file, second only to the CIDs nearly 4,000, accounted for its net decline. On this basis we might expect Cambridge to begin growing again in the near future. Note that the pattern in Boston for the importance of stationary establishments is similar to that in Cleveland: In every case those zones with declining employment in these establishments declined overall.

The composition of the zones with the greatest absolute growth is also of interest. Four of the five zones with the greatest growth (2, 8, 10, 17, and 18) are traditional manufacturing centers, although they are scattered about the area—one in ring I, one in ring II, two in III, and one in IV. No traditional zones in the Twin Cities displayed even relative growth; and in Cleveland, while two traditional zones grew, only the Berea area showed a substantial increase. In each of the five Boston-area

Table 4-6

Composition of the Net Change in Manufacturing Employment in Boston Area Analysis Zones, 1965 vs. 1968 (Number of Employees)

Number	Analysis Zone Description	1965 Base	Net Change	Movers At Origins	Movers At Destinations	Births	Deaths	Change in Stationary Establishments
	City of Boston							
1 [a]	CID	13,634	−5,910	1,486	430	164	3,950	−1,068
2 [a]	South Boston (I)	13,452	4,982	1,107	549	142	980	6,378
3 [a]	Charlestown-E. Boston (I)	15,742	961	366	561	20	992	1,738
4 [b]	Adjacent to CID (I)	17,175	−1,436	1,129	986	289	1,316	−266
6 [c]	CID waterfront (I)	5,109	32	593	388	39	301	499
5 [c]	Roxbury (II)	8,869	−1,857	523	194	29	1,100	−457
7 [b]	W. Boston-Dorchester (II)	18,620	263	849	583	152	2,931	3,308
	Boston total	92,601	−2,965	6,053	3,691	835	11,570	10,132
	Rest of Area							
10 [b]	Somerville-Everett (II)	22,464	1,967	904	1,614	729	910	1,438
11 [b]	Cambridge (II)	27,665	−689	2,367	1,413	437	3,253	3,081
13 [b]	Waltham-Newton (II)	35,720	−3,015	615	1,247	446	2,464	−1,629
9	Wakefield-Reading (III)	4,657	649	361	278	154	589	1,167
12	Woburn-Burlington (III)	18,896	−1,159	688	1,153	271	419	−1,476
14	Sudbury-Lexington (III)	8,173	455	288	173	15	29	584
16	Needham-Walpole (III)	9,241	1,796	331	228	145	222	584
17 [b]	Quincy-Braintree (III)	8,516	6,602	162	778	64	229	1,976
18	Norwood-Milton (III)	14,654	2,048	162	457	164	537	6,151
8 [b]	Peabody-Salem-Lynn (IV)	36,341	4,595	1,130	516	360	2,831	2,126
15	Framingham-Natick (IV)	9,158	477	348	513	86	208	7,680
19	Hingham-Stoughton (IV)	1,793	120	164	98	34		434
20 [b]	Brockton (IV)	8,239	336	425	141	144	588	152
	Total	298,118	11,217	13,998	12,300	3,884	23,849	32,880

Note: Roman numerals indicate distance from CID; for explanation, see Chapter 2, "Spatial Distribution of Major Industries in 1965."
[a] Traditional manufacturing area.
[b] Traditional manufacturing area; poverty area.
[c] Poverty area.

zones the change in stationary firms played an important role. Indeed, in three of the zones (2, 8, and 17) employment in these firms increased by over 6,000 jobs.[e] Whereas this certainly accounts for most of the net change, in two zones (Peabody-Salem-Lynn and Somerville-Everett) the establishment of new firms accounted for large increases in the number of employees. Likewise, three zones (in rings II and III) had sizable net in-migration.

The relocation pattern in Boston is somewhat different from that of the other SMSAs, in which there is a relatively simple pattern of movement from the central city to the suburbs, albeit with considerable cross migration and with the overall pattern being produced by a large number of short, but on balance outward, moves. In Boston, the majority of the moves are again short,[f] but there is considerable interchange among the traditional manufacturing areas. The basic pattern, though it is from the central city to Cambridge and Somerville-Everett (both in ring II) and then beyond, is still basically outward.

As found in Cleveland and the Twin Cities, the destinations of new establishments and relocating ones are roughly correlated. In the Boston area more than 200 employees of new firms were brought into six analysis zones over the observation period. Only the zone adjacent to the CID was in the central city. Two were adjacent to the central city (8 and 11), and the rest were separated from it by at least one analysis zone (8, 12 and 13). Of these, however, only the Woburn-Burlington zone was not a traditional manufacturing center. This is similar to the pattern found in Cleveland but not in the Twin Cities.[g]

The spatial distribution of the components of net change is summarized in Figure 4-2. The relatively inferior position of the Boston CID is evident. As in the Cleveland and Minneapolis cases the overall impression is of an upward slope to the right—the outlying areas gaining employment. The modest downturn in this process in the furthest ring was expected, given the presence of the older cities, Brockton and Peabody-Salem-Lynn,

---

[e] In South Boston 4,700 of these jobs were in the scientific instruments industry; in Peabody-Salem-Lynn 1,900 were in the transportation equipment industry and 1,100 in scientific instruments; in Quincy-Braintree 6,000 were in the transportation equipment industry, mostly in shipbuilding.

[f] The dominance of the short-move pattern of relocating establishments was first documented by Harold F. Williamson in his study of the determinants of the relocation decision of firms in the Chicago area. See "An Empirical Analysis of the Movement of Manufacturing Firms in the Chicago Metropolitan Area," Ph.D. dissertation, Yale University, 1969.

[g] In Minneapolis-St. Paul there were 4,300 jobs in new establishments apart from the 5,000 jobs provided by a single establishment in zone 10. Of the five zones receiving more than 300 of the jobs, only one, the Minneapolis CID, is a traditional zone. In Cleveland there were 7,708 jobs in new establishments. Six zones received more than 400 of these jobs. Five of these are defined as traditional areas; four of them, including the CID, are in the central city.

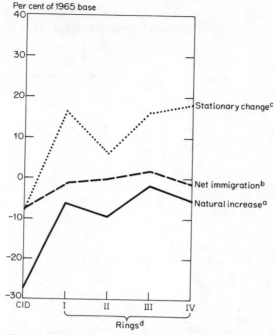

Per cent of 1965 base

Stationary change[c]

Net immigration[b]

Natural increase[a]

Rings[d]

[a] Equals employment of new establishments minus employment of establishments going out of business.
[b] Equals employment of in-migrating establishments minus employment of out-migrating establishments.
[c] Equals the change in employment of establishments that did not change their location over the period.
[d] Rings indicate distance from the CID; for explanation, see the section "Spatial Distribution of Major Industries in 1965" in chapter 2. The zones included in each ring are identified in Table 4-2.

Figure 4-2. Components of Change in the Spatial Distribution of Employment. Boston Metropolitan Area, 1965-68

in that ring. Interestingly, the area immediately adjacent to the CID did substantially better in terms of natural increase and stationary change than those slightly further away from the CID. The latter group includes Cambridge and Everett-Somerville. Finally, although not as strong as in some other cities, the decentralizing effect of migration is clear.

Importance of Industrial Structure

The same shift-share measures employed in the previous two chapters appear in Table 4-7 for the Boston area analysis zones. (These measures are described in Chapter 2, "The Process of Change.") The general rela-

Table 4-7

Shift-Share Measures for the Boston Metropolitan Area, 1968 Relative to 1965 (Per Cent)

Analysis Zone		Growth Relative to SMSA	Competitive Advantage	Comparative Industrial Structure
Number	Description			
	City of Boston			
1 [a]	Central industrial district	−45.09	−41.65	−5.89
2 [a]	South Boston (I)	24.71	23.31	1.68
3 [a]	Charlestown-E. Boston (I)	2.77	7.63	−5.00
4 [b]	Adjacent to CID (I)	−11.18	−2.78	−8.64
6 [c]	CID Waterfront (I)	−2.47	4.09	−6.46
5 [c]	Roxbury (II)	−23.37	−20.04	−4.16
7 [b]	W. Boston-Dorchester (II)	−1.70	2.41	−4.07
	Rest of Area			
10 [b]	Somerville-Everett (II)	5.14	0.05	5.07
11 [b]	Cambridge (II)	−5.83	−7.28	1.55
13 [b]	Waltham-Newton (II)	−11.33	−11.14	−0.20
9	Wakefield-Reading (III)	9.45	12.49	−3.36
12	Woburn-Burlington (III)	−9.02	−4.66	−4.57
14	Sudbury-Lexington (III)	2.27	7.07	−4.91
16	Needham-Walpole (III)	13.55	11.19	2.71
17 [b]	Quincy-Braintree (III)	41.88	27.20	20.15
18	Norwood-Milton (III)	9.48	11.50	−1.74
8 [b]	Peabody-Salem-Lynn (IV)	8.41	4.45	4.13
15	Framingham-Natick (IV)	1.94	−0.64	2.56
19	Hingham-Stoughton (IV)	3.30	6.46	−3.26
20 [b]	Brockton (IV)	0.87	8.03	−7.22

Note: Roman numerals indicate distance from CID; for explanation, see Chapter 2, "Spatial Distribution of Major Industries in 1965."
[a] Traditional manufacturing area; poverty area.
[b] Traditional manufacturing area.
[c] Poverty area.

tionship between the relative growth of an analysis zone and its comparative industrial structure is not very strong. In six cases the direction of growth predicted on the basis of the 1965 industry mix in the zone and industry growth rates would have been incorrect. This is better than the results for Cleveland but worse than those for the Twin Cities.

Earlier in this chapter it was stated that the industrial composition of Boston represents something of an amalgam of traditional and new industries. A relevant question is how the industry mix in zones that were traditional manufacturing locations has adjusted to this change. The measure of comparative industrial structure provides the basic information. Of the five central-city, traditional zones only South Boston has adjusted its structure toward the newer, growing industries. Surprisingly Peabody-Salem-Lynn, Cambridge, Somerville-Everett, and Quincy-Braintree have all adjusted their industrial composition to produce a favorable balance of growing industries. Only Brockton, still dominated by the shoe industry, and Waltham-Newton showed comparatively poor mixes. The Waltham-Newton result is something of a quirk, however, as it is dominated by the electrical machinery industry, which declined slightly over the period.

The competitive positions of central-city analysis zones varied sharply: The CID was the worst in the SMSA; South Boston was the second best. As expected Roxbury turned out to be an unattractive location, second only to the CID. However, none of the other three non-CID poverty areas was as unattractive as similar areas in Cleveland and Minneapolis-St. Paul. Outside the central city there were three zones (11, 12, and 13) adjacent to Boston proper, which were uncompetitive. The zones in the ring beyond them, though, were all attractive according to the competitive advantage measure. This kind of pattern is not repeated in the other SMSAs,[h] and seems to point up the continuing effects of the pattern of earlier development.

---

[h] Actually in Cleveland the East Cleveland-Shaker Heights zone had a competitive advantage measure of −0.90, which is considered to be negligible. Both Cleveland and the Twin Cities had noncompetitive zones at their periphery.

5 Phoenix

Any description of the historical patterns of industrial composition and location within the Phoenix Standard Metropolitan Statistical Area (SMSA) necessarily differs from that of the other cities included in this discussion because of the very recent advent of the Phoenix area as important industrially. In 1950 there were only 8,800 manufacturing jobs in Maricopa County; by 1965 this number had increased to nearly 50,000. The real impetus for industrial development of the Phoenix area came during the Second World War, when a major aluminum extruding plant was built in the area. At the same time Goodyear Aircraft and AiResearch Manufacturing Company opened sizable operations. During the 1940s the population of both the city of Phoenix and of Maricopa County nearly doubled to 106,800 and 331,800, respectively. The decade of real industrial growth, however, was to follow.

Industrial Composition

As shown in Chapter 1 the industrial composition of the Phoenix area as of 1963 is dominated by the two machinery-producing industries, the transportation equipment industry and the food-processing and printing and publishing industries. Table 5-1 shows the relative importance of these industries at intervals from 1954 to the present. Both the fraction of total manufacturing employment in each of these industries and the number of employees is given for the same five points in time. The employee figures demonstrate the tremendous growth that occurred during the 15-year observation period. For 1965 and 1968 employment figures based on both the Dun and Bradstreet (D&B) data and data from the Employment Security Commission are included because of some significant differences in the industrial distribution of employment shown by the two sources. While some of the divergence can be explained by variation in coverage,[a] the differences shown for the transportation equipment (SIC 37) and electronics (SIC 36) industries are too large to be attributed to this factor

---

[a] The Employment Security Commission only covers firms with four or more employees.

Table 5-1

Employment in Selected Manufacturing Industries, Phoenix Metropolitan Area, 1954-68

Industry	1954[a]	1958[a]	1963[b]	1965 D&B[c]	1965 ESC[a]	1968 D&B[c]	1968 ESC[a]
Employment as Fraction of Total SMSA Manufacturing Employment							
Electrical machinery	0.037	0.100	0.222	0.354	0.259	0.419	0.324
Machinery	.071	.094	.137	.161	.139	.157	.132
Transportation equip.	.235	.219	.138	.054	.117	.045	.132
Food products	.148	.194	.127	.091	.099	.074	.078
Publishing	.090	.078	.069	.057	.060	.047	.052
Fraction of total	0.581	0.685	0.694	0.717	0.674	0.742	0.718
Number of Manufacturing Employees							
Electrical machinery	536	2,411	8,985	18,697	12,518	28,134	21,029
Machinery	1,014	2,273	5,556	8,508	6,680	10,579	8,591
Transportation equip.	3,375	5,274	5,568	2,871	5,652	3,028	8,581
Food products	2,136	4,654	5,146	4,805	4,807	4,728	5,017
Publishing	1,293	1,879	2,802	2,998	2,885	3,199	4,910
Total	14,363	23,984	28,057	37,879	32,542	49,668	48,159

[a] Based on data provided by the Employment Security Commission of Arizona (ESC).
[b] *Census of Manufactures*, 1963, vol. III.
[c] Tabulations of Dun and Bradstreet data.

alone; it seems likely that differences in the classification of employment by the establishment's dominant output largely account for the differences in distribution.[b]

Probably the most striking aspect of these statistics is the phenomenal and accelerating growth in total employment that has occurred in recent years. The increase in the relative importance of the electrical machinery industry (SIC 36) over the period, viewed within this framework, is doubly impressive. This industry alone provides almost a third of all manufacturing jobs. It is also quite probably responsible for much of the employment in the production of instruments and scientific equipment, which accounts for about 5 per cent of total manufacturing employment in 1963.

Among the other major industries, only the nonelectrical machinery industry has been able to show consistent gains in importance. Although its share of jobs has fallen slightly since 1965, the increase in the number of jobs shows that it has shared in the general expansion of durable goods

---

[b] A quirk in the Standard Industrial Classification contributes to this confusion. Computers are classed under nonelectrical machinery (SIC 356) rather than electrical machinery. This problem is also important in the classification of employment in the Minneapolis-St. Paul area.

production observed in the other sample cities. The expansion has also given considerable impetus to the transportation equipment industry (SIC 37), which had stagnated from the mid-fifties until the beginning of the Vietnam build-up. The food and food-processing industry has declined the most precipitously. While the number it employs has remained relatively constant over the 15-year period beginning in 1954, its share of industrial employment has been practically halved, to about 8 per cent. The printing and publishing industry has fared little better.

Even with the amazing growth in manufacturing employment in the past decade, this sector still accounted for only 21 per cent of the area's jobs, although up considerably from 16 per cent in 1954. Wholesale and retail trade constitutes the largest single sector and combined with the service sector accounts for over 40 per cent of jobs—a share that has remained practically constant over the period. The relative importance of the governmental sector has increased only slightly, while the financial sector increased substantially to about 7 per cent of total employment by 1968. Consistent with the national experience, these gains were made at the expense of the construction and the transportation, communication, and public utility sectors.

Spatial Distribution of Major Industries in 1965

For our analysis the *Phoenix area* has been divided into 14 analysis zones. Ten of these are in the central city, which very much dominates the area. According to the criteria used for the other three sample metropolitan areas, then, about 15 per cent of an industry's employment must be located in a given analysis zone for the industry to be considered "concentrated" in that zone.[c] The analysis zones are shown on the map in Figure 5-1, and their formal definitions are given in Appendix Table C-4.

The major industries in Phoenix, like those in the other sample cities, display significant concentrations (see Table 5-2). The most heavily concentrated is the transportation equipment industry, with 65 per cent of all its jobs located in the Goodyear-Glendale area and an additional 21 per cent in Mesa-Tempe. The printing and publishing and nonelectrical machinery industries exhibit high employment concentrations. The former has over 80 per cent of its employment in or adjacent to the CID, reflecting the widely recognized need for quick communication between

---

[c] The criteria used to define the analysis zones and the definition of an employment concentration are given in Chapter 2, "Spatial Distribution of Major Industries in 1965." The use of "rings" to indicate distance from the CID is also discussed there.

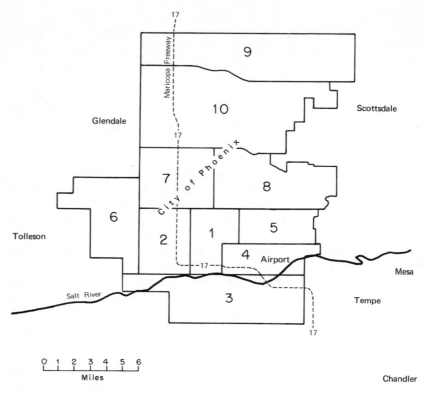

Figure 5-1. Map of Analysis Zones in the Phoenix Metropolitan Area

publishers and their clients; this pattern coincides closely with those observed in other cities. The major concentration of the nonelectrical machinery industry in the extreme north of Phoenix is in two large General Electric plants employing several thousand, although a large cluster of smaller, related firms is also present.

In the base year the electronics industry was concentrated in the two zones immediately east of the CID (4 and 5) and in Scottsdale (ring II). In two of these (zone 5 and Scottsdale) the jobs provided by the industry accounted for nine out of ten manufacturing jobs, while in the other it was only 15 per cent. The transportation equipment industry is concentrated in two zones, which together account for nearly 85 per cent of all the industry's employment in the Phoenix area. The Goodyear-Glendale area, to the west of the central city in ring III, houses more than 60 per cent of the industry's jobs, the single greatest concentration observed in any of the sample cities.

85

Table 5-2

Geographic Distribution of Employment in Major Manufacturing Industries, Phoenix Metropolitan Area, 1965

(Per Cent of Total SMSA Manufacturing Employment in the Industry)

Analysis Zone Number	Description	Food Products	Printing and Pub-lishing	Ma-chinery	Electrical Ma-chinery	Transpor-tation Equip-ment
	City of Phoenix					
1	Central industrial district	20.30	52.93	3.46	0.18	4.75
2	West of CID (I)	19.15	15.77	2.57	0.16	2.00
4	Southwest of CID (I)	19.37	6.17	15.80	24.33	3.74
5	East of CID (I)	9.20	0.43	1.66	36.36	0.10
7	Northwest of CID (I)	7.30	8.00	9.16	6.63	1.58
8	Northeast of CID (I)	6.43	3.94	3.06	——	0.25
6	West of CID (II)	2.81	1.23	——	1.33	0.03
10	North of CID (II)	0.43	3.57	——	0.01	——
3	South of CID (II)	1.68	0.86	0.98	——	0.22
9	North of CID (III)	1.71	——	59.83	——	——
	Rest of Area					
11	Scottsdale (II)	0.04	2.16	0.03	15.65	0.43
12	Tempe-Mesa (II)	7.53	4.90	2.94	1.53	21.60
13	Avondale-Buckeye (III)	0.08	0.04	0.12	——	0.03
14	Goodyear-Glendale (III)	3.68	0.80	0.90	4.01	65.00

Note: Roman numerals indicate distance from CID. For explanation, see Chapter 2, "Spatial Distribution of Major Industries in 1965."

Net Change in the Spatial Distribution of Total Manufacturing Employment

In discussing the distribution of jobs in the Phoenix area in recent years, we are departing from the format adopted for presentation of the other sample cities in that only the period 1965-68 is being considered explicitly. The reason for this is the great expansion of the boundaries of the city of Phoenix over the period 1950-65. As shown in Figure 5-2 Phoenix increased in area from 17.1 square miles in 1950 to 245.7 square miles by 1965. From 1965 to 1968 the area remained roughly constant. Another reason for considering this limited period is the small fraction of employment located outside of Phoenix in incorporated areas. Prior to the study period in 1963 only 13 per cent of total manufacturing employment was located in these areas; 78 per cent was in Phoenix; and the residual was in unincorporated areas.

The distribution of employment in 1965 and 1968 is presented in Table

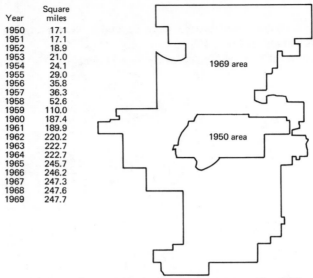

Year	Square miles
1950	17.1
1951	17.1
1952	18.9
1953	21.0
1954	24.1
1955	29.0
1956	35.8
1957	36.3
1958	52.6
1959	110.0
1960	187.4
1961	189.9
1962	220.2
1963	222.7
1964	222.7
1965	245.7
1966	246.2
1967	247.3
1968	247.6
1969	247.7

Source: Adapted from *Arizona Statistical Review,* Valley National Bank of Phoenix, 1969.

Figure 5-2. Growth of the Phoenix Incorporated Area, 1950-69

5-3.[d] The number of jobs in each zone as well as the fraction of total manufacturing employment accounted for by each zone are displayed in Table 5-3. Because of the tremendous growth of employment in the area, it is possible for a zone to lose a considerable portion of its share of total employment and still show an increase in the number of jobs there. A quick reading of the table shows that a substantial redistribution of industrial activity has occurred over the period. Interestingly, even with the greatly augmented size of the central city the fraction of employment outside of it increased by 2.7 per cent of the total, with the Tempe-Mesa area accounting for the increase. This single analysis zone is now the location of over 10 per cent of all manufacturing jobs.

The table also shows those zones classified as traditional manufacturing areas and poverty areas. Phoenix is the only sample SMSA that has any poverty areas outside of the central city, and here all of the poverty areas including the two in the central city are on the periphery. Actually Scottsdale is the only section along the central-city periphery that has not been

---

[d] Zones 4 and 5 contain a larger fraction of the total area manufacturing employment than is desirable for our analysis. However, each zone is a single zip code area, our smallest admissible geographical unit.

Table 5-3

Spatial Distribution of Manufacturing Employment, Phoenix Metropolitan Area, 1965 and 1968

(Fraction of Total SMSA Manufacturing Employment)

		1965		1968	
Number	Analysis Zone Description	Number of Manufacturing Employment	Fraction of SMSA Manufacturing Employment	Number of Manufacturing Employment	Fraction of SMSA Manufacturing Employment
	City of Phoenix				
1 [a]	Central industrial district	4,007	0.076	3,904	0.058
2 [a]	West of CID (I)	5,667	.107	7,372	.110
4 [a]	Southwest of CID (I)	8,680	.164	8,318	.124
5 [a]	East of CID (I)	7,574	.143	12,830	.191
7	Northwest of CID (I)	4,485	.084	4,323	.064
8	Northeast of CID (I)	3,170	.060	3,214	.048
6 [b]	West of CID (II)	705	.014	1,242	.018
10	North of CID (II)	1,247	.023	3,067	.046
3 [b]	South of CID (III)	803	.015	1,429	.021
9 [b]	North of CID (III)	5,430	.103	5,564	.083
	Rest of Area				
11	Scottsdale (II)	3,181	.060	3,460	.051
12 [b]	Tempe-Mesa (II)	3,422	.065	7,091	.106
13 [b]	Avondale-Buckeye (III)	119	.002	139	.002
14 [b]	Goodyear-Glendale (III)	4,326	0.082	5,171	0.077

Note: Roman numerals indicate distance from CID. For explanation, see Chapter 2, "Spatial Distribution of Major Industries in 1965."
[a] Traditional manufacturing area.
[b] Poverty area.

so classified. The reasons for this pattern, other than that Tempe and Mesa have long been Mexican centers, are not clear. However, the newness of the development of the metropolitan area in general may be a significant factor.[1] None of the poverty areas actually lost employment over the period, and they generally maintained their share of the SMSA's employment. In this light they stand in sharp contrast with similar areas in the other SMSAs. One reason for this may be the substantially lower density of settlement in those areas, which makes it possible for a firm to locate in these poverty areas but not to be too close to the more unpleasant aspects of such neighborhoods.

The traditional manufacturing zones were defined partially on the basis of a map, prepared by the Phoenix Chamber of Commerce, displaying the locations of new establishments with 20 or more employees in the Phoenix area over the 1948-57 period. The zones receiving the bulk of these establishments would, in this very young city, have to be considered traditional sites of manufacturing activity. Of the four zones classified as traditional, two have lost relative and absolute employment over the period. Both of these zones, the CID and zone 4 southwest of the CID, are centrally located. But others, which are also centrally located, have gained employment. Indeed, the increase in the share of total employment of the zone immediately east of the CID was almost enough to offset the share loss in the other two zones. By 1968, 19 per cent of all manufacturing jobs in the SMSA were in this single zone.

The Process of Change

The Composition of Net Change

There was a greater volume of locational activity within Phoenix over the observation period than in any of the other sample metropolitan areas (Table 5-4). The rates of births and deaths of establishments are higher in Phoenix than elsewhere, reflecting the interrelation of the two phenomena.[e] The fraction of firms relocating and the change in employment of relocating firms were lower in Phoenix than in the other SMSAs covered

Table 5-4

Numbers of Relocating, New, and Defunct Establishments and Employment in Phoenix: 1965-68

	Relocations		New		Defunct	
	Number	Percentage of 1965 Base	Number	Percentage of 1965 Base	Number	Percentage of 1965 Base
Establishments	106	8.9	290	24.4	240	20.2
Employment	2,465 [a]	4.7	6,380	12.1	2,821	5.3

[a] This is the employment of relocating establishments at their origin location.

---

[e] As mentioned in Appendix A, for Phoenix we were fortunate in having supplemental data providing very good information on new firms, and this in part explains the higher birth rate. In general, the Dun and Bradstreet data can be relied upon to reflect a firm's demise immediately. Our experience with the data, though, shows that there is a lag in entering new firms in the file. This means that our 1968 birth file (but not 1966 or 1967) in all the SMSAs initially contained about 65 per cent of the actual number of births. Our data checks permitted us to adjust this somewhat, but it is likely that this file is still incomplete, except for Phoenix.

in this study, possibly because many of the establishments had been at their initial location for only a relatively short time.

The basic data on the composition of net change are presented in Table 5-5. The feature most different in Phoenix from the other SMSAs is the lack of any consistent migration pattern. The CID and the zone to its immediate southeast are the only two centralized zones to show net out-migrations. Similarly, for the four noncentral-city analysis zones net migration is unimportant. Another distinctive feature is the relative importance of new firms; in nine of the 14 zones the net natural increase is positive. Again, it is only the CID and the zone to its southwest and the two zones immediately north of the CID (7 and 8) that show significant losses from the birth-death process. The opening of a large electronics plant in the Tempe-Mesa area (ring II) accounts entirely for this zone's spectacular growth over the period. The same thing occurred in the westernmost central-city zone (zone 6), resulting in a sizable net increase in employment over the period. With these two exceptions, net increases in employment of more than 500 are accounted for, in all the zones, by increases in employment of stationary establishments.

The spatial distribution of the components of net change has been summarized graphically for Phoenix in Figure 5-3. Net migration shows very little pattern and, if anything, favors the central city. However, both natural increase and employment change in stationary establishments exhibit a fairly strong decentralized pattern. The opening of the very large plant in ring II dominates the natural increase curve. The distribution of the increase in employment of stationary establishments favors non-CID central-city areas and the ring surrounding it and declines in the outermost ring.

Importance of Industrial Structure

The shift-share measures for the Phoenix area are presented in Table 5-6.[f] In general, as the number of areas included in a shift-share analysis decreases, the comparative differences tend to be magnified. This is what has occurred in the Phoenix data. For the Phoenix analysis zones there is little relation between the relative growth of a zone and its comparative industrial structure. If one looks at the five zones that had relative growth rates in excess of 20 per cent, it is seen that three (zones 3, 6, and 12) actually had negative scores for the measure of comparative industrial

---

[f] For definitions of the shift-share measures and a discussion of the rationale for using them here, see Chapter 2, "The Process of Change."

Table 5-5

Composition of Net Change in Manufacturing Employment, Phoenix Area Analysis Zones, 1965 vs. 1968
(Number of Employees)

Number	Analysis Zone Description	1965 Base	Net Change	Movers Origins	Movers Destinations	Births	Deaths	Change in Stationary Establish.
	City of Phoenix							
1 [a]	CID	4,007	−103	278	164	155	326	182
2 [a]	West of CID (I)	5,667	1,705	206	927	375	65	674
4 [a]	Southwest of CID (I)	8,680	−362	303	229	364	629	−23
5 [a]	East of CID (I)	7,574	5,256	4	6	23	8	5,239
7	Northwest of CID (I)	4,485	−162	80	198	374	644	−10
8	Northeast of CID (I)	3,170	44	64	69	185	271	125
6 [b]	West of CID (II)	705	537	35	—	880	120	−188
10	North of CID (II)	1,247	1,820	3	—	26	101	1,898
3 [b]	South of CID (II)	803	626	31	56	220	67	448
9 [b]	North of CID (III)	5,430	134	750	10	64	61	871
	Phoenix total	41,063	9,495	1,754	1,659	2,666	2,292	9,216
	Rest of Area							
11	Scottsdale (II)	3,181	279	678	680	58	10	229
12 [b]	Tempe-Mesa (II)	3,422	3,669	32	69	3,563	492	561
13 [b]	Avondale-Buckeye (III)	119	20	—	—	32	1	−11
14 [b]	Goodyear-Glendale (III)	4,326	845	1	1	61	6	789
	Total	52,816	14,308	2,465	2,406	6,380	2,801	10,789

Note: Roman numerals indicate distance from CID. For explanation, see Chapter 2, "Spatial Distribution of Major Industries in 1965."
[a] Traditional manufacturing area.
[b] Poverty area.

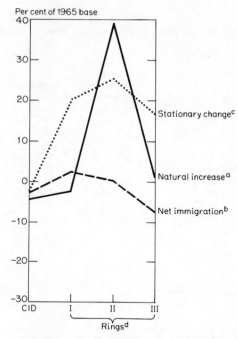

Per cent of 1965 base

a Equals employment of new establishments minus employment of establishments going out of business.
b Equals employment of in-migrating establishments minus employment of out-migrating establishments.
c Equals the change in employment of establishments that did not change their location over the period.
d Rings indicate distance from the CID; for explanation, see the section "Spatial Distribution of Major Industries in 1965" in chapter 2. The zones included in the rings are identified in Table 5-2.

Figure 5-3. Components of Change in the Spatial Distribution of Employment, Phoenix Metropolitan Area, 1965-68

structure. Only for zone 10, with its jobs almost completely concentrated in the production of scientific instruments, was the industrial structure of dominant importance.

Contrary to the findings for the other SMSAs five of the six analysis zones defined as poverty areas were found to be relatively attractive as

Table 5-6

Shift-Share Measures for Phoenix Metropolitan Area, 1968 Relative to 1965 (Per Cent)

Analysis Zone		Growth Relative to SMSA	Competitive Advantage	Comparative Industrial Structure
Number	Description			
	City of Phoenix			
1 [a]	Central industrial district	−23.34	−8.25	−16.44
2 [a]	West of CID (I)	2.30	21.85	−20.01
4 [a]	Southwest of CID (I)	−24.60	−26.45	2.46
5 [a]	East of CID (I)	24.97	13.95	12.81
7	Northwest of CID (I)	−24.16	−18.16	−7.30
8	Northeast of CID (I)	−20.22	−24.50	5.37
6 [b]	West of CID (II)	27.86	32.34	−6.60
10	North of CID (II)	48.33	2.62	46.92
3 [b]	South of CID (II)	28.58	44.92	−22.87
9 [b]	North of CID (III)	−19.37	−17.88	−1.82
	Rest of Area			
11	Scottsdale (II)	−14.41	−25.59	13.06
12 [b]	Tempe-Mesa (II)	38.67	41.75	−5.02
13 [b]	Avondale-Buckeye (III)	−8.09	23.50	−26.69
14 [b]	Goodyear-Glendale (III)	−5.95	1.46	−7.32

Note: Roman numerals indicate distance from CID. For explanation, see Chapter 2, "Spatial Distribution of Major Industries in 1965."
[a] Traditional manufacturing area.
[b] Poverty area.

locations for manufacturing activity (column 2). Only the northernmost central-city zone was unattractive, reflecting the out-migration of a large machinery-producing establishment. Finally, much of the relative decline of the CID can be attributed to its industrial mix. Compared with a number of the other central-city zones it remained relatively competitive as an industrial location over the period.

6

Summary of the Findings of Part I

The discussions of the location of manufacturing activity as reflected by employment in these four metropolitan areas have uncovered several interesting regularities that are discussed below.

Centralized Areas

Information on the growth of employment in the central cities and central industrial districts, contained in Table 6-1, offer the basis for several summary statements. The share of each area's manufacturing jobs present in the respective central cities declined in all the Standard Metropolitan Statistical Areas (SMSAs) save St. Paul. In St. Paul, however, the absolute level declined according to the Dun and Bradstreet (D&B) data even though the central city's share increased slightly. In Phoenix, by contrast, the number of jobs in the central city increased by about 9,500 inspite of a 2.4 percentage reduction in the central city's share of total area employment. It is important, however, to recall that these same data have demonstrated that there are areas within all of the central cities that have increased their share and level of manufacturing employment over the period. This finding offers a sharp contrast to statements deploring the lack of economic viability of all central-city locations. The data in Table 6-1 also show that of all the central industrial districts only that of Cleveland experienced a relative increase in importance as an industrial center. There have also been significant redistributions of employment within the central cities themselves, with areas in close proximity to the declining central industrial districts (CIDs), such as South Boston, the area southwest of the St. Paul CID, and the area to the east of the Phoenix CID, all experiencing large increases in employment. There is little question, however, that the dominant pattern in each of the SMSAs has been a shifting of manufacturing employment to less centralized locations.

Transportation Facilities

Based on individual-city observations, some casual observations on the influence of the proximity of airports and major highways in producing

93

Table 6-1

Manufacturing Employment in Central Cities and Central Industrial Districts of Four Sample Metropolitan Areas, 1965 and 1968

| | Manufacturing Employment | | | |
| | 1965 | | 1968 | |
	Number	Number as Fraction of SMSA Total	Number	Number as Fraction of SMSA Total
	Central Cities			
Cleveland	187,190	0.627	168,544	0.594
Minneapolis	58,262	.384	45,028	.315
St. Paul	44,073	.291	41,498	.299
Boston	92,601	.311	89,636	.289
Phoenix	41,063	0.777	50,558	0.753
	Central Industrial Districts			
Cleveland	44,319	0.148	43,338	0.153
Minneapolis	16,720	.110	13,491	.094
St. Paul	12,781	.084	8,799	.061
Boston	13,634	.046	7,724	.025
Phoenix	4,007	0.076	3,904	0.058

the existing locational pattern can be made. The importance of each area's major airport as a locational determinant is not easily discerned from the experience of these four areas. In Cleveland and the Twin Cities it appears to have had a significant positive effect. The situation of Boston and Phoenix is unclear owing largely to the location of these facilities in areas that contained substantial amounts of industrial activity prior to the emergence of airfields as a determinant of industrial locations.

The importance of limited-access highways seems to depend on the extent of congestion and the extensiveness of the highway system. The data in Table 6-2 provide some crude indication of the degree of peak-hour traffic congestion in the three largest sample SMSAs. J. R. Meyer, J. F. Kain, and Martin Wohl emphasize that these figures are swollen by the presence of vehicles passing through the central business district (CBD), so that in some sense they offer a more general indication of congestion than might be thought. In Boston and Cleveland, where congestion is relatively high and the highway system comparatively underdeveloped, the strength of major highways as a locational determinant is amply evident. But in Minneapolis and St. Paul, where the highway system has been extensively developed, and in Phoenix, where the system is small but the level of congestion relatively low, the apparent influence of major highways has been much less pronounced.

Table 6-2

Peak-hour Traffic Flows: Boston, Cleveland, Minneapolis-St. Paul, 1960

CBD	Number of Persons	Approximate Number of Persons Leaving CBD per Peak Hour in an Average Corridor, 1960
Boston	150,000 to 200,000	20,000 to 30,000
Cleveland	75,000 to 100,000	9,000 to 13,000
Minneapolis-St. Paul	50,000 to 75,000	6,000 to 9,000

Source: Adapted from John R. Meyer, John F. Kain, and Martin Wohl, *The Urban Transportation Problem*, Cambridge, Mass.: Harvard University Press, 1965, table 25. Copyright by the Rand Corporation, 1965. Reprinted with permission.

Poverty Areas

Areas within the SMSAs that were defined by the Bureau of the Census as poverty neighborhoods on the basis of 1960 data were generally shunned by manufacturing establishments. In the Cleveland and Minneapolis-St. Paul SMSAs the poor were concentrated entirely in zones that, after correcting for industrial-mix effects, were uniformly unattractive to manufacturing activity. Only the core zones in those cities in which the poor were concentrated increased their share of even central-city employment. In all other poverty areas in these two SMSAs the rate of growth of industrial employment was below that of the central city, and thus below that of the areas as a whole. Thus, in Cleveland and Minneapolis-St. Paul the poor were indeed concentrated in the areas least attractive to manufacturing activity within the SMSAs. As a matter of fact, in none of the poverty areas in these cities did the employment of manufacturers grow over the period. All lost some portion of their manufacturing employment.

In Boston the pattern survives in a somewhat modified form. The three heavily industrial and commercial zones that border on the bay and are classified by the census as poverty areas increased their share of employment over the period. One of these areas contains little population, however, and is best thought of as an industrial enclave. The other two areas, South Boston and Charlestown-East Boston, are largely populated by low-income, white ethnic groups and, therefore, differ sharply in character from areas like Roxbury and Hough. Also the location of Logan Airport in East Boston should not be overlooked. The pattern in Phoenix is completely different from that of the other three areas. The most striking difference is that all the suburban areas around the city, except those to the north, were poverty areas in 1960. Because of the extremely rapid growth occurring in Phoenix and the relative emptiness of these suburbs in 1960, it is to be expected that these areas may have changed a great deal by

1965. However, it is clear that these suburban areas were in fact quite attractive to manufacturers; and only one, to the west of the city, lost some portion of its very small 1965 share of manufacturing employment. All, of course, grew rapidly in absolute terms, as did those poverty areas within the central city.

Composition of Net Change

Several consistent patterns emerge from the discussion of the composition of the net change in employment. The components again, were (1) employment in moving establishments, (2) employment in establishments beginning business, (3) employment in establishments going out of business, and (4) change in employment of stationary establishments. For each of the SMSAs the rate of total movement (items 1-3) was found to be surprisingly high: On an annual basis between 5 and 10 per cent of the initial employment is associated with establishments relocating or beginning or ending business. Table 6-3 presents total net change, net immigration, net natural increase, and net change in stationary establishments for each SMSA for the central city and the rest of the SMSA. The importance of net change in employment of stationary establishments for both central cities and the rest-of-SMSA ring is evident from these data. Although

Table 6-3

Components of Net Employment Change in Central Cities and Rest of the Metropolitan Area, 1968 Relative to 1965 (Number of Employees)

	Total Net Change	Net In-migration [a]	Net Natural Increase	Net Change in Stationary Establishments
Boston				
Central city	−2,965	−2,362	−10,735	10,132
Rest of SMSA	14,182	664	−8,870	22,748
Cleveland				
Central city	−18,646	−4,441	−11,144	−3,061
Rest of SMSA	4,636	4,606	−4,240	4,383
Minneapolis-St. Paul				
Central city	−14,599	−2,764	−6,200	−5,635
Rest of SMSA	6,007	2,869	−1,446	4,422
Phoenix				
Central city	9,495	−86	374	9,216
Rest of SMSA	4,813	36	3,205	1,573

[a]The net number of jobs moving from central-city zones may not equal the number moving into SMSA-ring zones, because the employment count for "origin" firms is for 1965 while that for "destination" firms is for 1968.

there is no way of confirming our suspicion, it seems likely that the degree of importance of changes in employment of stationary establishments is related to the expanding national economy over the study period. In general, it is easier to expand output at an existing plant rather than open another. As the data presented in Table 6-4 indicate, this component of net change is not so dominant that the direction of net change could be consistently predicted by the direction of the change in employment in stationary establishments. On average the two changes moved together in about three-fourths of the analysis zones; in Boston they moved together in all but a single zone.

In general the pattern of net natural increase (employment associated with births minus deaths) favored the outlying areas; and, indeed, net

Table 6-4

Relationship between Employment Growth in Stationary Establishments and Overall Employment Growth in Analysis Zones of the four Metropolitan Areas

SMSA	Number of Analysis Zones	Number of Zones in Which Net Change in Employment and Change in Stationary Establishments Moved Together
Cleveland	18	13
Minneapolis-St. Paul	25	19
Boston	20	19
Phoenix	14	9

natural increase is at least as important in producing the overall outward shift of employment location as is net migration. This pattern is more evident in the data for individual zones than in the aggregate data in Table 6-3.

The overall locational process is demonstrated graphically in the first panel of Figure 6-1, which shows the natural increase in each SMSA by rings, going out from the CID. (The use of "rings" in this part of the book is described in Chapter 2, "Spatial Distribution of Major Industries in 1965.) Aside from Phoenix, which is dominated by one extremely large new plant in ring II, two patterns emerge. In Minneapolis and Cleveland the CIDs have relatively large increases compared with the areas adjacent to them, but their outlying areas also show increases. In Cleveland, though, only the final ring (IV) does better than the CID, while in Minneapolis all the rings after the first do better than the CID. The second pattern is exhibited by Boston and St. Paul, in both of which the CIDs do poorly relative to the areas adjacent to them (ring I); and ring I

98

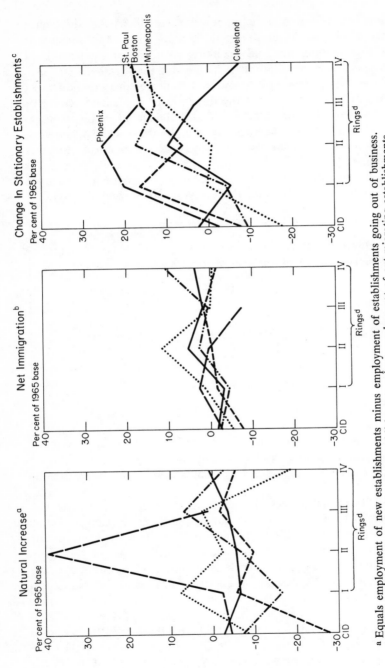

a Equals employment of new establishments minus employment of establishments going out of business.
b Equals employment of in-migrating establishments minus employment of out-migrating establishments.
c Equals the change in employment of establishments that did not change their location over the period.
d Rings indicate distance from the CID; for explanation, see the section "Spatial Distribution of Major Industries in 1965" in chapter 2. The zones included in the rings for Cleveland, Minneapolis-St. Paul, Boston, and Phoenix are identified in Tables 2-3, 3-2, 4-2, and 5-2, respectively.

Figure 6-1. Components of Change in the Spatial Distribution of Employment, Four Metropolitan Areas, 1965-68

also does better than ring II. Both lines again rise in ring III and then finally decline at the furthest ring (IV).[a]

The pattern of employment relocation generated by establishments moving within the SMSAs varied distinctly among the sample SMSAs. In Cleveland and Minneapolis-St. Paul the pattern was definitely one of shifting employment from the central cities to the suburbs, as mirrored by the data in Table 6-2. In Boston and Phoenix the patterns are less obvious, but the net movement is still definitely outward. In Boston the degree of cross migration is larger. In Phoenix there is little movement, and what has occurred has generally been confined within the central-city boundaries. The moves were generally short in each of the SMSAs, confirming the findings of Harold Williamson and of Robert A. Leone discussed in Chapter 2.

The overall decentralizing effect of migration is shown graphically, in the center panel of Figure 6-1, in the generally upward slope of the group of lines. Again the pattern for Cleveland and Minneapolis is the same—strong performance of the CID relative to the area adjacent to it. For the others the CID is the lowest point on the curve, except for ring IV in Phoenix. For most of the cities, however, it is ring II that experienced the largest net in-migration of employment.

It is interesting to contrast the three panels of Figure 6-1. Very clearly, the greatest force toward decentralization has been the change in employment in establishments stationary over the period. Except in Cleveland, the CID did least well of any area (ring) in terms of the net change in stationary employment. One might have expected quite the opposite given that the availability of rentable space in these areas should have made expansion there relatively easy. On balance, however, the slope of the figure is sharply upward to the right, reflecting the strong decentralizing influence. As outlined in the preceding paragraphs, there merge two distinct patterns (Cleveland-Minneapolis versus Boston-St. Paul) of natural increase and net in-migration among the cities. Little spatial pattern has been found in the behavior of employment associated with establishments ceasing operations.[b] As expected, however, a rough correlation was found between the destinations of relocating establishments and the initial location of new establishments. The actual simple correlation between the level of employment destinations and births was about 0.6 across all

---

[a] The large decline in ring IV of St. Paul should be discounted as this ring had a base-year employment of only 1,800.

[b] This is not strictly true. The incidence of employment death was generally lower at the periphery than in the CID, but the overall pattern was less systematic for deaths, on the basis of both this type of analysis and the statistical work, than for the other components of net employment change.

analysis zones of all the sample SMSAs. The data in Table 6-5, which show the number of zones in which the number of employees associated with new or in-migrating establishments is above average,[e] provide some additional information on this point. The pattern of births and destinations for expanding employment has tended to be reinforcing, especially in the Twin Cities and Boston.

Table 6-5

Relationship between Levels of Employment in New and in Inmigrating Establishments in Analysis Zones of the Four Metropolitan Areas

	Number of Zones of Above-average Employment Associated with		
	New Firms	In-migrating Firms	New plus In-migrating
Cleveland	5	8	1
Minneapolis-St. Paul	10	11	6
Boston	6	6	5
Phoenix	6	4	3

Spatial Distribution of Industry

The initial spatial distribution of the major industries [d] and the importance of the industrial structure in producing the net change in employment location over the period were also examined. Two strong and consistent regularities were observed in the spatial distribution of individual industries within metropolitan areas.[e] Without exception, the industries examined displayed substantial concentrations of employment within each metropolitan area. This observation is particularly striking when the range of ages of both the sample cities and the observed industries are considered. A related observation is that the concentrations in general tend to be in different sections of the area for each industry, although some analysis zones, usually in the central city, did have several industries concentrated in them.

---

[e] The average equals the total number of employees involved in the locational activity divided by the number of zones in the SMSA, except for new firms in Minneapolis-St. Paul and Phoenix. For these two the average excludes one extremely large firm in each. For further description, see the discussion for the individual cities.

[d] A major industry is defined as accounting for at least 5 per cent of total manufacturing employment in 1965.

[e] The criteria used to divide the SMSAs into analysis zones and the definition of a spatial concentration of employment in a single industry are set forth in Chapter 2, "Spatial Distribution of Major Industries in 1965."

Table 6-6 gives a rough idea of the type of area in which most of these concentrations occurred. At least half of the concentrations were in central cities and traditional manufacturing zones in each SMSA. The variation in the number of concentrations between the two types of area can be largely attributed to differences in the time period of industrial development. In Boston, the first to develop, heavy reliance was placed on water power at outlying locations in addition to the activity at the ocean's edge. In Cleveland its heavy metal works in Euclid were developed independently and later were linked with the central city. The Twin Cities and Phoenix were developed last, and there was plenty of room in the central

Table 6-6

Industrial Concentrations in the Central Cities and Traditional Manufacturing Zones of the Four Metropolitan Areas

	Number of Industries	Location of Concentrations (Number)		
		Total	Central City	Traditional Zone
Boston	7	20	10	16
Cleveland	5	16	11	14
Minneapolis-St. Paul	5	15	13	8
Phoenix	5	12	9	8

cities of these two areas for industrial development. The effect of these concentrations on the observed changes in locational patterns is discussed in Chapter 10.

Importance of Industry Mix in Net Change

Using several of the shift-share measures developed to study the composition of original employment changes,[f] the net change in manufacturing employment in each SMSA was examined. The overall relationship between the relative growth of aggregate manufacturing employment in a zone and its comparative industrial structure was found to be quite weak. As the data in Table 6-7 indicate, in the Minneapolis-St. Paul SMSA and in Cleveland, the measure of comparative industrial structure offers the best prediction of the *direction* of net change. It was much less effective in Boston and Phoenix, and overall the direction of net change and the industry share measure coincided only about two-thirds of the time. How-

---

[f] See Chapter 2, "The Process of Change," for a description of the shift-share measures. Their formal definitions are given in Appendix D.

Table 6-7

**Relative Employment Growth Rates and Industry Composition
of Analysis Zones in the Four Metropolitan Areas**

SMSA	Number of Analysis Zones	Number of Zones in Which Relative Change in Employment Was in Same Direction as Comparative Industrial Structure Measure
Cleveland	18	12
Minneapolis-St. Paul	25	19
Boston	20	13
Phoenix	14	7

ever, it is clear that this high correspondence was largely fortuitous, since in only 14 of the 77 zones was the comparative industrial structure measure larger than the measure of competitive shift. In spite of the shortcomings of industry mix as a predictor of net change, the measures did offer significant information regarding the relative attractiveness of various zones as locations of manufacturing activity (after controlling for industry mix) and were a useful indicator of a zone's industry mix.[g]

---

[g] The shift-share measures are used here strictly for description. They were never intended to be used for forecasting. The problems of using shift-share measures to predict employment changes even more aggregate than those presented here are substantial. See the discussion and analysis in H. James Brown, "Shift and Share Projections of Regional Economic Growth: An Empirical Test," *Journal of Regional Science*, 9 (1969): 1-18; and Franklin J. James and James W. Hughes, "A Test of Shift and Share Analysis as a Predictive Device," *Journal of Regional Science*, August 1973, pp. 223-31.

Part II
Behavioral Regularities and Hypotheses

7

Changes in the Location of Industry in Centralized Locations

Part I contained a great amount of detailed information concerning the location of the most important industries in each metropolitan area. The shift-share analysis presented in that section showed that knowledge of an analysis zone's industrial composition would rarely be sufficient to predict the net growth or decline in aggregate manufacturing employment in the zone even over a relatively short period such as the one used in this analysis. The data also show that knowledge of the industrial structure as reflected by the measure of comparative industrial structure of the central cities and central industrial districts (CIDs) provides an accurate indication of aggregate change only for the Boston central city. The purpose of this brief chapter is simply to determine if certain industries tend to be consistently located in the central cities and central industrial districts and whether they tend to do well in these locations.

A summary of the relevant data is presented in Table 7-1. (Appendix F contains the background data for this table.):

1. "Yes" in columns 1, 3, and 5 means that a given industry accounts for a greater fraction of total manufacturing employment in the central city, CID, or both areas than it does in the Standard Metropolitan Statistical Area (SMSA) as a whole in three or more of the sample SMSAs.

2. "Yes" in columns 2, 4, and 6 means that the industry grew more rapidly relative to its SMSA growth rate within three or more central cities or CIDs than did total manufacturing employment in the central city or CID relative to the rate of growth of total employment in the SMSA as a whole. The measure is thus a *relative* growth measure, and one that credits the industry with a "yes" for buoying central-city or CID employment.[a]

---

[a] To see this more clearly consider the following example.

Let $r20,c$ = growth rate of SIC 20 in the CID = 12 per cent

$r20,t$ = growth rate of SIC 20 in the SMSA = 10 per cent

$r_{t,c}$ = growth rate of all industries in the CID = 4 per cent

$r_{t,t}$ = growth rate of all industries in the SMSA = 8 per cent.

The formula for determining the classification of an industry, then is:

$$\frac{r20,c}{r20,t} \Big/ \frac{r_{t,c}}{r_{t,t}} \geq 1.$$

In our example, since $12/10 > 4/8$, the ratio is greater than 1. Consider now the case in which $r20,c = 8$; the ratio still exceeds 1 ($8/10 > 4/8$). Therefore, although the performance of the industry in the CID is below average, nevertheless, the rate of decline of the CID is being reduced.

Table 7-1

Concentration and Growth of Industries in Central Cities and Central Industrial Districts

		Industry Characteristics in Area Specified					
		Central City		Central Industrial District		Central City and CID	
SIC	Industry Description	Concentrated [a] (1)	Growing Faster [b] (2)	Concentrated [a] (3)	Growing Faster [b] (4)	Concentrated [a] (5)	Growing Faster [b] (6)
20	Food	yes	yes	yes	yes	yes	yes
22	Textiles	yes	no	no	no	no	no
23	Apparel	yes	yes	yes	yes	yes	yes
24	Lumber	no	no	no	no	no	no
25	Furniture	yes	yes	no	yes	no	yes
26	Paper	no	no	no	yes	no	no
27	Printing	yes	yes	yes	yes	yes	yes
28	Chemicals	no	yes	yes	yes	no	yes
29	Petroleum	no	yes	no	no	no	no
30	Rubber	no	yes	no	yes	no	yes
31	Leather	no	yes	yes	yes	no	yes
32	Stone	no	no	no	yes	no	no
33	Primary metals	yes	no	no	yes	no	no
34	Fabricated metals	yes	no	no	no	no	no
35	Machinery	no	no	no	no	no	no
36	Electrical machinery	no	yes	no	yes	no	yes
37	Transportation equipment	no	no	no	yes	no	no
38	Instruments	no	no	no	no	no	no
39	Miscellaneous Manufacturing	yes	no	yes	no	yes	no

[a] Industry accounts for greater fraction of total manufacturing employment in central city, CID, or both than it does for the SMSA as a whole in three or more of the SMSAs. Data are for 1965.
[b] See text for explanation. Data are for 1965-68.

Note that the criterion used for "concentration" is really much less stringent in the present analysis than that used in Part I or later in Chapter 10.

From columns 5 and 6 it is seen that three industries are relatively concentrated *and* growing relatively fast in both the central cities and CIDs across the sample cities—food products, apparel, and printing and publishing. The presence of the apparel and printing industries supports observations made on the basis of data for New York City by Raymond Vernon and by Robert Leone.[1] Vernon explained the presence of these industries in these centralized locations in terms of the need for rapid communication between buyers and sellers. The reasons for the consistent presence of the food-processing industry are less clear. In Boston the explanation may lie in the availability of wharf facilities nearby, and the rail yards and grain milling facilities in the Twin Cities provide a rationale in these areas; but in Cleveland and Phoenix the attraction to these locations is much less obvious. It is possible that centralized locations provide access to the large number of secondary workers generally required for food processing.

Interestingly, there are five industries that, although not dominantly located in both central cities and CIDs, grew relatively faster in these areas than elsewhere in the metropolitan areas. These industries (furniture, chemicals, rubber, leather, and electrical machinery) represent an extremely wide range of production technologies and input requirements. Of these only rubber and electrical machinery were not relatively concentrated in either the central cities or CIDs in 1965. Nevertheless, they, like the others, grew consistently more rapidly at the centralized locations. This may suggest a change in the land-use patterns of the innermost rings of metropolitan areas or at least a change in the type of industries locating in these areas. Only miscellaneous manufacturing was relatively concentrated in both locations and grew less rapidly in both.

Shifting focus to industry location and growth in the central cities, we see that only the furniture industry (in addition to SICs 20, 23, and 27) is both relatively concentrated and growing consistently in these areas. Three industries that were relatively concentrated in 1965 grew less rapidly than the SMSA average. Two of these are the heavy metals industries (SICs 33 and 34) and the third is textiles. All of the three growing, nonconcentrated industries in the central cities were among those listed in the same category for both central cities and CIDs. This leaves nine industries, nearly half of the total, which were neither relatively concentrated nor growing relatively rapidly in central cities. In short, in the following industries centralized locations within the sample SMSAs were consistently shunned—lumber, paper, petroleum, stone and glass, nonelectrical machinery, transportation equipment, and scientific instruments.

The situation in the central industrial districts is quite different from that in the central cities as a whole. For one thing every industry that was consistently concentrated in the CIDs in 1965 also contributed to the growth of the CID relative to that of the SMSA as a whole. Four industries are in this class—food products, apparel, publishing, and chemicals. There is another major difference between the two areas: Twice as many nonconcentrated industries were consistently growing relatively more rapidly in the CIDs than in the central cities. This is probably most accurately accounted for by the more generalized externalities available in the CID.[b] It may also suggest that the position of the CIDs is not as bleak as the raw data indicate. Of the total of 11 relatively prosperous industry groups now located in the CIDs, only four were dominantly located there in the past. This should signal that at least a significant holding action is taking place in the effort to retain manufacturing activity at these locations.[c]

Finally, six industries in the CIDs compared with nine in the central cities are neither concentrated nor growing in CID locations. The more interesting point, however, is that only four industries appear to shun both central cities and CIDs (i.e., are neither concentrated nor growing relatively rapidly on a consistent basis over the observation period). Three of these—lumber, petroleum, and nonelectrical machinery—require large sites to carry out production and storage functions and have little need for generalized external economies. The fourth, the scientific instruments industry, has few constraints, except that it locate relatively near the suburban residences of most of its employees.

From the above it is clear that there are very definite regularities in the location of specific industries in the central cities and central industrial districts of our four sample SMSAs. It is especially surprising, therefore, that the growth of these areas cannot be predicted on the basis of these regularities, and this finding reinforces our earlier observation that the "attractiveness" of particular locations as sites for manufacturing activity is a very important determinant of the growth of zones within metropolitan areas. In addition the data pinpoint those industries whose growth in metropolitan areas would be most likely to promote the growth of central cities in general and central industrial districts in particular.

---

[b] The industries are furniture, paper products, rubber products, stone and glass, primary metals, electrical machinery, and transportation equipment.

[c] Alexander Ganz also suggests that this is the case for both total and manufacturing employment in central cities. Unfortunately, his assertions are not strongly documented. See Alexander Ganz, "Our Large Cities: New Directions and New Approaches," mimeo, Cambridge, Massachusetts, M.I.T. Laboratory for Environmental Studies, December 1969.

8 The Incubator Hypothesis: A Test

The *incubator hypothesis* states that small, new establishments will be attracted to areas offering services essential to their operation that they, because of their small size and limited resources, would be unable to provide internally. Chief among these services are rentable production space and other types of physical capital, legal and financial services, and information on changes in demand or supply factors. These services are generally considered to be more readily available in the central industrial districts of central cities. Frequently, however, rentable production space and access to a trained labor force will be available in the traditional manufacturing centers in other parts of the city. It may be that a few of the traditional areas will produce near central industrial district (CID)-type conditions, for example, Euclid in the Cleveland area and Cambridge and parts of Peabody-Salem-Lynn in the Boston area.

The hypothesis was developed by Raymond Vernon and E. M. Hoover [1] on the basis of locational activity of manufacturing establishments in the New York metropolitan area and has recently been reconfirmed for the same area by Robert Leone.[2] In addition, Daniel Creamer has supported the hypothesis for three metropolitan areas in Pennsylvania.[3] Creamer, however, used the county of the principal city to define the centralized location, thereby making the geography of the hypothesis very broad. In brief, the hypothesis has received considerable empirical support to date.

The incubator hypothesis is important because it is one of the very few hypotheses advanced to date that could potentially account not only for the pattern of new-establishment locations but also for the variation in death and relocation rates. For example, new establishments can be expected to have a high incidence of death. On the other hand, as the surviving establishments grow they will eventually reach the point where the internal economies available from a large operation will outweigh the external economies available at incubation sites.

The purpose of the present analysis is to treat the validity of the hypothesis as part of a general theory of intraurban industrial location behavior. Consequently, the focus is the location of new establishments of all industries combined. It is recognized that it is quite possible for the hypothesis to hold for certain industries even if it were not supported for all industries combined.

109

The hypothesis would be supported using the data of this study if it were found that new establishments located in incubator-type areas at greater rates than they did in other types of areas. Therefore, the experience of three incubator areas in each of the sample metropolitan areas was analyzed—the central industrial districts, central cities as a whole and traditional manufacturing locations. Table 8-1 presents the percentage distribution of 1965 base and new manufacturing establishments and base year and new-firm employment located in each of these areas. The hy-

Table 8-1

Distribution of Base Year and New Establishments and Employment in Central Industrial Districts, Central Cities, and Traditional Manufacturing Locations, Four Sample Metropolitan Areas (Figures are Percentages of Corresponding SMSA Totals)

	Central Industrial District		Central City		Traditional Manufacturing Locations	
	1965 Base	Births	1965 Base	Births	1965 Base	Births
Establishments						
Boston	6.58	5.08	37.14	22.32	80.64	77.96
Cleveland	21.75	17.46	68.43	55.39	66.24	59.24
Minneapolis	12.97	5.91	45.86	29.68	42.21	23.53
St. Paul	5.91	2.41	21.02	11.23		
Phoenix	16.21	10.68	77.39	70.00	46.72	37.58
Employment						
Boston	4.57	4.26	31.07	21.69	73.52 [a]	83.51
Cleveland	14.87 [a]	29.34	62.82 [a]	65.96	74.08 [a]	74.36
Minneapolis	11.10	4.02	38.69	12.96	41.75	10.25
St. Paul	8.48	1.44	29.27 [a]	59.34		
Phoenix	7.58	2.42	79.08 [a]	81.83	49.07	14.35

[a] Percentage of births in area is greater than percentage of base establishment or employment.

pothesis is supported if the percentage of Standard Metropolitan Statistical Area (SMSA) births located in an area exceeds the percentage of SMSA base-year establishments located there.

For establishments there is not a single instance in which the hypothesis is supported. For employment some support is evident. All three Cleveland areas are shown to be incubators. Actually, in only three of the analysis zones was the incidence of births higher than average—the CID, the zone southwest of the CID (zone 4), and the central-city zone adjacent to Euclid (zone 13). In Cleveland incubation is apparently a central-city phenomenon. The central cities of St. Paul and Phoenix also appear to be incubators. For both of these cities the high employment rate for new firms was produced by the opening of a single very large branch establishment. Finally, the traditional areas in Boston display a higher incidence of births than base employment. An examination of the underlying data shows the establishments involved to be of more than average size, but none are enormous. Only one of the zones with a higher incidence of births is a central-city zone.[a] There is, on balance, then, little support for the hypothesis.[b]

In searching for the cause for the rather dramatic differences between the findings for the New York area and the four SMSAs included in the present study, the possible variation in industry mix between centralized and suburban locations offered a reasonable potential explanation. The large variations in the locational patterns of individual industries was demonstrated in Part I, and an examination of the data reveals substantial variation among industry birth rates as well. The same type of shift-share measures used in Part I to study the importance of industry mix for total net employment change was employed to analyze industry effects on new-establishment employment.[c] Two shift-share measures are presented in Table 8-2 for the CID and the other traditional manufacturing zones in all four of the SMSAs. The first measure, "births relative to the SMSA," tells whether the zone received more or less new establishment employment than it would have received if it had received a fraction of the total proportional to its base employment.[d] The second measure is similar to the first except that new-establishment employment in the zone is adjusted for industry mix. The data in Table 8-2 show that this adjustment changed below-average zones into above-average zones in only three cases, and these were all in the Cleveland and Boston areas. The adjustment made a truely dramatic difference in the Berea-North Olmstead area in Cleveland, and smaller but significant changes were effected in the Peabody-Salem-Lynn and Waltham-Newton areas in Boston. The one Boston central-city zone that was an incubator according to the unadjusted figures lost this status after the data were adjusted for industry mix. On balance, the results

---

[a] The zones with a high incidence of births are Somerville-Everett, Cambridge, and Brockton outside of Boston, and zone 4 adjacent to the CID in the central city.

[b] These results are consistent with some recent results obtained by Gordon Cameron for Clydeside, United Kingdom, conurbation for the 1958-68 period. For details, see "Metro Urban Location and the New Plant," Glasgow, University of Glasgow Urban and Regional Studies Discussion Paper No. 5, 1972, Tables 4 and 5.

[c] This analysis has only been conducted for employment, since the growth rate for establishments as used in shift-share analysis had little meaning in the present context.

[d] It provides the same information as the ratio of the two columns in Table 8-1, except that a ratio of unity there is equivalent to a zero in Table 8-2.

Table 8-2

**Birth Shift-Share Measures for Traditional Manufacturing Zones,
All Sample Metropolitan Areas, 1965-68 (Per Cent)**

Analysis Zone		Births	
Number	Description	Relative To SMSA	Standardized for Industry Mix
	Boston		
1 [a]	CID	−6.8	−24.7
2 [a]	South Boston	−18.1	−29.6
3 [a]	Charlestown-E. Boston	−90.1	−88.1
4	Adjacent to CID	23.3	−11.9
7	W. Boston-Dorchester	−36.7	−49.0
8	Peabody-Salem-Lynn	−23.2	0.4
10	Somerville-Everett	60.2	60.4
11	Cambridge	17.8	17.4
13	Waltham-Newton	−2.8	4.3
17	Quincy-Braintree	−41.7	−10.0
20	Brockton	26.2	19.3
	Cleveland		
1 [a]	CID	49.4	50.5
2 [a]	Hough	−70.4	−69.6
3	Southeast of CID	−52.1	−29.0
4 [a]	Southwest of CID	16.6	18.7
13	Northeast of CID, ring II	30.3	17.2
7	Berea-N. Olmstead	−20.5	53.4
14	Euclid	−28.9	−4.9
	Minneapolis-St. Paul		
	Minneapolis		
2	East of Miss. R., N.	−86.4	−90.0
3	CID	−50.7	−54.6
4	Southwest of CID	−71.5	−71.9
	St. Paul		
8	CID	−76.9	−70.0
12	Northwest of CID	−69.4	−67.1
	Phoenix		
1	CID	−67.9	−40.5
2	West of CID	−45.2	−9.5
4	Southwest of CID	−65.2	−72.0
5	East of CID	−97.5	−98.5

[a] Poverty area.

of the adjustment for industry mix do little to increase support for the hypothesis.

If the incubator hypothesis does not explain the distribution of new establishments and their employment within the four metropolitan areas,[e]

---

[e] It was thought possible that the lack of above-average birth rates in these areas might have occurred only recently and that the rest of the process suggested by the incubator hypothesis might still be working itself out. In general, the zones that best provide for the incubation function would be characterized by (1) a relatively

then what factors do? We were led by this question to carry out a simple regression analysis on the rates of new-establishment employment to determine what factors systematically influence the initial location of these establishments. Employment in new establishments in each zone, expressed as a percentage of the 1965 base employment in the zone, was regressed on the following independent variables: (1) total manufacturing employment in the zone in 1965; (2) the "competitive advantage" shift-share variable, reflecting the recent industrial attractiveness of the zone; (3) the average level of employment of establishments in the zone; (4) dummy variables for three of the sample SMSAs (relative to Cleveland); and (5) dummy variables identifying the zone as a CID, a central-city zone, and/or a traditional manufacturing area.

Total employment in a zone is expected to be positively associated with employment in new firms since, after controlling for firm size, it should reflect the presence of other industrial activity, some of it presumably complementary to that of the new firms. Likewise, new firms are expected to be positively associated with unusually high growth in a zone (variable 2), as such areas represent expanding markets and are probably competitive locations. On the other hand, new establishments are expected to be inversely related to the size of the establishments already in the zone; big operations will typically have little need for small suppliers and may not wish to provide products, especially customized products, to small producers. The signs of the coefficients of the location variables (5) will reflect the higher or lower average attractiveness of these locations for new firms compared to other locations, after controlling for the factors captured by the other variables.[f]

---

high rate of establishment birth; (2) a relatively high rate of death, since new establishments are presumably unstable; (3) a net out-migration of successful, sufficiently matured establishments; and (4) a positive net increase in the employment levels of existing establishments as they matured. The data (in Part I) on the composition of net employment change in each city showed that the last three parts of the process occurred in a number of central-city zones. However, the overall pattern was not sufficiently consistent to support a view that the dynamics in these cities is such that the entire process had applied until recently.

[f] Using the central-city, CID, and traditional zone dummy variables together in the same regression did not cause a significant problem of linear dependence among these variables, a condition that could have biased the results of the analysis. The simple correlation coefficients among these variables are CID: traditional zone 0.267 and central-city zone 0.288; Traditional Zone: traditional zone 1.000 and central-city zone 0.423. In this analysis a 0.20 level of significance (corresponding to a t-value of about 1.3) is considered significant because of the basically exploratory nature of the analysis. Since the regression model being estimated is not based on a well developed theoretical model, there is little guidance as to functional form or variable specification. A low level of significance criteria is warranted to preclude prematurely eliminating variables from further analysis in this area. Finally, the regression model reported in Appendix G excludes the many large branch establishments in St. Paul and Phoenix noted in the text, as they represent truly extreme observations. The dummy variable for the Twin Cities was insignificant, and it was dropped from the analysis.

The results, which are given in Appendix G and only summarized here, are generally consistent with expectations.[g] Holding a number of zonal characteristics constant, employment in new establishments is attracted to zones with large numbers of manufacturing employees, zones that are competitive, and zones with manufacturing establishments of below-average employment size. The results also suggest that, in general, new establishments are attracted to central-city zones but repulsed by traditional manufacturing centers, relative to other areas, again after controlling for several zonal characteristics. Each of these findings can be interpreted as consistent with the incubator hypothesis. The central-city and employment concentration effects reflect the attraction of general external economies. The average-employment-size effect simply indicates that for a number of reasons the zones that contain small firms are good incubators. The repulsion of traditional manufacturing areas probably indicates that these areas are better suited for the larger, already established or new branch establishments of large corporations.

The results lead to two conclusions: The first is that the incubator hypothesis as broadly formulated here—that new establishments tend to locate dominantly in highly centralized locations—is not supported for the four sample SMSAs. However, it appears that a more complex version of this hypothesis may be viable. The results of the regression analysis suggest that new establishments are attracted to areas having some of the characteristics of incubators but that other factors, including the recent overall attractiveness of a zone as an industrial site, may be of equal importance. The possibility of the complex incubator hypothesis is pursued in some detail in Chapter 10 in the context of the importance of spatial clustering of individual industries in the locational decision.

---

[g] Appendix G also contains similar analyses for the other employment locational change components—outmovers, inmovers, and deaths.

9 Manufacturing Activity in Poverty Areas

As was noted in Part I, manufacturing employment levels declined in most poverty areas within the sample metropolitan areas, and employment declined in each of the central cities except Phoenix. There is great and valid concern among students of the city and policy makers at all levels of government that the continued movement of manufacturing establishments to suburban locations will exacerbate the problems of the urban poor in finding productive employment.[1] The general argument is that as manufacturing jobs move away from the city it becomes increasingly more difficult for inner-city residents to commute to them, given the current configuration of urban transit facilities. Further, even where the jobs are accessible, the cost of commuting may be so high that low-skilled jobholders are little better off than if they were receiving welfare payments or taking whatever work is available in the inner city.

In contrast to this line of reasoning, the findings of projects providing low-cost bus service from inner-city poverty areas to suburban industrial areas consistently indicate that providing transportation is not enough. A significant unfilled demand for low-skilled labor does not seem to exist at suburban job sites. In addition, though heavily subsidized in many of these projects, transportation from the inner city to suburban jobs is still sufficiently time-consuming and costly to reduce greatly the attractiveness of those jobs that are available.[2] Though one can argue that training *and* transportation must be provided to offer a fair test of the need for these special bus routes, the more relevant point in this context is that the unfilled suburban demand for unskilled labor can easily be exaggerated.

The question to be addressed in this chapter is the degree to which employers are adjusting to the concentration of a low-skilled labor force in core areas of poverty. The establishment-level analysis zone data upon which this study is based permit us to identify in considerable detail the types of industry that are located in poverty areas. More importantly, it allows identification of those industries that have grown in these areas over the observation period. The simple process of identification will, it is hoped, provide the basis for formulating hypotheses that future studies can test in detail. Unfortunately, our data do not provide any information on the area of residence of employees whose jobs are located in poverty areas. This information is critical for testing any hypothesis regarding employment in poverty areas. It is evident, for example, that to the extent that industries located in poverty areas provide jobs almost exclusively to non-poverty-area residents, government programs aimed at attracting employment into these areas fail to meet their objectives.[3]

Insight into the effects of poverty concentrations on industry location must be sought in the behavior of specific industries. The characteristics of industries attracted to poverty areas offer insight into relationships linking concentrated poverty and patterns of industrial growth. Basic information on two groups of industries is presented in Table 9-1. The first group

Table 9-1

Characteristics of Industries with Initial or Increasing Employment Concentrations in Poverty Areas, 1965

SIC[a]	Per Cent of Total Industry Employment in Poverty Areas, 1965[b]	Payroll[c] Per Employee Per Year	As Per Cent of Value Added	Value Added Per Employee
Boston				
20[d]	52.7	$5,340	50.0	$10,650
23[d]	32.6	3,900	60.0	6,500
24[e]	15.1	N.A.	N.A.	N.A.
25[d]	35.8	5,010	69.5	7,200
27[d]	52.7	6,080	66.8	9,080
28[f]	28.9	6,640	39.4	16,900
29[e]	6.3	6,040	37.6	16,040
33[f]	48.3	5,950	64.3	9,250
34[d]	57.5	5,930	58.9	10,070
35[d]	31.8	6,610	76.3	8,660
36[e]	9.7	6,310	89.9	7,800
39[d]	35.8	4,830	N.A.	N.A.
All industries	28.4	$6,030	73.0	$ 8,250
Cleveland				
20[d]	73.5	$5,990	48.0	$12,480
22[d]	83.9	4,320	64.7	6,670
23[f]	88.8	4,410	38.1	11,570
24[e]	21.7	5,010	69.2	7,240
26[d]	53.8	6,190	60.0	10,400
27[d]	84.6	6,710	53.7	12,490
29[d]	69.2	7,050	31.5	22,410
30[e]	20.8	5,560	60.4	9,210
31[d]	98.5	N.A.	N.A.	N.A.
32[e]	30.5	6,080	48.1	12,640
36[e]	35.6	6,490	48.8	13,280
38[d]	49.8	N.A.	N.A.	N.A.
39[d]	67.7	5,030	53.7	9,360
All industries	38.3	$6,810	56.5	$12,050

Table 9-1 (continued)

SIC [a]	Per Cent of Total Industry Employment in Poverty Areas, 1965 [b]	Payroll [c] Per Employee Per Year	As Per Cent of Value Added	Value Added Per Employee
Minneapolis-St. Paul				
20 [d]	37.1	$6,340	47.7	$13,290
22 [d]	78.9	4,470	85.4	5,230
23 [f]	79.3	3,820	55.3	6,910
24 [e]	7.8	6,060	48.1	12,590
26 [d]	30.1	5,670	51.6	10,990
27 [d]	55.3	6,130	61.7	9,930
28 [f]	42.6	6,740	20.9	32,200
31 [f]	50.7	N.A.	N.A.	N.A.
33 [e]	6.2	6,200	61.7	10,060
36 [e]	11.3	6,720	55.8	12,050
37 [e]	2.5	7,240	41.2	17,590
All industries	27.5	$6,450	54.0	$11,900
Phoenix-Central City Poverty Zones Only				
25 [e]	11.7	$4,780	62.5	$ 7,640
26 [e]	47.4	N.A.	N.A.	N.A.
30 [e]	16.3	N.A.	N.A.	N.A.
32 [f]	20.3	5,890	44.8	13,130
33 [e]	9.3	N.A.	N.A.	N.A.
34 [e]	7.9	5,640	55.9	10,090
35 [d]	60.8	6,600	74.2	8,890
39 [e]	6.5	4,850	63.2	7,670
All industries	13.1	$6,190	58.3	$10,630

[a] Industry codes are

20 Food products	28 Chemicals	33 Primary metals
22 Textiles	29 Petroleum	34 Fabricated metals
23 Apparel	30 Rubber and rubber products	36 Electrical machinery
24 Lumber	31 Leather and leather products	37 Transportation equipment
25 Furniture	32 Stone, clay, and glass	39 Miscellaneous manufacturing

[b] From tabulations of revised 1965 DMI file.
[c] From *Census of Manufactures*, 1963. Industry characteristics were ascertained for each individual SMSA.
[d] Industry accounts for greater fraction of total manufacturing employment in poverty areas than it does in the SMSA as a whole.
[e] Industry grew faster in poverty area than in SMSA as a whole.
[f] See notes d and e above.

comprises those industries that accounted for a greater fraction of 1965 employment in poverty areas than for the Standard Metropolitan Statistical Area (SMSA) as a whole. In the second group are industries that grew faster in the poverty areas over the period than in the SMSA as a whole. Both geographic concentration and rapid growth performance are potential indices of the attractiveness of poverty areas to industries. Industries attracted to these areas should appear in one or the other of these groups.

It is apparent that some individual industries are doing quite well in poverty areas. At least five industries in each SMSA grew more rapidly in poverty areas than in the rest of the SMSA. In seven cases in the four areas industries were both concentrated and rapidly growing in poverty areas.

This growth performance need not be in response to the presence of a low-skilled labor force. Other characteristics of the zones may be operative in determining this growth. This seems especially likely because, except in Phoenix, the poverty areas include the central industrial districts (CIDs) of the metropolitan areas. In addition, it is quite possible that the zones are areas of poverty as a result of the presence of manufacturing activity, and not vice versa. Manufacturing is often dirty, noisy, and ugly, and often congests traffic. Such side effects of manufacturing may make an area so unattractive for residential use that only poor households perforce live in the area.[a]

One group of industries especially likely to cause undesirable neighborhood effects are the so-called nuisance industries. Edgar M. Hoover and Raymond Vernon, in their study of the New York region, classified several industries as nuisance industries on a four-digit SIC basis. These industries, aggregated to a two-digit basis, are listed in Table 9-2, and those that are

Table-9-2

Nuisance Industries Located or Growing in Poverty Areas

Industry	Boston	Cleveland	Minneapolis-St. Paul	Phoenix
Chemicals and products (SIC 28)	yes	no	yes	no
Petroleum and products (SIC 29)	yes	yes	no	no
Primary metals (SIC 33)	yes	no	yes	yes

concentrated on growing in the poverty areas of the four SMSAs are identified.[b] This listing suggests that these industries are to some extent attracted to poverty areas, though not unusually so. The other, less noisome industries are either growing or concentrated in poverty areas to essentially the same extent. However, three of the seven instances of an industry both

---

[a] It is also possible that because of the concentrations of poor households in the areas, local authorities are less likely to "zone out" these nuisance activities. No actual causality can be inferred from these data.

[b] In food and food products (SIC 20), only meat products (SIC 201) was classified as a nuisance; so SIC 20 was omitted from the aggregated list.

growing and concentrated in poverty areas are in this group of nuisance industries. This does perhaps suggest a special attraction of nuisance industries to poverty areas.

The basic hypothesis that residence in core areas of poverty results in lack of information about and access to the growing job demands in suburban areas appears to imply that wages paid to residents of these areas by core-area employers may be lower than those they would receive if employed at comparable tasks in suburban plants. At a minimum it would seem core-area manufacturers must pay core-area residents at least what they would receive in suburban plants, minus an allowance for job search and commuting costs required to obtain and hold a job in suburban areas. At a maximum, they will be paid their potential suburban wage plus the increment in wages necessary to attract suburban residents to core-area jobs. The secular decline in manufacturing activity in core areas and the scattered reports of large increases over the last decade in reverse commuting suggest that the lower limit is at present the effective constraint on core-area wage rates in production activities.[4] Furthermore, because these are areas of poverty, it seems reasonable to presume that residents in the labor force have relatively low job skills.[e]

Following this line of reasoning, it is possible to go somewhat further in the classification and description of industries located in poverty areas using data contained in the Census of Manufactures for each industry in each SMSA: payroll per worker, payroll as a percentage of total value added, and value added per worker. These data provide a basis for testing the validity of the hypothesis that industry is locating in poverty areas to take advantage of low-wage labor that may be available there. The census data can be used in the following way:

1. Payroll per worker is a measure of industry wage level. It may be expected that low-wage industries would be attracted to these areas because they may be presumed to employ low-skilled and semiskilled workers to a larger extent than do high wage industries.

2. Payroll as a percentage of total value added is a measure of the labor intensity of the industry. The more labor-intensive the industry, the greater might be the attractiveness of these areas because the effect of core-area residence may be expected to depress the wage level of persons of all skill levels who are resident in the area. In the data this effect might easily be clouded, however, by the presence of low-wage, moderately labor-intensive industries that in terms of this measure would appear to be nonlabor-intensive.

---

[e] This supposition is reinforced by the fact that the skill status of adults was one of several factors employed to define areas of poverty.

3. Value added per worker, derived from the two preceding measures,

$$\frac{payroll}{number\ of\ workers} \bigg/ \frac{payroll}{total\ value\ added} = \frac{total\ value\ added}{number\ of\ workers}$$

is a composite measure. Since the attractiveness of poverty areas is expected to be inversely related to the industry's wage level and directly related to its labor intensiveness, the attractiveness should be inversely related to the ratio of these values. This measure suffers from the same potential ambiguity as the labor-intensity measure.

In Table 9-1 the basic census data are presented for each industry located or growing in poverty areas together with the average of all industries in each SMSA. A summary of the comparisons of each industry with the SMSA average for all industries is provided in Table 9-3. In the summary table for each SMSA the industries are divided into the two categories used in the main table. Only industries for which all data were available have been included in the summary. The pattern for payroll per worker is much stronger than for the other two items. Over two-thirds of the industries attracted to poverty areas pay wages below the average manufacturing wage paid in the SMSA as a whole. All but two of the industries included in the analysis for Cleveland and the city of Phoenix paid relatively low wages. The pattern is evident in Boston, where just over half fit the pattern. However, in Boston two of the high-wage industries—chemicals and petroleum products—are nuisances, and have grown more rapidly in poverty areas than elsewhere in the SMSA. Likewise, in Minneapolis-St. Paul the chemical industry is a relatively high-wage industry that was both relatively concentrated and expanding in the poverty areas. In the Twin Cities seven of ten industries pay lower than average wages. If one excludes from consideration the nuisance industries in the Boston and Twin Cities poverty areas as being constrained to such locations or as an agent producing neighborhood decline, the correspondence between low wages and poverty-area locations is almost one to one.

The comparisons of labor intensiveness and value added per worker of the poverty-area industries with the SMSA average offer little real pattern, and the reason would seem to rest in the "softness" of the labor-intensity measure outlined above. Likewise, it is difficult to observe differing patterns in the wage levels and labor-intensity of industries relatively concentrated in poverty areas in 1965 and those which have grown more rapidly at these locations. Only in Boston and the Twin Cities is any differentiation possible, and in three cases the growing industries are definitely high wage, although in over half of the cases they are nuisance types.

On balance, these results support the basic hypothesis that low-wage industries do find core poverty areas attractive as manufacturing sites. In

Table 9-3

Characteristics of Industries Located in Poverty Areas Compared with Characteristics of All Manufacturing Industries in Each Metropolitan Area, 1968 Relative to 1965

Area (SMSA)	Total Number	Number of Industries		
		Payroll Per Worker is Less Than	Ratio of Payroll to Total Value Added is More Than	Value Added Per Worker is Less Than
			SMSA Average	
Boston				
All industries [a]	10	5	2	3
Relatively concentrated [b]	8	5	1	2
Relatively growing [c]	4	1	1	1
Cleveland				
All industries [a]	11	10	4	6
Relatively concentrated [b]	7	6	2	4
Relatively growing [c]	5	5	2	3
Minneapolis-St. Paul				
All industries [a]	10	7	5	5
Relatively concentrated [b]	6	5	3	4
Relatively growing [c]	6	3	3	2
Phoenix (city only)				
All industries [a]	5	4	3	4
Relatively concentrated [b]	2	1	1	1
Relatively growing [c]	4	4	2	3
All SMSAs				
All industries	36	26	14	18
Relatively concentrated	23	17	7	11
Relatively growing	19	13	8	9

[a] Only industries with complete information on payrolls and value added were included in these tabulations.
[b] Industry accounts for greater fraction of total manufacturing employment in poverty areas than it does in the SMSA as a whole in 1965.
[c] Industry grew faster in poverty area than in SMSA as a whole.

several instances high-wage industries were located and growing rapidly in poverty areas. Often, however, these were nuisance industries. These findings strongly suggest that further analysis could profitably be done on the impact of poverty areas on industrial location. Several obvious questions are raised by this analysis: The first concerns the degree to which the constraints on job opportunities imposed by core-area residence might be relaxed by locational adjustments of employers to take advantage of the labor force available in these areas. Is the growth of low-wage industries in poverty areas observed in this analysis to any extent the result of the attractiveness to employers of the resident labor force? How powerful is this mechanism in shielding core-area residents from their inability to participate in suburban labor markets?

The growth of high-wage industry in poverty areas is especially important, of course. The data base of this analysis offers no insight into the characteristics of the employers of these establishments. What explains the growth of these industries in core areas of poverty? Are factors such as historical growth patterns of the industries, orientation toward the CID, or zoning or other controls on locational choice determining their growth in poverty areas, or do they find the resident labor force an attraction? Whatever their motives, do establishments in these industries offer significant employment opportunities for poverty-area residents? Unfortunately, definitive answers to these important questions must await future research.

10 Industrial Concentrations and Changes in the Location of Industrial Employment

In Part I it was found that individual industries in each of the sample metropolitan areas were clustered spatially to a significant degree and that each industry exhibited a distinctive locational pattern within the metropolitan area. In this chapter we explain the spatial distribution of these industries in 1965 and then test the general hypothesis that the concentration of industries in specific locations influences the locational decisions of establishments in these and other industries.

The locational decision of an individual manufacturer is a much-studied phenomenon and one that is demonstrably complex. At a very general level the firm seeks to locate so as to maximize its profit and market potential or minimize its costs, such as labor and transportation. A theory of the types of trade-off involved in this process has been proposed by Alfred Weber and August Lösch; Walter Isard and others have attempted to apply the proposals to actual situations. The presence of an individual manufacturer in a given metropolitan area, however, implies that many of the most fundamental decisions have already been made. This being the case, local variations in tax rates, neighborhood characteristics, legal restrictions, availability of specialized facilities, and economies possible from locating near other firms in the same or other industries become the important locational determinants. In this chapter the focus is upon the last of these factors, which will be referred to as external economies. It should be clear from the outset, however, that this is a very broad label.[a]

The problem of defining externalities in the real world has long been a vexing one for economists. Regional economists have concentrated on

---

[a] The strongest argument against the assertion that external economies have been an important locational factor might be termed the *physical constraint argument*. The thesis is that the requirment for certain natural resource inputs (e.g., water) or complementary facilities (e.g., railroads) by industries so constrains their locational possibility set that they have only a few areas in which to locate; and they concentrate there. This argument certainly has strength for industries like primary metals, which require heavy transportation facilities for their inputs and finished products and great quantities of water and other utility inputs obtained through their own sources or public utilities with adequate capacity. However, the force of this argument is diminished when it is observed that the electrical machinery industry, which has really emerged only since the end of the Second World War and which is not constrained significantly and by the need for specialized facilities, has tended to agglomerate within metropolitan areas much like other industries.

what Weber termed *economies of urbanization*—economies that accrue to a firm from the level of overall economic activity in an area. Urban economists (with exceptions discussed below) have paid little attention to external economies, either economies of urbanization or *economies of localization* that accrue to firms of a given industry from the number and functions of firms of that industry present in a given area.[1] This is surprising, given the numerous examples of externalities available in the metropolis. Firms of different industries may locate in close proximity to minimize transportation costs. Recall, for example, that in Cleveland the primary metals industry was concentrated in two separate zones with fabricated metals producers spread out between them. In addition, the need for consultation between firms producing specialized machinery and their clients may encourage the grouping of industries. Firms of the same and different industries can minimize their search costs for replacements in their labor force by being located where a large pool of workers exists, some of whom will be searching for a different job. Firms of the same industry may also aggregate to reduce the transportation costs to intermediate products.[b] This argument is supported by a quick look at the fraction of direct interindustry inputs that industries (defined on a two-digit basis) receive from themselves, as shown in Table 10–1. For some

Table 10-1

Intra-Industry Input-Output Linkages for Major Industries in the Four Metropolitan Areas

SIC	Fraction	SIC	Fraction
20	0.173	34	0.052
23	0.149	35	0.219
27	0.110	36	0.149
31	0.120	37	0.195
33	0.287		

Source: *Survey of Current Business*, November 1969.

industries locating together may provide the leverage necessary to obtain special utility rates or to have specialized loading facilities provided. Several studies for the New York area have documented the importance of marketing and production aspects in causing establishments of the apparel and printing and publishing industries to locate together.[c]

---

[b] Table 10-1 gives these fractions for the major industries (i.e., those accounting for more than 5 percent of total manufacturing employment) concentrated in one or more of the sample cities.

[c] These studies include E. M. Hoover and Raymond Vernon, *Anatomy of a Metropolis,* Cambridge, Massachusetts, Harvard University Press, 1956; Raymond Vernon,

Attempting to identify external economies and their locational effects would be difficult enough if that represented the only aspect of the problem. However, whereas individual firms may enjoy the benefits of these external economies, they certainly incur costs in doing so. If the market for urban land were operating perfectly one would expect that at the margin the value of these economies would be reflected in site rents. Because of the relatively higher rents at such locations the firm may be forced to conserve on land. Given the comparatively greater efficiency of single-level plants for continuous processing and material handling, conservation of land will impose a production cost on the firm. Thus, there is a trade-off between internal and external economies.[d] Another type of cost imposed on the firm locating to obtain external economies may be the increasing importance of external diseconomies at such locations. This type of cost is probably best thought of as congestion costs: an overabundance of trucks in an area of limited loading facilities and narrow streets; a dearth of parking places for employees' cars; inadequate storage area for inputs and finished products, causing purchasing and shipping to be made at above-minimum rates; and a general lack of space for expansion. From the above examples, the complexity of the problem of isolating the posi-

---

Metropolis 1985, Cambridge, Massachusetts, Harvard University Press, 1960; and Robert Leone, *Location of Manufacturing Activity in the New York Metropolitan Area,* New York, National Bureau of Economic Research, forthcoming. The nature of the external economies that have been discussed as influencing the locational decision differ basically from those referred to by Vernon. According to Vernon's view, externalities and centrality of location are highly correlated, and the reason for a central location is to provide a high degree of access to services provided by other industries or access to customers. For this reason he lists industries such as high fashion apparel, printing and publishing, and military electronics as prime candidates for centralized locations. Although these types of externality undoubtedly are factors influencing highly centralized locations, the concentrations of firms and employment of a particular industry in an area outside the central business district (CBD) indicates that other favorable externalities may be available from such groupings.

[d] The idea that external economies available at some locations may be offset by internal economies available to larger plants at other locations is not new. The striking point, though, is the limited extent to which external economies in any form have been explicitly introduced into analytical models of industry location. Such treatment is absent from the standard Lösch, Weber, and Heinrich von Thunen models, and their refinements of recent years. Several exceptions might be noted. Michael Goldberg in his *Intrametropolitan Industrial Location: Plant Size and Theory of Production* (Berkeley, University of California Center for Real Estate and Urban Economics, 1969) has introduced the trade-off between external and internal economies to a limited degree in the firm's production function. A more general formulation of the problem has been by Nurudeen Alao, "An Approach to Intraurban Location Theory," *Economic Geography* No. 2 1974, pp. 59-69. On balance, though, extremely little has been done to incorporate external economies into theoretical models of industry location, owing largely to mathematical intractableness of the resultant models.

tive effects of external economies in the face of offsetting forces can be appreciated. In brief, the presence of significant and substantial external economies may be more than offset by the costs of external diseconomies and foregone internal economies. Thus, a reduction over the observation period in the level of manufacturing activity in the zones offering the greatest external economies is not unexpected. It is possible that at the present time (as perhaps over the past two decades) the level of industrial activity in concentrated zones is adjusting to congestion costs of somewhat different types from those existing when the maximum concentration of activity was reached. If this were the case, an eventual "final" (equilibrium) adjustment with a reduced but substantial level of activity remaining in these areas could be expected.

Before proceeding further it is reasonable to ask why the existence of external economies of the kind described might be important in approaching some of the problems of cities. The evidence in Part I showed that the central cities in the sample Standard Metropolitan Statistical Areas (SMSAs) contained a large number of the concentrations of manufacturing industry and thus apparently enjoyed a comparative advantage in the presence of these economies. Since any departure of industry from the central city erodes the local tax base and increases the commuting distances for central-city poor,[e] it is vital to determine whether localization economies are continuing to effect the locational decision of firms. If they are, one immediate policy implication for the central cities is to work at improving the public services provided to the concentrated areas in order to maintain the competitive advantage of these locations (i.e., to enhance the economies and reduce the diseconomies) rather than devoting great energy and expense to attracting into the city new firms that may move to a peripheral location in a relatively short time.

On another level it is evident that localization economies have served as the implicit basis for the industrial location sectors of a number of land use-transportation models developed for individual metropolitan areas. In these models future growth of a given industry has frequently been allocated proportionately to those areas in which the industry is located at

---

[e] The main evidence on decentralization is from the estimation of density gradients for manufacturing employment at different points over the past 70 years. They have been done by Ed Mills in his *Studies in the Structure of the Urban Economy,* Baltimore, The Johns Hopkins Press, 1969. For additional estimates and a critique of such functions, see P. Kemper and Roger Schmenner, "The Diversity Gradient for Manufacturing Industry," *Journal of Urban Economies* 1 (1974): 410-17. A strong counter argument against this evidence on decentralization in the 1960s as well as a substantial clarification of the meaning of decentraliaztion is given by Bennett Harrison in the early chapters of his *Urban Economic Development: Suburbanization, Minority Opportunity, and the Condition of the Central City,* Washington, D.C., The Urban Institute, 1974.

the time of the study.[2] These modeling efforts have been sharply criticized for using this method of prediction, but the importance of external economies has never been documented; so the conditions under which this procedure might have theoretical validity remain unknown. The present analysis should provide information germane to such a test.

Definitions and Approach

A number of operational definitions must be adopted in order to test the hypothesis that locational activity within metropolitan areas is being influenced by the clustering of industry at specific locations and the externalities that accompany such concentrations. The first and most important definition concerns externalities. Three distinct types of externality can be identified as being available at a given location in a metropolitan area (analysis zone): (1) those available from special facilities, such as docks and piers, over which a firm has virtually no locational control; (2) those from the general type of activity in the zone or the zone's general location, including the characterization of the area as a traditional site of manufacturing activity and the location of the zone in a relatively centralized location; and (3) those resulting from the concentration of firms of a single industry or different industries, discussed earlier. Although the first two types are conceptually quantifiable in relatively simple ways, they make isolation of the third type more complex. The third type is the most difficult to quantify but of greatest interest to us. For this work the presence of one or more concentrated industries in an analysis zone will be considered indicative of the third type of external economy.

The definition of *concentration* employed here is the same as that used in Part I (described in "Spatial Distribution of Major Industries in 1965," Chapter 2). Two aspects of that definition require clarification in this context: use of employment as the classifying variable and use of a discrete level of employment. The use of employment instead of number of establishments to indicate clustering can be defended on two grounds. The first is simply that use of employment instead of number of establishments does not significantly alter the results. In Chapter 2 (and Appendix H) it was shown that only half of the zones would have the same industry concentrated in them using both employment and establishments as classifying variables. At the same time, almost universally there were a substantial number of establishments located in zones classified as having an industry concentrated in it in terms of employment. In addition, since the types of external economies being discussed are basically production economies, the use of employment to define concentration, which weights the larger establishments more heavily, is appropriate because larger establishments can probably place more emphasis on such economies than could smaller ones. The use of employment as the classifying variable is defensible on a second ground. The definition of localization economies set out earlier included both the number of firms *and* their functions; presumably larger firms carry out a broader range of productive operations.

The other dimension of the definition to be examined is that it is essentially a threshold definition, that is, in each city a given percentage of an industry's employment must be located in a zone for a concentration to be defined as existing in that zone. Leaving aside the issue of the level at which the threshold has been defined, the advantage of using this approach is that it largely eliminates the problem of attributing external economies of the third type to an area when a relatively small amount of industrial activity of a specific type is located there. A small amount of such activity may be clustered on a random basis.[f] The limitation of this definition, on the other hand, is that the threshold has in some sense been arbitrarily defined. In this type of exploratory research it is not evident that this is a significant limitation. The external economies accruing within a given industry or among several industries at a given location, then, are to be represented by the amount of employment in the industries defined as being spatially concentrated in that location.

For our purposes *locational activity* in a zone of a city will be represented by the net change in employment in that zone over the observation period. It is obvious that this simply summarizes the in- and out-migration of some firms, the birth or death of others, and the expansion or contraction of employment of firms not involved in other categories of change. These individual categories of change are examined for the same "locational influence" hypothesis in the second section of this chapter, and reinforce the findings presented below. The same broad two-digit Standard Industrial Classification of industry is used here as in the preceding chapters. This means that several distinct products and processes are being carried out at a single plant complex, implying that internal economies from joint production are accruing to the firm. Such internal economies should not, as argued earlier, effect the external economies available to firms of the same or different industries that locate together.

It is difficult to isolate the effect of concentration of activity of a given industry on the locational behavior of individual firms and thus on the growth of the industry in particular locations. Ideally one would like to know what the change in the level of activity would have been in the

---

[f] Thus far, by implication, a clustering of employment has connoted the presence of the third type of external economy. More formally, such clustering, beyond some minimal (random) level, is taken to be a sufficient but not necessary condition for the presence of such external economies.

absence of the concentrations of the industry that were present at the beginning of the period. If these influences can be isolated, the hypothesis that external economies associated with the clusterings of industry are exerting influence on the locational decision of firms will be supported if the growth rate of an industry at different locations in a metropolitan area are being differentially affected by these economies.

Conceptually, there appear to be two ways of isolating the effect of external economies associated with the spatial clustering of industry: The first would be to examine the growth of a single industry at different locations within the SMSA and, after controlling for other factors influencing the competitive position of each location, to determine statistically if the concentration of the industry in some locations significantly affects the growth rate. However, it is, in fact, not possible accurately to measure all the factors that affect the attractiveness of a particular location as a site for manufacturing activity. We have, therefore, focused our efforts on a second approach in which we examine the growth rates of concentrated and nonconcentrated industries within a single analysis zone. Thus, the attributes of the zone are held constant while the types of industry within it (concentrated and nonconcentrated) are examined. In particular, the specialized facilities and the location of the zone vis-à-vis other economic phenomena in the area are kept fixed while it is determined whether the clustering of industry exerts a significant influence. Evidently, the comparison of the two types of industry might be heavily influenced by the overall regional growth rates of industries included in each class. For this reason, in some of the analysis, the measure of competitive advantage described in Chapter 2, "The Process of Change," is used to take account of area-wide growth of each industry.

Differences in Aggregate Locational Change

The classification of all the manufacturing industries in a zone as concentrated or not concentrated is the same as the classification used in Part I. Table 10-2 presents basic data on the results of this classification for the 65 zones in which both types of industry are found. The data in columns 2 through 5 are intended to provide an idea of the absolute size of the base and change involved in each area. Columns 6 and 7, on the other hand, give the percentage change in employment of the concentrated and nonconcentrated industries adjusted for the industry mix in the zone in the base year, using the shift-share measure presented in Part I. This adjustment has been made so that observed differences between the two types of industry are not distorted by the overall growth rate of the individual industries in each city. A cursory examination of these data shows

Table 10-2

Changes in Employment of Concentrated and Nonconcentrated Industries within Analysis Zones, All Areas, 1968 vs. 1965

City and Analysis Zone [a]	Concentrated Industries [b] (SIC Code) (1)	1965 Employment		1965-68 Change in Employment		Per Cent Change Adjusted for Industry Mix, 1965-68	
		Concentrated Industries (2)	Non-concentrated Industries (3)	Concentrated Industries (4)	Non-concentrated Industries (5)	Concentrated Industries (6)	Non-concentrated Industries (7)
			Cleveland Area				
City of Cleveland							
CID (Central Industrial District) [d]	20, 22, 23, 24, 26, 27, 28, 29, 31, 32, 36, 38, 39	28,505	15,814	1,581	−2,562	5.65	−11.70
Ring 1, Northeast of CID	20, 22, 23, 25, 29, 34, 35, 36, 37, 38, 39	32,501	5,384	−7,347	−939	−20.10	−3.40
Ring 1, Southeast of CID	25, 29, 32, 33, 34	20,883	12,962	−987	−433	0.84	4.40
Ring 1, Southwest of CID	20, 23, 26, 27, 29, 30, 33, 34, 38	20,308	10,799	−4,631	−899	−20.68	−3.88
Ring 1, West of CID	26	825	15,743	−62	−2,606	−8.73	−11.92
Ring 2, Northeast of CID	25, 34, 35, 36	15,984	6,605	−2,051	2,290	−13.60	34.95
Rest of Area							
Berea-Olmstead Falls	37	11,162	5,907	1,330	3,527	21.36	42.48
Brecksville-Strongsville	24	193	229	−14	228	10.81	46.57
Maple and Garland Heights	36	3,808	6,758	−1,272	1,601	−31.51	22.21
E. Cleveland-Cleveland Heights	24	256	11,357	−253	−686	−98.58	0.87
Euclid	33, 35, 37	29,154	11,056	−2,436	1,581	−2.72	29.15
Bedford-Solon	25, 26, 30, 32, 34	7,046	7,602	483	75	4.33	8.63
Wickliffe-Willoughby	22, 30, 38	2,840	5,981	−741	2,736	−34.17	33.58

Table 10-2 (continued)

City and Analysis Zone [a]	Concentrated Industries [b] (SIC Code) (1)	1965 Employment		1965-68 Change in Employment		Per Cent Change Adjusted for Industry Mix, 1965-68	
		Concentrated Industries (2)	Non-concentrated Industries (3)	Concentrated Industries (4)	Non-concentrated Industries (5)	Concentrated Industries (6)	Non-concentrated Industries (7)
Painsville	28	7,602	1,252	-2,757	-30	-19.79	0.17
			Boston Area				
City of Boston							
CID	23, 27, 35, 39	9,437	4,197	-4,764	-1,146	-48.33	-22.65
South Boston	27, 34	6,409	7,043	-281	5,263	-3.11	41.33
Charlestown-E. Boston	20, 34	12,638	3,104	844	117	9.09	-0.94
Adjacent to CID	23, 27, 31, 39	13,296	3,879	-1,089	-347	-1.24	-7.89
Roxbury	27	2,367	6,502	-257	-1,600	-5.40	-25.26
W. Boston-Dorchester Rest of Area	22, 23, 25, 39	5,746	12,875	-1,113	1,376	-14.14	8.56
Peabody-Salem-Lynn	26, 28, 29, 31, 32, 35, 36, 37	31,077	5,264	2,506	2,089	-1.97	28.36
Somerville-Everett	22, 24, 25, 26, 28, 30, 32, 33, 37	11,488	10,976	927	1,040	-13.10	10.92
Cambridge	20, 25, 28, 30, 33, 34, 38, 39	16,724	10,941	-2,034	1,345	-21.82	14.08
Woburn-Burlington	36	13,590	5,306	-2,965	1,806	-18.35	21.89
Waltham-Newton	22, 29, 30, 32, 35, 36, 38	29,064	6,518	-4,590	1,560	-16.99	17.25
Sudbury-Lexington	36	6,893	1,280	797	-342	14.16	-36.68
Framingham-Natick	26	2,805	6,353	48	429	-3.75	-1.29
Needham-Walpole	22, 29, 38	5,089	4,050	-570	2,338	-23.15	37.28
Quincy-Braintree	37	4,031	4,485	5,982	620	36.79	11.71
Norwood-Walpole	22, 30	5,244	9,410	306	1,742	4.62	13.52
Hingham-Norwell	32	297	1,496	2	118	12.91	4.41
Brockton	24,31	4,547	3,692	-170	456	4.11	12.09

Table 10-2 (continued)

City and Analysis Zone [a]	Concentrated Industries [b] (SIC Code) (1)	1965 Employment		1965-68 Change in Employment		Per Cent Change Adjusted for Industry Mix, 1965-68	
		Concentrated Industries (2)	Non-concentrated Industries (3)	Concentrated Industries (4)	Non-concentrated Industries (5)	Concentrated Industries (6)	Non-concentrated Industries (7)
Minneapolis-St. Paul Area							
City of Minneapolis							
East of Miss. River, South	25, 33, 34, 39	2,562	3,826	−489	−319	−18.35	−5.34
East of Miss. River, North	20, 24, 29, 33, 34, 35, 36, 37, 38, 39	12,094	1,110	−3,097	9	−22.08	2.96
CID	20, 23, 25, 27, 31	11,563	5,157	−1,841	−1,388	−1.54	−28.15
Southwest of CID	23, 31	3,322	5,663	−1,588	−1,890	−12.08	−33.26
Northwest of CID	22, 29, 30	607	3,904	−199	−735	−27.44	−16.69
Southeast of CID	33, 34, 39	2,867	4,869	−1,717	−29	−58.04	−0.54
City of St. Paul							
CID	20, 22, 23, 26, 27, 28, 29, 31	9,965	2,816	−3,091	−891	−20.47	−29.30
East of CID	36	1,508	2,092	−1,498	1,632	−99.07	38.92
Southwest of CID	27, 37	3,609	3,083	495	6,853	17.39	65.72
Northwest of CID	25, 26, 27, 28, 32, 33, 34, 36, 37, 38, 39	14,722	3,316	−3,719	231	−13.59	3.45
Rest of Area							
Columbia Heights-Findley	33	336	1,409	230	174	30.85	14.38
North and West St. Paul suburbs	24, 30, 38	1,437	4,894	7	607	−9.31	10.13
St. Louis Park	24, 30, 31, 32	1,231	4,681	61	−96	8.54	5.24
Golden Valley-Robbinsdale	38	3,035	4,031	106	161	−12.15	12.27
Bloomington	33, 35	3,023	1,253	91	624	−9.97	41.31
Richfield-Intl Airport	30	437	1,644	−113	182	−29.76	17.14
Mahtomedi-Bayport	24, 31	1,290	536	−225	201	0.67	32.37
Newport-St. Paul Park	20, 28, 29	8,303	864	295	839	3.93	53.53
Hopkins-Mound	37, 39	1,360	4,047	205	108	13.48	0.22

Table 10-2 (continued)

City and Analysis Zone [a]	Concentrated Industries [b] (SIC Code) (1)	1965 Employment		1965-68 Change in Employment		Per Cent Change Adjusted for Industry Mix, 1965-68	
		Concentrated Industries (2)	Non-concentrated Industries (3)	Concentrated Industries (4)	Non-concentrated Industries (5)	Concentrated Industries (6)	Non-concentrated Industries (7)
City of Phoenix							
CID	20, 22, 24, 27, 28, 31, 34, 39	3,285	722	-99	-4	-5.96	-16.3
West of CID, Ring 1	20, 24, 25, 27, 28, 29, 30, 33, 34, 39	5,288	379	101	1,604	4.65	76.5
South of CID	25, 32	324	479	353	273	54.05	37.40
Southwest of CID	20, 25, 28, 29, 30, 32, 34, 35, 36, 39	8,268	412	-507	145	-29.24	18.50
East of CID	36	6,800	724	5,202	54	14.74	3.30
West of CID	26	250	455	-250	787	-100.00	60.00
Northwest of CID	22, 23, 24, 25, 26, 30, 33, 34, 39	1,746	2,739	102	-264	2.79	-30.70
Northeast of CID	32, 36	2,237	933	-167	211	-36.63	7.30
North of CID, Ring 3	30, 35	5,141	289	109	25	-17.91	-23.90
North of CID Ring 2	38	1,100	147	1,900	-80	7.46	-57.40
Rest of Area							
Scottsdale	31, 36	2,931	250	181	98	-29.42	18.26
Tempe-Mesa	23, 28, 29, 30, 32, 33, 34, 37	2,204	1,218	88	3,581	-6.96	69.93
Avondale-Buckeye	29	20	99	-20	40	-100.00	36.46
Goodyear-Glendale	23, 26, 27	3,277	1,049	604	241	2.58	-9.10

[a] Analysis zones that did not have one or more industries concentrated in them in 1965 are omitted.

[b] Concentrations are defined as being greater than or equal to twice the amount of employment of a given industry in an analysis zone than would be present if employment in that industry were evenly distributed across all analysis zones in that area. The industry codes are identified in Table 9-1, note a.

[c] For a formal definition of this measure, see Appendix D. This measure is discussed in Chapter 2, section "The Process of Change."

[d] The central industrial district is best thought of as a substantially enlarged central business district.

that the separation of employment into concentrated and nonconcentrated classes leaves a number of zones with very few employees in one class or the other. In addition, the statistical results for the Phoenix analysis zones were not significant. Phoenix is, therefore, omitted from the following analysis, as are those zones in other areas with few employees in either of the classes.

An examination of the percentage change figures for the 51 remaining zones is highly suggestive. In only a quarter of the zones (14) the concentrated industries show changes greater than (or less negative than) those of the nonconcentrated industries; and of these over half were in the four central cities, although only 23 of the 51 comparison zones are central-city zones. A further examination of these central-city zones shows that 7 of the 8 zones in which the concentrated industries have done relatively better are traditional manufacturing areas; none of the more rapidly growing, concentrated zones outside of the central cities are traditional areas. This suggests that such concentrations continue to be relatively more important in more centralized locations perhaps implying the presence of external economies general to many industries rather than the industry-specific economies posited by Raymond Vernon. (See note c.)

Differing patterns of employment growth between concentrated and nonconcentrated industries are also evident. The level of net change is higher for the nonconcentrated industries than for the concentrated ones (22 versus 16 per cent). Likewise, as detailed in the next section, these net change figures understate the amount of locational activity ongoing in the two types of industries. On average over the three SMSAs, nearly twice as much employment was associated with migrating establishments or with establishments beginning or ending business for nonconcentrated industries as for concentrated.

To test the hypothesis that the locational decisions of concentrated and nonconcentrated industries at the same location are differentially affected by external economies, the net change in employment has been regressed on several factors reflecting special characteristics of the location. Because the two types of industry are in all cases located in the same zone, most of the factors affecting the competitiveness of the zone as a location are held constant. This leaves us free to examine the importance of several factors reflecting external and internal economies. Table 10-3 contains most of the variables included in the actual analysis and shows the phenomena that were to be included and the manner in which they were actually measured. Each of these is elaborated later in the text with the discussion of the results. Not included in this list is a measure of the external economies available as a result of the location of firms and functions of a single industry in one area. As explained below, the significance of such economies will be evident indirectly from the regression results.

Table 10-3

Definitions of Quantitative Measures of Factors Influencing Industry Location Choices

Phenomenon	Measure
External diseconomies resulting from congestion	Square of total manufacturing employment in zone, divided by one million
Internal economics available from large-scale operations	Average establishment employment
General externalities present due to location or history of location	Zone type: central city of traditional site of manufacturing activity
General recent prosperity of zone as site for industrial activity	"Comparative industrial structure" of zone (see Part I), which shows industry mix to be growing faster or slower than expected
Specific industry effects, e.g., presence of the apparel and printing industries might indicate special capital effects and their decline might indicate the availability of space; also controls broadly for industry type: market oriented, footloose, or input-oriented	Additive dummy variables for concentrated industries important in all the sample SMSAs

There are two conceptually equivalent ways of estimating a regression model in which the goal is to differentiate between two classes of response in the dependent variable. One is to pool the observations from the two groups and in the simplest case to include a dummy variable to distinguish between them. (In the present case a dummy variable for concentrated observations could be included.) The case at hand is not this simple. Since, for reasons already discussed, a firm located in an area with significant potential external economies may alter its production process or size of operation as a result of these externalities, the inclusion of a simple dummy variable is insufficient. Since the slopes of each of the independent variables might be affected, the addition of a multiplicative dummy variable for each independent variable is required. The second approach is to estimate a model separately for each type of differentiated response (concentrated versus nonconcentrated). If the coefficients differ significantly between the two models, the differential response is confirmed. The second method of estimation has been used here basically to conserve on degrees of freedom. To sum up, significant differences in the estimated coefficients between the models for concentrated and nonconcentrated industries would demonstrate that the two types of industry are responding differently to the same economic factors. Further, since the regressions hold other zonal characteristics constant for the analysis, the differences in the coefficients between the concentrated and nonconcentrated models will also *in part* indicate differences in the importance of external economies arising from the clustering of the firms and functions of individual and groups of industries. Because in two-thirds of the zones more than one industry is concentrated, it is not possible to assume a close correspondence between the importance of these economies in general and their importance for a single industry.[g]

Before reviewing the empirical results a final restatement of the hypothesis is in order. The hypothesis is that firms of manufacturing industries at locations at which they are concentrated respond differently in their location decisions to certain economic factors from other firms of those industries which are not concentrated together. Part of the explanation of the differences is in the importance of external economies to those firms in each industry that have grouped themselves into concentrations.

Empirical Results

Two different dependent variables are used in both regression models. The variables are the simple change in employment in the industry type (concentrated or nonconcentrated) between 1965 and 1968 in an analysis zone and the same change expressed as a percentage of base-year employment and weighted for the SMSA-wide growth rates of the industries included.

The estimated regression models are presented in Table 10-4. The fit for the concentrated model was markedly superior when the unweighted change in employment was used as the dependent variable, while the nonconcentrated model was superior when the net change in employment was weighted for industry mix and expressed as a percentage. These results provide some information on the extent to which scale effects, that is, the absolute size of the change in employment, influence the functional relationship with the independent variables.[h] The greater explanatory power of the unweighted-change form for concentrated locations compared to unconcentrated ones suggests the reinforcing nature of external economies for the concentrated industries.

---

[g] If only a single industry were concentrated, with a minimum of other industrial activity in the zone, the effect of economies accruing to the firms of the industry could be unambiguously inferred. Where more than one industry is concentrated and/or there are substantial amounts of other industrial activity, the form of the economies and determination of the industries to which they accrue are much less clear. The effort in the current work is to isolate the individual-industry effects to the greatest extent possible. In the statistical work that follows, the isolation is accomplished through the traditional and central-city dummy variables, which are intended to account for "general industrial activity." However, the problem of interpreting the results when more than one industry is concentrated in a zone is not fully resolved by these devices.

[h] A dependent variable that was the same as the second form just described except that it was not standardized for SMSA-wide industry growth was also tested. The results compare favorably with those shown in Table 10-4, except that, as expected, this "comparative industrial structure" variable is stronger in the model for concentrated industries.

Table 10-4

Regressions for Change in Employment, All Industries, Concentrated vs. Nonconcentrated Locations, 1968 Relative to 1965
(Figures in parentheses are t Ratios)

| Independent Variables | Dependent Variable: Change in Employment, 1968 vs. 1965 | | | |
| | Concentrated Locations | | Nonconcentrated Locations | |
	Actual Change	Industry-weighted Per Cent Change	Actual Change	Industry-weighted Per Cent Change
Constant	−802.10	−15.15	454.06	24.06
Area dummy				
Boston	1,057.50	13.75	118.10	−10.95
	(1.88)	(1.45)	(0.20)	(1.28)
Minneapolis-St. Paul	−24.50	5.84	−47.60	−1.51
	(0.04)	(0.56)	(−0.07)	(0.16)
Traditional	1,072.00	44.09	——	——
	(1.82)	(1.47)		
Central city	——	——	−665.30	−14.22
			(1.44)	(2.08)
Comparative industrial structure ^{a}	0.54	0.006	0.004	−0.004
	(2.99)	(1.90)	(0.02)	(1.58)
Average firm size	2.51	0.012	−0.75	−0.005
	(4.76)	(1.26)	(1.44)	(0.48)
(Total manufacturing employment)^2/10^6	−1.98	0.003	0.190	0.008
	(2.48)	(0.23)	(0.27)	(0.75)
Industry dummy ^{b}				
SICs 20, 21, 22	−1,143.00	−10.58	257.50	−1.62
	(2.21)	(−1.22)	(0.55)	(0.23)
SICs 23, 27	−1,882.00	−8.05	−871.30	−18.85
	(2.98)	(0.76)	(1.63)	(2.34)
SICs 35, 36	−1,624.00	−21.44	230.00	−5.01
	(3.03)	(2.60)	(0.51)	(0.74)
R^2	0.783	0.520	0.460	0.576

^{a} See Appendix D for definition.
^{b} Industry codes are 20, food products; 21, tobacco products; 22, textiles; 23, apparel; 27, printing and publishing; 35, nonelectrical machinery; 36, electrical machinery. Variable has a value of 1 if industry is concentrated in the zone and is zero otherwise.

A t-test of the equality of the coefficients common to both models for each of the dependent variables shows that with only two exceptions the coefficients are significantly different at the 0.05 level.[i] This supports the

---

[i] In the models for the level of the dependent variable, the coefficients of the dummy variable for Minneapolis–St. Paul did not differ significantley in the concentrated and nonconcentrated models. In the models for the industry-weighted form of the dependent variable, the coefficients of the congestion variable (the square of employment divided by 10^6) were not significantly different.

hypothesis that the two types of industry are responding differently to the same economic factors. The second general point concerns the level of significance of the individual coefficients. In this exploratory analysis, the minimum acceptable level of significance for a two-tailed test is 0.20; the corresponding value of the t-statistic is about 1.28.

The additive dummy variables for the SMSAs relative to Cleveland were included to account for general differences in net employment change between the sample cities. Different dummy variables for zone types were included in the concentrated (traditional versus nontraditional) and nonconcentrated (central city versus other) models simply because each performed better in the particular model. The difference in these variables and their signs implies that concentrated industries do comparatively well in traditional manufacturing areas in which they are concentrated and which may also be in the central city, while employment growth of the same industries in central-city locations in general, including nontraditional areas, is relatively poor.

The variable for comparative industrial structure, which was developed in Part I, was included to control for the general industrial well-being of the analysis zone. Its coefficient is positive and significant in both models for concentrated industries and insignificant in one of the nonconcentrated models and significant but with a negative sign in the other. For concentrated industries these results show these industries grow and decline with the area: as the area becomes less attractive, they leave it, making the area still less attractive to the firms remaining by further reducing the external economies available there. From the data displayed in Table 10-2, it is evident that concentrated industries are not dominantly responsible for the overall industrial growth in most zones; so we are not explaining growth in terms of itself. For nonconcentrated industries the industry mix of the zone does not seem to make much difference; if anything, these industries are attracted to areas with little rapidly growing industry, possibly areas in which formerly occupied buildings are now available.

Average firm size was included to account crudely for the strength of internal economies as an offset to the external economies of concentrated locations. To support this use of the variable, after controlling for congestion (reflected by the square of total employment), the sign of the coefficient should have been negative for concentrated industries and positive for nonconcentrated ones. The results are just the opposite. This probably is caused by the use of employment to measure the presence of concentrations, with larger firms contributing heavily to the classification of industry as concentrated. At the same time, it may be that some localization economies accrue to the largest firms, while as a class have a lower propensity to move. Such economies might include the presence of specialized loading facilities on rail spurs or dock facilities from which these large firms reap disproportionate benefits because of their higher volume of inputs and outputs. The positive effect of firm size on concentrated industries and its negative effect on the nonconcentrated ones, combined with the findings for comparative industrial structure suggest another hypothesis: Firms of concentrated industries are willing to bid up land rents as they expand, forcing out those with relatively less economic reasons for remaining.

Congestion is measured here by the square of the total manufacturing employment in the analysis zone. The squaring of the number reflects the nonlinear nature of the increase in congestion costs.[j] The variable is significant only in the first of the two estimated models for concentrated locations, where it has a negative effect on the growth of concentrated industries. The poor performance in the other concentrated regression is attributed to the way in which we measure congestion. In the present form of the measure no account is taken of the congestion created by commercial and residential activities that in some areas is clearly more important than that generated by manufacturing enterprises. The lack of significance for the nonconcentrated industries does, however, bear out expectations. They gain less from the external economies of locating or expanding in highly congested areas. Therefore, their growth rate is not adversely affected, since they simply can locate elsewhere. The concentrated firms presumably would, given increased demand, like to expand in the same zones; and for them congestion costs become a factor retarding expansion.

Finally, the results for the dummy variables for specific concentrated industries are of interest. Except for the variable for the printing and publishing and apparel industries, the results show little relation between changes in a specific concentrated industry and nonconcentrated industries in general. For apparel and publishing, however, their decline appears to have caused a decline in employment of complementary, nonconcentrated industries. In one respect this result can be interpreted as reflecting the artificiality of our classification of concentrated versus nonconcentrated. In general, it was believed that the vacating of space by a declining major industry would leave room for nonconcentrated industries, thus producing a positive relation in the nonconcentrated regression. If, as some of the other results indicate, larger establishments are bidding up rents at concentrated locations, then the actual results for specific industry dummy variables is understandable.

---

[j] The nonlinear form performed generally better than the linear form in these tests. The use of a more general congestion variable based on all types of employment was theoretically available from Census data. However, because zip code boundaries (used in defining the analysis zones) and census tract boundaries are completely independent, it would have required a great deal of on-site observation to determine accurately in which analysis zones much of the employment was in fact located.

Summary and Conclusion

From the above analysis it is evident that firms at the two types of location (concentrated and nonconcentrated) are responding differently to the same economic factors. In addition, this indirectly indicates that external economies that accrue when firms locate together are more important to the firms located in concentrated areas, which are presumably located there in part to capture these economies, than to firms in nonconcentrated locations. Several reasons can be advanced to explain this differential response within the same industries. One has been alluded to above; it may be that firms of the same industry differ significantly in their technology between the two types of location, the more land-extensive operations permitting greater internal economies in nonconcentrated areas. A more basic reason may be that the employment at the two types of location is producing for different markets and, therefore, is constrained in different ways. Within all manufacturing industries there are firms that are definitely producing for highly localized markets. The production location constraints of these firms are generally the same set as those found by their counterparts producing for national markets but they must simultaneously be much more sensitive to local market considerations as well. Finally, it is possible that the difference in response between the two types of location can be partly attributed to firm size, those at concentrated locations being about 10 per cent larger on average.

Differences in the Components of Locational Change

Certain systematic differences in the locational behavior of firms in the same industry at concentrated and nonconcentrated locations as measured by net change in employment were found in the previous section. The purpose of this section is to test the central hypothesis of the chapter and to pursue the findings of the previous section, using the data on the individual components of locational change (movers and new and dying establishments).

Changes in employment that result from locational change entail a change in the physical position of the establishment involved. It is recognized that the pattern of industrial employment is heavily influenced by the net changes in employment of firms whose physical location remains fixed, as demonstrated in Part I. These changes are not included in this analysis because our confidence in these data, particularly on a disaggregated basis, is not as great as for the other data. (This point is amplified in Appendix A.)

Background

Some insights into the processes that have led to the consistently different growth rates for industry at concentrated and nonconcentrated locations can be obtained from the summary data contained in Table 10-5. The data are reported for concentrated and nonconcentrated industries separately. These labels refer respectively to the employment across all manufacturing industries in zones in which these industries are concentrated and those in which they are not.[k] The first two columns give the number of employees involved in locational changes—in- or out-migrations and births and deaths of establishments—and this number as a percentage of the total base-year employment. These data give an idea of the amount of locational activity involved. For example, an equivalent of about 17 per cent of base-year industrial employment at concentrated locations was involved in locational shifts over the 1965-68 period. Note that this is only an equivalent percentage; employment of industries migrating into areas in which they are concentrated may not come from other concentrated areas, and employment by new firms definitely does not.[1]

It is very clear from the statistics in column 2 that the rate of locational activity relative to base-year employment for nonconcentrated employment is substantially larger (almost twice on average) than for employment at concentrated locations. This would be expected to a certain degree from our definition of concentration, since the largest firms practically constitute concentrations by themselves and, in addition, have a lower propensity to move than the smaller firms. The extent of the difference between the two types of location, however, is much greater than anticipated a priori. An occasional move by one of these large establishments would suffice to offset the flurry of activity of small firms shown in the employment data.

Each locational-change component is expressed as a percentage of the total locational change (column 1), to abstract from the level of locational activity in each zone. These percentages for the four elements are presented in columns 3 to 5 of the table. A number of fairly clear patterns are discernible from the data. For firms located where their industries are concentrated, employment in these firms moving away from these locations has in all cases exceeded that migrating in. Likewise, employment of firms going out of business has substantially exceeded that of new establishments. In fact, deaths were the largest locational change in all the cities

---

[k] These data are on the same basis as those contained in Table 10-2, that is, on a basis to facilitate *within*-zone comparison of industries that are and are not concentrated in each zone.

[1] For the moment we ignore the issue of whether deaths in one area and births within the same industry in other areas are related phenomena.

Table 10-5

Locational Change in Employment, All Industries, Concentrated vs. Nonconcentrated Locations, 1968 Relative to 1965

	Total Manufacturing Employment in Moving, New, or Defunct Establishments, 1968		1968 Mfr. Employment in Specified Establishments as Percentage of Col. 1			
	Number (1)	As Fraction of 1965 Employment in Same Set (2)	Outmovers (3)	Inmovers (4)	New (5)	Defunct (6)
Boston						
Concentrated industries [a]	22,948	12.69	23.46	18.61	5.46	52.45
Nonconcentrated industries	28,413	26.46	27.31	25.78	8.46	38.44
Cleveland						
Concentrated industries [a]	30,097	16.62	26.49	23.63	14.32	35.54
Nonconcentrated industries	32,697	29.60	26.49	27.97	9.73	35.79
Minneapolis-St. Paul						
Concentrated industries [a]	19,750	23.71	25.85	20.16	5.68	48.28
Nonconcentrated industries	27,399	46.28	21.97	25.86	27.02	25.13
Phoenix						
Concentrated industries [a]	6,043	12.20	34.53	19.51	15.83	30.11
Nonconcentrated industries	8,542	85.89	10.27	14.39	63.48	11.83

[a] For definition of concentration, see Chapter 2, "Spatial Distribution of Major Industries in 1965."

except Phoenix, where emigration caused the greatest change in employment. The locational change of firms located where their industries are not concentrated is quite different: The amount of employment moving in exceeded that emigrating everywhere except in Boston, and deaths were larger than births only in Boston and Cleveland. Some further differences in the locational changes of the two types of firms can be noted. Except for Phoenix, in-migrating employment was more important (as a share of total locational change) for nonconcentrated firms in those areas. Also the importance of employment of new establishments was much greater for the nonconcentrated firms except in Cleveland, where this pattern was reversed. Since one would imagine the industry-specific external economies available to new firms to be greatest in the areas in which its industry is concentrated, this result at face value is somewhat surprising. Finally, a larger share of employment in defunct establishments is found among firms located where their industry was grouped. Again the exception is in Cleveland, where such firms show a lower loss from the birth-death process than to firms located away from their industries' concentrations.[m]

From the foregoing it is evident that not only do the levels of locational activity of the same industry differ depending on whether the firms being examined are part of a concentration of the industry, but also the relative importance of the locational components differ in their effect on net change in employment. The issue is whether the various components of locational change for industry differ significantly in their response to economic factors with the presence of concentration as we found to be the case for net change in employment. In trying to discern the effects of various factors on these components a regression analysis has again been employed.

Empirical Results

The dependent variable in each case is the number of employees in the locational component for a given analysis zone divided by the number of employees in the industries concentrated or not concentrated in that zone in 1965. The independent variables in the reported regressions are the same as those used in the net change analysis (presented in Table 10-4), and so we do not discuss them individually again. In Table 10-6 it is seen that the multiple correlation coefficients for the various rates of locational activity of industry have greater explanatory power for concentrated cases than for nonconcentrated ones. The difference is especially striking for

---

[m] The same type of table was constructed for traditional-nontraditional zones. Examination of the patterns in the tables did not show substantive differences between the two types of zone in this respect.

Table 10-6

Regression Results for Employment in Locational Change Components of All Industries at Concentrated and Nonconcentrated Locations, Cleveland, Boston, and Minneapolis-St. Paul (Figures in Parentheses are t Ratios)

Independent Variable	Dependent Variable: Employment in Specified Establishments as Fraction of 1965 Employment							
	Outmovers		Inmovers		New		Defunct	
	Con-centrated	Non-concentrated	Con-centrated	Non-concentrated	Con-centrated	Non-concentrated	Con-centrated	Non-concentrated
Constant	0.141	0.186	0.318	0.286	0.065	0.152	−0.081	0.191
Area dummy								
Boston	−0.292	−0.042	−0.344	−0.113	−0.100	−0.030	0.114	−0.009
	(1.90)	(0.42)	(2.42)	(0.88)	(1.57)	(0.17)	(0.83)	(0.07)
Minneapolis-St. Paul	−0.154	−0.103	−0.266	−0.166	−0.136	0.123	0.244	−0.087
	(0.91)	(0.94)	(1.72)	(1.18)	(2.02)	(0.63)	(1.66)	(0.65)
Central city	0.131	−0.016	0.004	−0.060	−0.016	−0.193	0.034	−0.002
	(0.88)	(0.20)	(0.03)	(0.55)	(0.26)	(1.35)	(0.26)	(0.09)
Comparative industrial structure [a]	0.0001	−0.0001	0.0001	−0.0001	0.0001	0.0001	−0.0001	0.0001
	(0.94)	(0.20)	(0.016)	(0.02)	(1.00)	(0.27)	(0.75)	(0.76)
Average firm size	−0.0005	−0.0001	−0.0003	0.0001	0.0001	−0.0001	−0.0003	−0.0002
	(3.21)	(0.68)	(1.99)	(0.04)	(1.61)	(0.13)	(2.59)	(1.5)
(Total manufacturing employment)^2/10^6	0.0007	0.0001	−0.0004	−0.0001	−0.0002	0.0002	0.0006	0.0003
	(3.67)	(1.19)	(2.20)	(0.34)	(2.25)	(0.72)	(3.34)	(1.8)
Industry dummy [b]								
SICs 20, 21, 22	0.054	0.137	0.032	0.287	0.077	−0.169	−0.124	0.186
	(0.39)	(1.65)	(0.27)	(2.69)	(1.36)	(1.12)	(1.03)	(1.83)
SICs 23, 27	0.24	−0.040	0.103	−0.200	0.094	0.132	−0.094	−0.070
	(1.31)	(0.43)	(0.62)	(1.64)	(1.25)	(0.78)	(0.58)	(0.61)
SICS 35, 36	−0.22	−0.071	−0.181	−0.028	−0.050	−0.176	0.069	−1.181
	(1.71)	(0.89)	(1.51)	(0.28)	(0.94)	(1.20)	(0.60)	(1.84)
Employment in dying establishments as fraction of 1965 base					0.410	0.146		
					(11.84)	(0.72)		
Employment in new establishments as fraction of 1965 base							1.87	0.069
							(11.50)	(0.72)
R^2	0.708	0.427	0.553	0.422	0.910	0.476	0.916	0.498

[a] See Appendix D for definition.
[b] See Table 10–4, note b.

births and deaths. The combination of the lack of correlation with these independent variables and the greater levels of locational activity for industry in nonconcentrated cases would seem to add credibility to the hypothesis that more of this activity may be random essentially in nature where the industry is not concentrated.

Turning first to the results for employment in establishments moving out of or locating in each analysis zone (columns 1-4), it is seen that aside from individual industry effects the main differences between the estimates for firms in the two circumstances are in firm size and in total manufacturing activity. In the models for concentrated employment the greater the average firm size the lower the rate of movement—as one would expect. At the same time, however, the larger the establishments in the zone in the base period the lower the rate of in-movement of establishment employment in the industries concentrated in a zone. There is no similar effect for establishments not concentrated in the zones. Also, as might be expected, the variable for total amount of activity, which reflects congestion costs, was positively associated with outmovers' employment and negatively associated with in-movers' employment for firms in industries in locations at which they were concentrated. For the firms located where the industries were not concentrated, increased congestion affects only the rate of origins.

The industry dummy variables display an interesting pattern in their own right. The rate of outmoving employment has been significantly greater in apparel and in printing and publishing than in other industries, but the establishments have tended to relocate in the same types of places. Likewise, establishments in the food-processing industry have been shifting among areas in which the industry is not concentrated. The machinery industries, on the other hand, have on net moved away from areas where they were concentrated, but there is still movement to the areas in which these industries are concentrated. Together these results suggest that external economies remain important for the apparel and printing and publishing industries, unimportant for food processing, and are declining in importance for the two machinery industries.

In general, these data have shown a very high correlation between the rates of employment at establishment origins and destinations for individual zones. In fact, the addition of the complementary rate as an additional explanatory variable in the regressions just discussed greatly increases the amount of explained variance. This high correlation is, however, in some sense spurious because the data on origins only indicates that the moving employment originated in the zone not that it left the zone. Earlier work with these data as well as work by Harold Williamson have shown the majority of industry moves to be relatively short, so they frequently begin and end in the same zone.[3] The other reason for this correlation is that there actually has been a substantial amount of cross-migration both in aggregate and by industry for all the sample cities.

The regression models in which birth (death) rates are the dependent variables include the rate of change of employment in (new) defunct establishments among the independent variables. The discussion of the interrelatedness of these events, which was presented with the aggregate data in Part I, made it clear that birth and death rates should not be considered to be independent. In fact, with a more complete set of explanatory variables it would be profitable to consider the two rates statistically as simultaneously determined. A surprising result in the estimated models is the lack of significance of the birth rate variable in the death rate equation and vice versa for the firms located away from their industries' concentrations. This confirms what the raw data show, namely, that the births and deaths are taking place in different zones among the nonconcentrated firms, with births particularly infrequent in central-city locations. A strong relation exists between births and deaths among the zones where the industry was concentrated, after accounting for variations in congestion, industrial composition, and average firm size. The elasticities of birth rates with respect to death rates and vice versa at the mean are quite high—approximately 1.6 and 0.46.

This result in the birth regression tends to support a substantially more complicated incubator hypothesis than that advanced by Raymond Vernon and tested in Chapter 8. The process observed here shows the relation between rentable production space in process of creation, a possible but not necessary fall in the rent level, and the in-movement of employment of new establishments belonging to the industries concentrated there. The fact that the results are so strong for the concentrated industries underscores both the importance of the particular externalities available and importance of limited capacity of *suitable* production space at such locations. Thus, it would appear that the incubator hypothesis cannot be supported outside of New York City because it has been formulated too simply; other factors must be controlled before the test can be fairly made.

Conclusions

One truly important point stands out from this fairly crude, exploratory analysis. Firms belonging to industries that are concentrated and nonconcentrated at the same location are responding differently to the same economic factors. This differential behavior is *in part* attributable to the importance of external economies resulting from firms of the same and other industries locating together, although other factors may also be important. This finding has two important implications: First, in a policy context, it suggests that central cities might do well to improve the services they provide their industrial enclaves in order to exploit the comparative advantage of external economies they currently enjoy. Such aid might extend even to facilitating land assembly for expansion and other forms of assistance beyond the simple tax incentives now used. Second, in a research context, the results imply a potentially powerful dichotomy for predicting future industrial location. Given the greater stability and the consistent responses to economic forces of firms at concentrated locations, resources should be expended primarily on predicting the locations of the nonconcentrated firms, since the latter are apparently more influenced by changes in transportation facilities (access provided by highways and airports), locational shifts in local markets, and "neighborhood effects." This dichotomous relationship clearly needs to be explored more fully, and, if possible, exploited.

Appendixes

Appendix A
Method Used to Prepare DMI Data for Studying Metropolitan Industrial Location

The first step in the preparation of the data was to machine-match the 1965 and 1968 files using the DUNS numbers "Structure of This Study," Chapter 1. Figure A-1 presents a simplified flow chart of the program used.

For each of the metropolitan areas, five files of establishments were created. For all establishments that could be located in both the 1965 and 1968 files the physical address field in its Duns Market Identifier (DMI) record was compared; and if the data in this field were identical the establishment was coded into the file of nonmoving establishments (File A). If the address fields were not identical the establishment was tentatively coded as a moving establishment (File B). If an establishment in the 1965 files could not be found in the 1968 files it was included in the file of dying establishments (File C). If an establishment in the 1968 file was not located in the 1965 file and its date of formation was after 1965 it was included in the file of new establishments (File E). If its date of formation was missing or occurred before 1966 it was included in the additions-to-coverage file (File D). The initial breakdown of establishments among these files, for each of the four areas, and their percentage distribution are presented in Table A-1.

The first step taken in our testing of these data was to verify that the machine-identified moving establishments were in fact movers. The machine identification of moving establishments was made on the basis of the address of the physical location of the establishment. If in the two records of the establishment the fields allocated by Dun and Bradstreet for the entry of the address were not identical, the establishment was entered into the file of moving establishments. A large number of establishments were falsely identified as movers, because of spelling changes in the field, etc. Verification of this movers file was done with a simple hand check of the records of each establishment machine-identified as a mover. If on inspection the differences between the two addresses of the establishment could be convincingly attributed to a simple spelling change, format change, or some simple error, the establishment was deleted from the sample of moving establishments. If not, then it remained in the file of moving establishments. Almost one-half of the preliminary identifications of establishments as movers were incorrect.

After these operations, however, the data remained to some extent un-

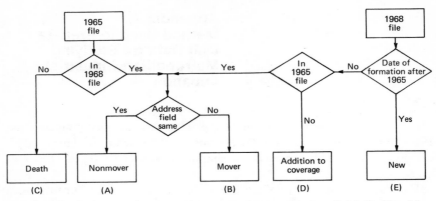

Figure A-1. Schematic Presentation of Methods Used to Initially Partition Establishments in the Four Metropolitan Areas

satisfactory. Figure A-2 suggests some of the more important reasons why this is so. The four boxes on the left side of the diagram, labeled NEW, MOVER, DIE, and NONMOVER, correspond to the files E, B, C, and A of Figure A-1, which would have resulted had the DMI files been perfectly designed and executed for the purpose of this study. Thus, *Mover* is the population of establishments that have changed location in each of the four metropolitan areas; *Death* is an exhaustive list of every establishment that died or left the areas; etc. In Figure A-1 the boxes labeled *New,*

Table A-1

Initial Classification of Establishments

SMSA	Total Establishments 1965	Total Establishments 1968	Address Changers (B)	Deaths (C)	New Establish-ments (E)	Additions to Cov-erage (D)
		Number of Establishments				
Cleveland	4,178	4,598	728	820	447	793
Boston	5,131	5,590	865	1,039	482	922
Minneapolis-St. Paul	2,624	3,199	833	653	422	816
Phoenix	983	1,208	143	344	280	294
Total	12,916	14,595	2,569	2,856	1,631	2,825
		Establishments as Percentage of 1965 Total Establishments				
Cleveland	100.00	110.05	17.42	19.63	10.70	18.98
Boston	100.00	108.94	16.86	20.24	9.39	17.97
Minneapolis-St. Paul	100.00	121.91	31.74	24.89	16.08	31.10
Phoenix	100.00	122.88	14.54	34.99	28.48	29.90
Total	100.00	112.99	19.89	22.11	12.63	21.87

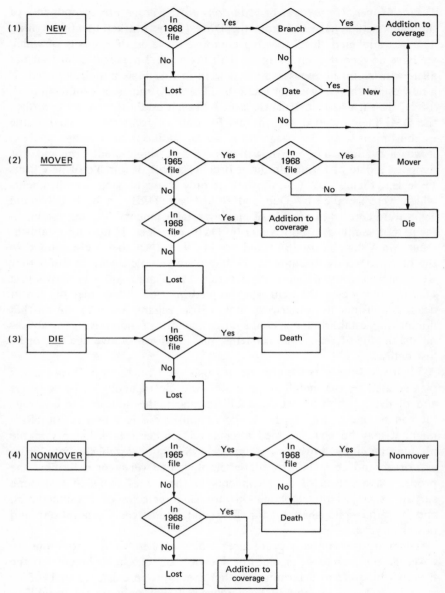

Figure A-2. File Matching Logic

Death, Mover, Nonmover, or *Additions to Coverage* are components of the fields actually derived from the DMI (Duns Market Identifier) files. The boxes labeled "lost" together comprise those establishments of which we have no record at all. Diagram 1 in Figure A-2 makes it clear that not all new firms in the areas examined were in File E as initially created. If a new establishment was not found by Dun and Bradstreet ("not sampled, '68"), then it was lost. If it was a new branch establishment its record in the DMI files included no variable for date of formation, and thus the establishment would be assigned to File D, additions to coverage. Only if it was a headquarters of a new firm or a new single-plant firm and was assigned a date of formation did it become a part of our file of new firms (File E). Figure A-2 (2) shows that only those moving establishments which were sampled by Dun and Bradstreet (D&B) in both 1965 and 1968 were entered in our file of moving establishments. Moving establishments not sampled in both years by D&B were lost. If moving establishments were sampled in 1965 and not in 1968, then they were entered in the file of dead establishments; if they were sampled only in 1968 they were entered in the additions-to-coverage file. Figure A-2 (3) shows that only if a dying establishment was sampled in 1965 did it enter the file of dead establishments; otherwise, it was lost. Figure A-2 (4) shows that nonmoving establishments could enter the file of nonmoving establishments, the file of dead establishments, the additions-to-coverage file, or be lost entirely.

Figure A-3 presents the obverse of Figure A-1 for the most problematic files created by the matching program—the file of additions to coverage and of dead establishments. Establishments in the additions-to-coverage file can be one of four types: If the establishment is a branch establishment, it may be new (formed after 1965); other establishments in the file may be either movers or nonmovers. Similarly, establishments, movers, or nonmovers. The procedures employed to verify or determine the proper classification of establishments in these files included telephone surveys; searches of telephone directories, directories of manufacturers, and materials published by the Dun and Bradstreet Corporation; and postal surveys.

The purpose of these procedures when applied to the additions-to-coverage file was to determine the location of all establishments in the files in 1965, and to determine whether they were in existence in 1965 or were in fact new. It should be emphasized that only branch establishments in the files might be new. The report on the establishments in the additions-to-coverage file included only data current in June 1968. Three techniques were used to determine the correct classification of establishments in the additions-to-coverage file: First establishments in the file were sought, when possible, in directories of manufacturers that contain

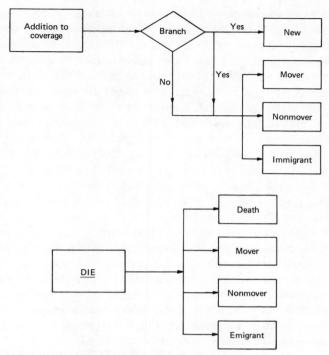

Figure A-3. Logic of Data Verification

data collected around 1965. Establishments in the Cleveland area additions-to-coverage file were sought in the 1965 *Ohio Directory of Manufacturers*. Establishments in Phoenix were sought in the 1965 *Directory of Manufacturers in the Phoenix Area*. The 1967 *Minnesota Directory of Manufacturers* was used with the Minneapolis-St. Paul additions-to-coverage file. No useful directory was available to us for our work with the Boston data.

Typically, these directories contained several pieces of data on each establishment, which when taken together made the identification of establishments in our files with establishments in the directories fairly straightforward. The data in the listings of establishments in these directories generally included the address of the physical location of the establishment, the number of employees or employment-size class of the establishment, and four-digit SIC data. In all cases, of course, new-address data obtained from the directories were inserted in the 1965 records of the found establishments. Where possible, current employment data from the directories were also substituted.

After the manufacturing directory checks, the number of establishments in the additions-to-coverage file that were left unclassified in each area was still very large. For this reason it was decided to search through the appropriate 1965 telephone directories for the remaining establishments. Telephone directories were much less valuable than directories of manufacturers because the data they offered were less useful in identifying establishments. On the other hand, they could be expected to include a far more complete list of establishments than could be found in the directories of manufacturers. The identification of establishments listed in the telephone directories with establishments in the additions-to-coverage file was done with some caution. This was particularly true for branch establishments of multiplant firms. In general, branch establishments in the additions-to-coverage file were identified in telephone directories only if the name, address, and telephone number of the establishments were identical.

Different procedures had to be used to identify new establishments in the additions-to-coverage file. As has been pointed out, only branch establishments could be unidentified new firms. In Cleveland those branches still unidentified after the manufacturers' and telephone directory searches, were telephoned, and personnel were asked about the status of the establishment in 1965. In Minneapolis unidentified branch establishments were surveyed by mail. Establishments identified by asking their personnel were added to the file of new establishments (File E).

The procedure used to identify new establishments in the Phoenix additions-to-coverage file was somewhat different. The 1968 *Directory of Manufacturers in the Phoenix Area* for each manufacturing establishment listed a date of formation. Establishments in the 1968 *Directory* with dates of formation after 1965 that were either not in the 1968 DMI files or were listed but had not been identified as new were entered in the new-establishment file, and where appropriate in the 1968 Phoenix DMI files.

The procedures used to partition the additions-to-coverage file in Boston differ completely from those used in the other metropolitan areas. Because Boston is relatively close to New York City, it was economical simply to telephone establishments in the Boston additions-to-coverage file. This telephone survey was supplemented by a search through 1965 telephone directories.

Of the additions-to-coverage establishments located using these various techniques, a considerable number were movers. When a moving establishment was located in a directory of manufacturers offering establishment employment data, or by a telephone contact from which it was possible to elicit 1965 employment estimates, the moving establishment was entered into the movers file at this 1965 employment figure. When it was impossible to obtain such an estimate, the establishment entered the file at its 1968 employment level.

Because of the techniques used by Dun and Bradstreet to update the DMI file, no single DMI file is complete. Establishment records containing incorrect information or that require updating are deleted entirely from the file. This, of course, implies that the files of dead establishments are artificially expanded. The Dun and Bradstreet *Code Book*—an alphabetical listing of the entire DMI file—giving for each establishment its name, address, and DUNS number, was employed to eliminate those establishments in the death file that, in fact, were in operation in 1968 in the four metropolitan areas. Establishments found in the *Code Book* were deleted from the death files, and merged into the 1968 files. Some of these establishments were found to have moved between 1965 and 1968, and these were merged into the movers file at their 1965 DMI employment figures.

One final procedure was employed that affected primarily the file of new and dead establishments. Figure A-1 showed that all establishments in the 1968 DMI file with dates of formation after 1965 entered the file of new establishments. Under some circumstances an establishment date of formation can change, but the DUNS number of the establishment remains unchanged, approximately one-fifth of the establishments in the new-establishment file could be identified by name and DUNS number in the file of dead establishments. These establishments were deleted from both files.

The geographic areas used in this analysis are groups of zip code zones. In the DMI files whenever an establishment had a mailing address different from the address of its physical location, the zip code reported in the record of the establishment referred to the mailing address. In addition, because the zone improvement plan of the United States Postal Service that resulted in the present system of zip codes was relatively new in October 1965, a considerable number of establishments in the 1965 DMI files were not assigned zip codes. Only those central cities that we sorted into zip code zones would be affected by this problem. Because this problem would introduce geographic biases if it were not corrected and because a considerable number of establishments, in fact, lacked zip codes in both the 1965 and 1968 files, establishments for which no zip code was reported and establishments with mailing addresses were assigned zip codes using the 1969 *Zip Code Directory*.

Appendix B
Coverage of Census of Manufactures and DMI Employment and Establishment Data, by Industry

Table B-1

Census and DMI Employment Data, Four Sample Metropolitan Areas, 1963-68 [a]

Industry SIC [b]	Number of Manufacturing Employees				Average Annual Percentage Change	
	1963 Census [c]	1965 DMI [d]	1967 Census [c]	1968 DMI [d]	Census [c]	DMI [d]
Boston						
20	24,813	25,198	22,800	22,950	−2.0	−3.0
21	——	——	——	——	——	——
22	4,693	5,641	5,100	5,262	2.2	−2.2
23	21,069	21,599	20,400	19,899	−0.8	−2.6
24	2,015	2,155	1,900	2,158	−1.4	0.0
25	3,530	4,367	3,200	4,402	−2.3	0.3
26	10,439	10,168	10,100	10,746	−0.8	1.9
27	23,472	22,019	25,200	20,751	1.8	−1.9
28	7,368	10,616	7,700	15,426	1.1	15.1
29	899	554	600	496	−8.3	−3.5
30	17,133	17,442	16,800	17,834	−0.5	0.7
31	18,294	22,211	16,700	20,603	−2.2	−2.4
32	2,964	2,920	3,100	2,561	1.1	−4.1
33	3,975	3,963	3,700	5,090	−1.7	9.5
34	17,603	25,664	19,600	26,539	2.8	1.1
35	26,832	28,249	32,800	29,544	5.6	1.5
36	47,522	57,211	53,400	54,784	3.1	−1.4
37	16,354	14,514	23,500	22,789	10.9	19.0
38	17,105	17,873	22,300	21,703	7.6	7.1
39	5,624	5,754	5,600	5,650	−0.1	−0.6
Total [c]	271,704	298,118	294,500	309,335	2.1	1.3
Cleveland						
20	12,038	11,144	11,600	7,657	−1.0	−10.4
21	——	——	——	——	——	——
22	3,620	5,975	3,200	7,884	−2.7	10.6
23	8,424	7,708	7,400	8,749	−3.0	4.5
24	950	1,158	300	958	−17.2	−5.8
25	3,393	4,278	3,600	4,850	2.0	4.5
26	5,306	4,694	4,600	4,757	−3.2	0.4
27	14,243	14,135	17,800	15,445	6.2	3.1
28	12,856	23,063	15,100	18,326	4.4	−6.8
29	1,721	1,900	1,200	1,653	−7.5	4.3
30	6,167	4,576	6,700	3,879	2.2	−5.1
31	92	590	——	73	——	−29.2

Table B-1 (continued)

Industry SIC [b]	Number of Manufacturing Employees				Average Annual Percentage Change	
	1963 Census [c]	1965 DMI [d]	1967 Census [c]	1968 DMI [d]	Census [c]	DMI [d]
32	4,292	3,370	4,800	3,554	3.0	1.8
33	37,064	41,684	37,100	36,398	0.0	−4.2
34	32,496	40,327	45,300	41,454	9.8	0.9
35	40,321	54,037	51,900	54,554	7.2	0.3
36	22,132	25,835	25,400	25,124	3.8	−0.9
37	45,493	46,698	39,500	41,097	−4.2	−4.0
38	3,603	2,842	3,800	3,686	1.2	9.9
39	4,250	3,978	4,200	3,875	−0.2	−0.9
Total	258,461	297,992	288,200	283,973	2.9	−1.6
Minneapolis-St. Paul						
20	19,955	23,474	18,900	22,851	−1.3	−0.9
21	——	——	——	——	——	——
22	1,384	840	1,400	570	0.3	−10.7
23	4,840	7,688	4,000	4,646	−4.3	−13.2
24	2,425	2,630	2,400	2,289	−0.3	−4.3
25	1,743	1,856	2,000	1,987	3.7	2.4
26	5,460	8,454	——	6,687	——	−7.8
27	17,221	14,896	18,700	12,535	2.1	−5.3
28	4,461	7,353	4,900	8,155	2.5	3.6
29	1,239	1,670	1,400	1,297	3.2	−7.4
30	——	3,273	3,600	3,455	——	1.9
31	——	617	——	363	——	−13.7
32	5,994	1,750	——	1,626	——	−2.4
33	2,490	2,645	3,800	3,081	13.2	5.5
34	10,289	12,900	13,900	11,750	8.8	−3.0
35	28,331	30,893	40,800	35,300	11.0	4.8
36	16,207	14,460	19,600	10,343	5.2	9.5
37	6,931	3,910	7,300	4,079	1.3	1.4
38	7,738	5,278	8,100	6,218	1.2	5.9
39	3,869	6,004	5,600	5,867	11.2	−0.8
Total	149,604	150,591	181,000	143,099	5.2	−1.7
Phoenix						
20	5,146	4,805	4,900	4,728	−1.2	−0.5
21	——	——	——	——	——	——
22	——	37	——	12	——	−22.5
23	2,082	2,459	2,800	3,276	8.6	11.1
24	604	887	700	711	4.0	−6.6
25	757	1,080	700	944	−1.9	−4.2
26	253	527	——	435	——	−5.8
27	2,802	2,998	3,300	3,199	4.4	2.2
28	530	824	700	611	8.0	−8.6
29	43	117	——	75	——	−12.0
30	244	460	——	604	——	10.4
31	6	28	——	39	——	13.1
32	1,885	1,048	1,500	1,053	−5.1	0.2
33	1,970	2,922	——	2,543	——	−4.3
34	1,951	2,621	2,800	3,436	10.9	10.4
35	5,556	8,508	13,200	10,579	34.4	8.1

Table B-1 (continued)

Industry SIC [b]	Number of Manufacturing Employees				Average Annual Percentage Change	
	1963 Census [c]	1965 DMI [d]	1967 Census [c]	1968 DMI [d]	Census [c]	DMI [d]
36	8,985	18,697	18,400	28,134	26.2	16.8
37	5,568	2,871	1,400	3,028	−18.7	1.8
38	1,499	1,285	——	3,243	——	50.8
39	343	642	400	474	4.2	−8.7
Total	40,970	52,816	59,300	67,124	11.2	9.0

[a] Definitions of the Boston, Cleveland, and Minneapolis-St. Paul regions used in the analysis of the DMI data differ from census definitions of the SMSAs. See Part I of this report for detailed explanations.
[b] See Table 7-1 for definitions of the industry SIC codes.
[c] From *Census of Manufactures*, vol. III. Central administrative and auxiliary employment is not included in area total, and not tabulated by industry.
[d] See Table 7-1 for definitions of the industry SIC codes.

Table B-2

Census and DMI Establishment Data, Four Sample Metropolitan Areas, 1963-68 [a]

Industry SIC [b]	Number of Establishments				Average Annual Percentage Change	
	1963 Census [c]	1965 DMI [d]	1967 Census [c]	1968 DMI [d]	Census [c]	DMI [d]
Boston						
20	487	411	405	378	−4.2	−2.7
21	1	2	——	2	——	——
22	92	149	88	128	−1.1	−4.7
23	644	558	556	520	−3.4	−2.3
24	124	125	111	120	−2.6	−1.3
25	196	283	170	269	−3.3	−1.6
26	138	152	133	152	−0.9	0
27	758	765	776	773	0.6	0.3
28	265	374	241	352	−2.3	−2.0
29	30	21	——	22	——	1.6
30	138	149	139	164	0.2	3.4
31	315	378	265	352	−4.0	−2.3
32	123	131	125	124	0.4	−1.8
33	83	97	84	97	0.3	0
34	560	568	516	549	−2.0	−1.1
35	617	659	639	682	0.9	1.2
36	352	414	364	445	0.9	2.5
37	84	68	71	65	−3.9	−1.5
38	139	228	175	224	6.5	−0.6
39	212	281	206	278	−0.7	−0.4
Total	5,358	5,813	5,085	5,696	−1.3	−1.7

Table B-2 (continued)

| Industry SIC [b] | Number of Establishments | | | | Average Annual Percentage Change | |
	1963 Census [c]	1965 DMI [d]	1967 Census [c]	1968 DMI [d]	Census [c]	DMI [d]
Cleveland						
20	262	234	232	208	−2.8	−3.7
21	——	——				
22	39	36	35	36	−2.5	0
23	117	132	114	125	−0.5	−1.8
24	79	69	——	63	——	−2.9
25	107	126	91	133	−3.8	+1.9
26	61	76	68	82	2.8	+2.6
27	523	568	473	556	−2.5	−0.7
28	254	360	226	325	−2.8	−3.2
29	41	61	44	57	1.8	−2.2
30	96	119	105	122	2.2	+0.8
31	14	10	——	11	——	+3.3
32	145	152	144	146	−0.2	−1.3
33	206	229	208	234	0.2	+0.7
34	712	773	711	781	0	+0.3
35	909	1,059	1,027	1,164	3.2	+3.3
36	182	249	184	256	0.5	+0.9
37	105	111	98	107	−1.8	−1.2
38	53	81	59	80	2.8	−0.4
39	139	211	131	192	−1.5	−3.0
Total	4,046	4,656	4,042	4,678	0	+0.1
Minneapolis-St. Paul						
20	255	232	219	225	−3.5	−1.0
21	——	——	——	——	——	——
22	13	18	12	21	−1.9	5.6
23	137	131	118	121	−3.5	−2.5
24	87	90	84	92	−0.9	0.7
25	96	142	88	135	−2.1	−1.6
26	73	70	——	70	——	0
27	416	452	408	485	−0.5	2.4
28	132	186	122	173	−1.9	−2.3
29	19	27	——	22	——	−6.2
30	92	119	91	132	−0.3	3.6
31	10	17	——	19	——	3.9
32	88	93	——	95	——	0.7
33	61	62	67	66	2.5	2.2
34	299	386	324	391	2.1	0.4
35	457	543	524	646	3.7	6.3
36	117	139	121	160	0.9	5.0
37	62	55	61	64	−0.4	5.5
38	49	85	58	101	4.6	6.3
39	132	197	128	209	−0.8	2.0
Total	2,596	3,044	2,606	3,227	0.1	2.0
Phoenix						
20	133	130	118	131	−2.8	0.3
21	——	——	——	——	——	——
22	1	6	——	4	——	−11.1

Table B-2 (continued)

Industry SIC [b]	Number of Establishments				Average Annual Percentage Change	
	1963 Census [c]	1965 DMI [d]	1967 Census [c]	1968 DMI [d]	Census [c]	DMI [d]
23	51	45	49	48	−1.0	2.2
24	44	47	48	45	2.3	−1.4
25	57	68	52	60	−2.2	−3.9
26	7	10	——	13	0.2	10.0
27	161	178	162	183	0.2	0.9
28	46	54	45	64	−.5	6.2
29	4	8	——	5	——	12.5
30	21	41	——	45	——	3.3
31	4	6	——	8	——	11.1
32	67	60	65	58	−0.7	−1.1
33	13	31	——	20	−11.5	−11.8
34	90	126	107	146	4.7	5.3
35	114	158	161	213	10.3	11.6
36	43	64	52	81	5.2	8.9
37	52	56	50	69	−1.0	7.7
38	9	18	——	25	——	13.0
39	47	84	55	69	4.3	−6.0
Total	965	1,190	1,045	1,287	2.1	2.7

[a] Definitions of the Boston, Cleveland, and Minneapolis-St. Paul regions used in the analysis of the DMI data differ from census definitions of the SMSA. See Part I of this report for detailed explanations.

[b] See Table 7-1 for definitions of the industry SIC codes.

[c] From *Census of Manufactures*, vol. III. Central administrative and auxiliary establishments are not included in the area total, and not tabulated by industry.

[d] From tabulations of adjusted DMI file.

Appendix C
Description of Analysis Zones

Table C-1

Description of Analysis Zones, Four Sample Metropolitan Areas

Zone	Description	Definition (Zip Code or Town Name)
Cleveland		
1	Central industrial district	44113, 44114, 44115
2	Northeast of CID, ring I	44103, 44104, 44106
3	Southeast of CID, ring I	44105, 44127
4	Southwest of CID, ring I	44102, 44109, 44144
5	West of CID, ring I	44107, 44111, 44135
13	Northeast of CID, ring II	44108, 44110
6	Bay Village-Westlake	44116, 44120, 44145
7	Berea-Olmstead Falls	44138, 44142, 44017, 44070
8	Parma-Independence	44129, 44131, 44134
9	Strongsville-Brecksville	44136, 44139
10	Maple Heights-Garfield Heights	44125, 44128, 44137
11	E. Cleveland-Cleveland Heights-Shaker Heights	44112, 44118, 44122
12	South Euclid	44121, 44124, 44143
14	Euclid	44117, 44119, 44123, 44132
15	Bedford-Solon	44141, 44146
16	Wickliff-Willoughby	44060, 44092, 44094
17	Painesville	44077, 44045
18	Madison-Perry	44057, 44081, 44040, 45612
City of Minneapolis		
1	East of Mississippi River, South	55414
2	East of Mississippi River, North	55413, 55418
3	Central Industrial District	55401, 55402, 55415
4	Southwest of CID	55403, 55404, 55405
5	Northwest of CID	55411, 55412
6	Southeast of CID	55406, 55407, 55408
7	South of CID, ring II	55409, 55410, 55417, 55419
City of St. Paul		
8	Central Industrial District	55101
9	East of CID	55106, 55119
10	Southwest of CID	55105, 55102, 55116
11	South of CID	55107
12	Northwest of CID	55103, 55104, 55108, 55114
13	Columbia Heights, Findley	55421, 55432
14	North and West St. Paul Suburbs	55109, 55110, 55112, 55115, 55113, 55117
15	Mendota-West St. Paul	55118, 55111
16	Edina	55436, 55424, 55435
17	St. Louis Park	55426, 55416
18	Crystal-Brooklyn Park	55428, 55429, 55430

Table C-1 (continued)

Zone	Description	Definition (Zip Code or Torn Name)
19	Golden Valley-Robbinsdale	55422, 55427
20	Bloomington	55431, 55430
21	Richfield-International Airport	55423, 55430
22	Anoka-Hugo	Anoka, Champlin, Osseo, Cedar, Rogers, Hugo, Circle Pines
23	Mahtomedi-Bayport	Mahtomedi, Willennie, Stillwater, Lake Elmo, Bayport, Scandia, Forest Lake
24	Newport-St. Paul Park	St. Paul Park, Newport, Inven Grove, Rosemount, Farmington, Lakeville, Castle Rock, Hastings, S. St. Paul
25	Hopkins-Mound	Hopkins, Minnetouka, Wayzata, Spring Park, Mound, Long Lake, Excelsior, Loretto, Maple Plains
Boston		
1	Central industrial district	02108, 02109, 02113, 02114, 02116
2	South Boston	02110, 02127
3	Charlestown-East Boston	02128, 02129
4	Adjacent to CID	02111, 02118, 02116
5	Roxbury	02119, 02125
6	CID Waterfront	02210
7	Rest of city	All other zip codes in Boston
8	Peabody-Salem-Lynn	Peabody, Salem, Lynn, Nahant, Swampscott, Marblehead, Danvers
9	Wakefield-Reading	Revere, Winthrop, Melsrose, Saugus, Stoneh, Wakefield, Lynnfield, Reading, N. Reading
10	Somerville-Everett	Arlington, Somerville, Medford, Malden, Everett, Chelsea
11	Cambridge	Cambridge
12	Woburn-Burlington	Burlington, Woburn, Wilmington, Winchester
13	Waltham-Newton	Brookline, Waltham, Watertown, Newton, Easton
14	Sudbury-Lexington	Maynard, Sudbury, Wayland, Weston, Lincoln, Concord, Bedford, Lexington, Belmont
15	Framingham-Natick	Framingham, Natick
16	Needham-Walpole	Wellesley, Needham, Dover, Medfield, Walpole, Westwood, Dedham, Foxborough, Sharon, Hanover
17	Quincy-Braintree	Quincy, Braintree
18	Norwood-Milton	Norwood, Canton, Stoughton, Avon, Milton, Randolph, Holbrook

Table C-1 (continued)

Zone	Description	Definition (Zip Code or Town Name)
19	Hingham-Norwell	Weymouth, Hingham, Cohasset, Hull, Scituate, Norwell, Rockland
20	Brockton	Brockton
Phoenix		
1	Central industrial district	85007, 85003, 85004, 85006
2	West of CID, ring I	85009
3	South of CID	85040, 85041
4	Southwest of CID	85034
5	East of CID	85008
6	West of CID, ring II	85031, 85033, 85035
7	Northwest of CID	85013, 85015, 85017, 85019
8	Northeast of CID	85012, 85014, 85016, 85018
9	North of CID, ring III	85021, 85029
10	North of CID, ring II	85022, 85020, 85028, 85032
11	Scottsdale	Scottsdale
12	Tempe-Mesa	Tempe, Mesa, Chandler, Gilbert
13	Avondale-Buckeye	Avondale, Buckeye, Gila Bend
14	Goodyear-Glendale	Goodyear, Glendale, Peoria, Lichtfield, Tolleson

Appendix D
Definition of Shift-Share Measures

The following notation is employed:

X_{si} = value in 1965 of industry i in zone s

X_{sI} = value in 1965 of all industries I in zone s

X_{Si} = value in 1965 of industry i in the SMSA, S

X_{SI} = value in 1965 of all industries I in the SMSA, S

Y_{si}, Y_{sI}, Y_{Si}, and Y_{SI} represent the same values in the terminal year, 1968. Also,

$$H_{sI} = X_{sI} \frac{Y_{SI}}{X_{SI}} \qquad H_{si} = X_{si} \frac{Y_{Si}}{X_{Si}} \qquad H'_{sI} = \sum_i H_{si}$$

$$B_{sI} = Y_{sI} \frac{X_{SI}}{Y_{SI}} \qquad B_{si} = Y_{si} \frac{X_{Si}}{Y_{Si}} \qquad B'_{sI} = \sum_i B_{si}$$

Definitions:

(1) Growth relative to SMSA $= \dfrac{Y_{sI} - H_{sI}}{Y_{sI} \text{ or } H_{sI}}$

(2) Competitive change $= \frac{1}{2}\left[\dfrac{Y_{sI} - H'_{sI}}{Y_{sI} \text{ or } H'_{sI}} + \dfrac{B'_{sI} - X_{sI}}{B'_{sI} \text{ or } X_{sI}}\right]$

(3) Comparative industrial structure $= \frac{1}{2}\left[\dfrac{H'_{sI} - H_{sI}}{H'_{sI} \text{ or } H_{sI}} + \dfrac{B_{sI} - B'_{sI}}{B_{sI} \text{ or } B'_{sI}}\right]$

**Appendix E
Percentage Distributions
of 1965 and 1968 Base
Employment and
Employment in Relocating,
New, and Dying
Establishments for Each
Analysis Zone in Each
Sample Metropolitan Area**

Table E-1

Percentage Distribution of Employment, Four Sample Metropolitan Areas

| Analysis Zone [a] | Total Employment | | Movers | | New Establish- ments | Defunct Establish- ments |
	1965	1968	At Origin	At Desti- nation		
Boston						
1 [b]	4.57%	2.49%	10.61%	3.50%	4.22	16.56%
2 [b]	4.51	5.96	7.90	4.47	3.66	4.10
3 [b]	5.28	5.40	2.61	4.57	0.51	4.15
4 [b]	5.76	5.09	8.06	8.03	7.44	5.51
5 [b]	2.97	2.26	3.73	1.58	0.75	4.61
6 [b]	1.71	1.66	4.23	3.16	1.01	1.26
7 [b]	6.24	6.10	6.06	4.75	3.91	12.29
8	12.19	13.24	8.07	4.20	9.27	11.87
9	1.56	1.71	2.57	2.26	3.96	2.46
10	7.53	7.90	6.45	13.12	18.77	3.81
11	9.28	8.72	16.90	11.49	11.25	13.64
12	6.34	5.73	4.91	9.37	6.98	1.75
13	11.98	10.57	4.39	10.14	11.48	10.33
14	2.74	2.79	2.05	1.41	0.38	0.12
15	3.07	3.11	2.48	4.18	2.21	0.87
16	3.10	3.57	2.36	1.85	3.73	0.92
17	2.85	4.89	1.15	6.34	1.66	0.96
18	4.91	5.40	1.15	3.72	4.22	2.25
19	0.60	0.61	1.17	0.79	0.88	0.00
20	2.76	2.77	3.03	1.14	3.71	2.46
Cleveland						
1 [b]	14.87%	15.26%	20.82%	15.74%	29.34%	14.58%
2 [b]	13.01	10.74	16.23	10.24	3.84	15.62
3 [b]	11.35	11.41	12.14	6.36	5.42	8.29
4 [b]	10.43	9.00	10.61	5.15	12.48	9.05
5 [b]	5.55	4.89	15.26	10.63	4.02	9.56
6	0.50	0.63	0.13	1.96	1.37	1.81
7	5.72	7.72	2.26	13.73	4.54	2.22
8	0.76	1.20	2.33	2.56	0.83	0.25
9	0.14	0.22	0.63	1.34	0.98	0.08
10	3.54	3.83	3.44	8.06	3.19	3.37

Table E-1 (continued)

Analysis Zone [a]	Total Employment		Movers		New Establish-ments	Defunct Establish-ments
	1965	1968	At Origin	At Desti-nation		
11	3.89	3.75	1.39	2.40	5.66	4.68
12	0.37	0.37	0.35	0.28	0.12	0.51
13 [b]	7.56	8.02	2.96	3.96	10.84	13.14
14	11.14	11.39	4.43	3.42	7.90	6.33
15	4.91	5.35	3.76	7.16	4.91	7.88
16	2.96	3.80	2.20	6.00	4.12	2.29
17	2.97	2.13	0.95	0.92	0.31	0.25
18	0.23	0.19	0.01	0.01	0.06	0.00
Minneapolis-St. Paul						
1 [b]	4.24%	3.89%	5.91%	3.81%	0.78%	2.77%
2 [b]	8.76	7.06	4.46	3.84	0.87	15.18
3 [b]	11.10	9.42	10.07	6.60	4.02	9.44
4 [b]	5.96	3.86	9.55	6.45	1.24	13.03
5 [b]	2.99	2.49	7.82	1.40	3.49	4.40
6 [b]	5.13	4.19	8.61	4.18	2.36	6.30
7 [b]	0.47	0.51	0.27	0.27	0.17	0.23
8 [b]	8.48	6.14	16.73	11.29	1.44	7.02
9 [b]	2.39	2.60	0.00	0.47	0.19	0.90
10 [b]	4.44	9.81	2.15	2.04	54.21	0.24
11 [b]	1.96	1.10	1.96	1.48	0.80	1.62
12 [b]	11.97	10.16	7.71	10.82	2.68	15.07
13	1.15	1.50	0.96	2.56	0.72	2.83
14	4.20	4.85	0.22	5.50	3.16	2.11
15	0.68	0.73	0.68	2.19	0.36	0.68
16	1.47	2.54	2.05	5.59	2.99	0.27
17	3.92	4.10	8.39	7.73	1.79	3.78
18	0.95	1.63	5.47	1.44	3.23	0.04
19	4.69	5.12	1.59	7.57	1.85	2.27
20	2.83	3.48	2.59	7.63	1.77	2.65
21	0.50	0.74	0.36	0.83	0.70	0.21
22	1.38	1.50	0.40	0.66	0.97	3.61
23	1.21	1.25	0.44	0.35	0.43	2.34
24	6.08	7.19	0.40	0.32	3.78	0.71
25	3.59	3.99	1.09	4.87	5.89	2.16
Phoenix						
1 [b]	7.58%	5.81%	11.27%	6.80%	2.42%	11.63%
2 [b]	10.72	10.98	8.35	38.48	5.87	2.32
3 [b]	1.52	2.12	1.25	2.32	3.44	2.39
4 [b]	16.43	12.39	12.29	9.50	5.70	22.45
5 [b]	14.34	19.11	0.16	0.24	0.36	0.28
6 [b]	1.33	1.85	1.41	0.00	13.79	4.28
7 [b]	8.49	6.44	3.24	8.21	5.86	22.99
8 [b]	6.00	4.78	2.59	2.86	2.89	9.67
9 [b]	10.28	8.28	30.42	0.41	1.00	2.17
10 [b]	2.36	4.56	0.12	0.00	0.40	3.60
11	6.02	5.15	27.50	28.22	0.90	0.35
12	6.47	10.56	1.29	2.86	55.84	17.56
13	0.22	0.20	0.00	0.00	0.50	0.03
14	8.19	7.70	0.04	0.04	0.95	0.21

[a] For description of zones, see Appendix C.
[b] Central-city zone.

Appendix F
Regularities in the Location of Industries in Central Cities and Central Industrial Districts

Table F-1

Percentage Distribution of Manufacturing Employment Among Industries in Central Cities and Metropolitan Areas (SMSAs), 1965

Industry SIC [a]	Boston City	Boston SMSA	Cleveland City	Cleveland SMSA	Minneapolis-St. Paul City	Minneapolis-St. Paul SMSA	Phoenix City	Phoenix SMSA
20 [b]	15.71 [e]	8.45	5.17	3.74	13.76 [e]	15.59	10.20 [e]	9.10
22 [b]	1.80	1.89	2.73 [e]	2.00	0.82 [e]	0.56	0.09	0.07
23 [b]	18.53	7.24	4.00 [e]	2.59	6.51 [f]	5.11	1.35 [f]	4.66
24	0.43 [e]	0.72	0.23 [f]	0.39	0.81	1.75	1.77	1.68
25 [c]	2.04 [f]	1.47	1.83 [f]	1.44	1.39 [e]	1.23	2.43	2.04
26 [d]	2.00 [f]	3.41	1.91	1.58	6.88 [e]	5.61	0.86	1.00
27 [c]	14.96 [e]	7.39	6.81 [e]	4.74	13.02 [e]	9.89	6.58 [e]	5.68
28	2.01 [f]	3.56	5.97 [f]	7.74	4.50 [f]	4.88	1.67	1.56
29 [d]	0.01 [e]	0.19	0.87	0.64	1.34	1.11	0.14	0.22
30	0.93 [f]	5.85	0.76 [f]	1.54	1.13 [e]	2.17	0.95 [f]	0.87
31 [d]	4.76 [e]	7.45	0.31	0.20	0.32 [f]	0.41	0.06 [e]	0.05
32	0.67	0.98	0.94 [f]	1.13	1.01	1.16	2.10	1.98
33 [b]	1.17 [f]	1.33	15.52	13.99	1.81	1.76	6.11	5.53
34 [c]	14.67 [e]	8.61	14.17	13.53	8.92	8.57	5.26 [e]	4.96
35	8.79	9.48	15.86	18.13	18.37 [e]	20.51	19.66 [f]	16.11
36	5.70 [f]	19.19	8.53 [f]	8.67	10.35 [e]	9.60	35.28	35.40
37	0.47	4.87	11.75	15.67	3.04 [e]	2.60	1.08 [f]	5.44
38	2.27	6.00	0.84 [f]	0.95	1.70	3.50	2.98 [f]	2.43
39 [c]	3.09	1.93	1.78	1.33	4.35	3.99	1.44 [e]	1.21

[a] See Table 7-1 for identification of industry SIC codes.

[b] The fraction of central city manufacturing employment in the industry in 1965 was greater than the fraction of SMSA employment in the industry in three of the four SMSAs.

[c] The fraction of central city manufacturing employment in the industry in 1965 was greater than the fraction of SMSA employment in the industry in all four SMSAs.

[d] The fraction of central city manufacturing employment in the industry in 1965 was greater than the fraction of SMSA employment in the industry in two of the four SMSAs.

[e] The industry grew more rapidly within the central city relative to its SMSA growth rate than total manufacturing employment in the central city grew relative to the rate for total employment in the SMSA (see Chapter 7 for amplification).

[f] The industry grew more rapidly within the central city than it did in the SMSA outside the central city (the SMSA ring), a substantially more stringent test in most cases than that expressed in footnote e.

Table F-2

Percentage Distribution of Manufacturing Employment Among Industries in Central Industrial Districts (CIDs) and Metropolitan Areas (SMSAs), 1965

Industry SIC [a]	Boston CID	Boston SMSA	Cleveland CID	Cleveland SMSA	Minneapolis-St. Paul CID (Minn)	Minneapolis-St. Paul CID (SP)	Minneapolis-St. Paul SMSA	Phoenix CID	Phoenix SMSA
20 [b]	11.49 [e]	8.45	6.73 [f]	3.74	23.58	17.17 [f]	15.59	24.41 [f]	9.10
21	——	——	——	——	——	——	——	——	——
22	0.30	1.89	7.33 [f]	2.00	0.39 [e]	4.19	0.56	0.10	0.07
23 [c]	17.74 [e]	7.24	5.89 [f]	2.59	9.58 [f]	9.65 [e]	5.11	0.85 [e]	4.66
24	0.09 [e]	0.72	0.44 [f]	0.39	0.17	0.62	1.75	3.94	1.68
25	1.69	1.47	0.46 [f]	1.44	0.92 [f]	0.13 [e]	1.23	1.72	2.04
26 [d]	1.14 [e]	3.41	1.66	1.58	1.11 [f]	16.24	5.61	0.30 [f]	1.00
27 [d]	17.79 [e]	7.39	17.35	4.74	34.32 [f]	12.30	9.89	39.61 [e]	5.68
28 [d]	2.09	3.56	8.59	7.74	2.26 [e]	14.75 [f]	4.88	2.89 [e]	1.56
29	0	0.19	1.22	0.64	0.00	2.82	1.11	0	0.22
30	0.28 [e]	5.85	0.50 [f]	1.54	1.56 [e]	0.05	2.17	0.12	0.87
31 [d]	0.10 [f]	7.45	1.30	0.20	0.76 [f]	0.86 [e]	0.41	0.52	0.05
32	0.81 [f]	0.98	1.03 [f]	1.13	0.15 [f]	0.14	1.16	1.67	1.98
33	0.18 [e]	1.33	8.35 [f]	13.99	0.70 [f]	0 [f]	1.76	1.12	5.53
34 [d]	10.46 [e]	8.61	7.26 [f]	13.53	3.32	1.84	8.57	7.79	4.96
35	29.09	9.48	10.55 [e]	18.13	12.00	9.22	20.51	7.36 [f]	16.11
36	0.54 [f]	19.19	7.37 [f]	8.67	4.51	6.26 [f]	9.60	0.87 [f]	35.40
37	0 [f]	4.87	8.57	15.67	0.00 [f]	0.41 [f]	2.60	3.29	5.44
38	1.62 [e]	6.00	1.53	0.95	2.25	0.20	3.50	0.70 [e]	2.43
39 [b]	4.60 [e]	1.93	3.87	1.33	2.44	3.17	3.99	2.72 [e]	1.21

[a] See Table 7-1 for identification of industry SIC codes.

[b] The fraction of central city manufacturing employment in the industry in 1965 was greater than the friction of SMSA employment in the industry in all four SMSAs.

[c] The fraction of central city manufacturing employment in the industry in 1965 was greater than the fraction of SMSA employment in the industry in three of the four SMSAs.

[d] The fraction of central city manufacturing employment in the industry in 1965 was greater than the fraction of SMSA employment in the industry in two of the four SMSAs.

[e] The industry grew more rapidly within the central city relative to its SMSA growth rate than total manufacturing employment in the central city grew relative to the rate for total employment in the SMSA (see Chapter 7 for amplification).

[f] The industry grew more rapidly within the central city than it did in the SMSA outside the central city (the SMSA ring), a substantially more stringent test in most cases than that expressed in footnote e.

Appendix G
Regression Analysis of Incidence of Marginal Employment in Analysis Zones

Table G-1 presents the regression results for employment of out-movers, in-movers, new firms, and defunct firms for all four metropolitan areas combined, using the form of dependent variable and the independent variables outlined in Chapter 8. Additive dummy variables are included for three of the metropolitan areas, with the Cleveland Standard Metropolitan Statistical Areas (SMSA) serving as the base. The portion of the total variance of the four dependent variables explained by the regressions across the four areas is highest for employment of movers classified by destination and for new employment (R^2 of 0.590 and 0.650, respectively). This reinforces earlier findings that the geographic distribution of variation of these phenomena is more systematic than variation in the rates for movers classified by origin and for deaths. In general, these regressions tell a coherent tale, in spite of their very rough structure.

Four variables in the regressions are used to measure the broad level of industrial activity or attractiveness within a zone. First is the central-city dummy variable. After controlling for the influence of the other independent variables, the results of the regressions using all the cities suggest the following: (1) The movement rate of the employment of establishments located within the central city in 1965 was not significantly different from area-wide movement rates; (2) however, given that an establishment within a metropolitan area moved, it was quite significantly less likely to move to central-city locations than would be expected if movement rates were simply proportional to 1965-base employment; (3) new employment, by contrast, which has been shown to be more dispersed from the central city than employment of out-migrating firms, appears to be significantly attracted to central-city locations; (4) deaths in the central city occur at rates no higher than elsewhere in the SMSA.

The obvious measure of the level of industrial activity in a zone is the total number of manufacturing employees located there. This variable is subject to a number of possible interpretations because a high level of manufacturing activity implies, at the same time, that (1) the area at some time has been attractive to manufacturers; (2) the supply system of inputs into the manufacturing process and that for the disposition of output will be highly developed; but also (3) the level of congestion will very likely also be high. The coefficient of this variable will, therefore, reflect the net effects of these countervailing forces. Although the simple correlation be-

175

Table G-1

Regression Analysis of Incidence of Marginal Employment in Analysis Zones (Figures in Parentheses are t Ratios)

Independent Variable	Dependent Variable: Percentage Rate of Employment of Specified Establishments			
	Out-movers	In-movers	New	Defunct
1965 employment (hundreds)	−0.0119 (−0.9298)	−0.0260 (−1.9498)	0.0477 (1.6243)	−0.0076 (−0.6502)
Average establish-ment employment	−0.0305 (−1.6147)	−0.0427 (−2.1788)	−0.0534 (−1.2377)	−0.0561 (−3.2555)
Competitive advantage shift variable	0.0071 (.1525)	0.0778 (1.6061)	0.5537 (5.1988)	−0.0731 (−1.7165)
Central city	0.8231 (0.3982)	−4.4547 (−2.0728)	8.2146 (1.7377)	1.2512 (0.6621)
CID	3.8266 (1.0687)	1.7266 (0.4638)	2.6651 (0.3255)	−0.0507 (−0.0155)
Traditional zone	0.8586 (0.3303)	4.2413 (1.5696)	−10.6803 (−1.7968)	2.6861 (1.1306)
Boston	−1.6818 (−0.7220)	−6.3087 (−2.6051)	−0.7779 (−0.1460)	−1.3988 (−0.6570)
Phoenix	−3.8395 (−1.2553)	−1.7041 (−0.6561)	5.4299 (0.9504)	−2.6064 (−0.9323)
Minneapolis	2.4985 (0.3083)	−6.9625 (−2.1897)	—— ——	1.5091 (0.6608)
R^2	0.380	0.590	0.650	0.514

tween employment level and growth over the period in a zone is negative (−0.25, significant at the 95 per cent level), the regression analysis suggests that after taking the other variables into account the different components of the variable are important for different components of locational change. The employment rates for movers, in or out, and for defunct firms are negatively related to the level of employment, possibly reflecting congestion costs. Only the employment birth rate is positively correlated with the employment level and presumably indicates the importance of external economies available at such sites.

Another measure of a particular type of attractiveness is the dummy variable for traditional zones. In each metropolitan area a number of zones were identified roughly as having been for some time centers of manufacturing activity within the area. This variable appears to affect marginal establishments somewhat differently than do the other measures of centrality. This difference shows up most obviously in the dichotomy between the effect of the variable on the rate of employment of movers by destination (positive) and the employment rate of new firms (negative).

It may indicate that established firms are attracted more to areas in which the external economies available differ from those to be had in the "incubator" zones.

The final measure of centrality in the regressions is the central industrial district (CID) dummy variable, which is marginally statistically significant only in the out-migration model where it indicates a higher average rate of out-movement from the CIDs than from other zones.

The only variable available to account for the current industrial attractiveness of a zone was the "competitive advantage" variable, but it involves serious identification problems because it is based on the net change in employment in the zone over the period. As expected, it performs well in the regressions. It is positively related to employment rates of in-movers and of new firms, negatively related to rates of out-movers and of defunct firms. This indicates a higher death rate, ceteris paribus, in unattractive zones, including most poverty areas.

The final variable in the regressions was average size of establishment. This variable is significantly and inversely related to the incidence of all the components of locational change. The meaning of this result generally is that larger establishments move and die at lower rates than smaller ones and that moving establishments and new firms are not attracted to zones in which the establishments are above-average in size. The implications of these results for the incubator hypothesis are discussed in Chapter 8. To a limited extent, they do support the "flight from the central city" hypothesis, which envisions firms as moving out of centralized locations.[1] Only two variables were significantly related to variation in the incidence rate of out-movement of employment, namely, the average employment size of establishments in the zone and the CID dummy. The interpretation of the first of these is, as has been suggested, that the costs of the movement of an establishment are an increasing function of establishment size. To the extent that the returns to establishment movement are not an increasing function of establishment size or, rather, do not increase as rapidly with establishment size, a lower rate of movement will be observed of larger establishments and in zones with larger establishments, when other important characteristics of the zone that affect movement rates are controlled for. The central industrial district coefficient implies that the rate of gross out-movement of employment is 3.8 per cent higher in CIDs than in non-CID zones.

Appendix H
Concentration of Major Industries by Zone: Classification Based on Employment Compared with Classification Based on Establishments

Table H-1

Number of Establishments in Major Industries and Industry Concentration,[a] by Analysis Zone and Metropolitan Area, 1965

Analysis Zone [b]	Number of Establishments				
	Primary Metals	Fabricated Metals	Machinery	Electrical Machinery	Transportation Equipment
Cleveland					
1	34 [c]	128 [c]	140 [c]	35 [d]	17 [c]
2	46 [c]	125 [d]	113 [e]	49 [d]	15 [d]
3	34 [d]	85 [d]	80	12	7
4	23 [e]	98 [d]	126 [c]	12	12 [c]
5	14	69	114	30 [c]	13 [c]
6	2	15	22	13	1
7	8	20	36	8	10 [e]
8	1	14	24	5	2
9	——	3	8	0	1
10	15	30	46	17 [e]	5
11	3	29	36	18	5
12	1	4	15	5	0
13	10	38	80 [e]	12 [e]	5
14	19 [d]	35	60 [e]	5	5 [e]
15	11	40 [e]	62	15	8
16	6	32	83	10	2
17	2	5	11	0	3
18	——	3	3	3	——
Total	229	773	1,059	249	111

Analysis Zone [b]	Number of Establishments				
	Food Products	Publishing	Metals	Machinery	Electrical Machinery
Minneapolis-St. Paul					
1	8	5	17 [e]	19	4
2	14 [e]	7	34 [d]	45 [d]	13 [d]
3	34 [d]	121 [d]	26	51 [c]	11 [c]
4	16	51 [c]	23	34	9
5	18	18	16	30	10
6	27 [c]	29	40 [d]	56 [c]	7
7	——	10	5	11	3

Table H-1 (continued)

| Analysis Zone[b] | Number of Establishments | | | | |
	Food Products	Publishsng	Metals	Machinery	Electrical Machinery
8	13 [e]	58 [d]	13	14	5
9	1	8	3	8	3 [e]
10	11	13 [e]	9	11	5
11	6	3	9	10	0
12	24 [c]	29 [c]	37 [d]	38	11 [d]
13	2	6	13	21	1
14	8	10	24	14	6
15	3	1	4	3	2
16	——	6	4	5	2
17	8	15	18	45 [c]	16 [c]
18	2	5	12	20	6
19	3	11	18	17	7
20	3	13	22	26 [e]	5
21	4	6	14	13	1
22	4	5	7	14	3
23	3	6	5	7	2
24	11 [e]	6	2	5	——
25	9	10	11	26	7
Total	232	452	386	543	139

| Analysis Zone[b] | Number of Establishments | | | | | | |
	Food Products	Apparel	Publishing	Leather Products	Fabricated Metals	Machinery	Electrical Machinery
Boston							
1	43 [c]	45 [e]	94 [d]	1	22	16 [e]	11
2	15	34	84 [d]	7	29 [e]	26	8
3	24 [e]	13	7	2	14 [e]	7	5
4	19	237 [d]	56 [e]	61 [d]	21	11	7
5	18	9	11 [e]	5	27	10	9
6	14	16	88 [c]	11	6	10	4
7	44 [c]	58 [d]	63	9	62 [c]	52	33
8	38	26	48	155 [d]	53	90 [d]	41 [d]
9	14	5	27	9	4	19	20
10	64 [c]	32	56	15	94 [c]	62	27
11	39 [e]	15	50	10	41 [e]	54	48 [c]
12	9	3	14	6	35	44	35 [e]
13	22	28	56	2	66 [c]	116 [d]	84 [d]
14	2	——	10	——	3	7	13 [e]
15	10	9	13	5	11	12	18
16	5	2	25	1	7	29	14
17	8	3	22	2	29	34	7
18	18	5	14	5	28	37	20
19	——	1	5	3	4	6	1
20	5	17	22	69 [d]	12	17	9
Total	411	558	765	378	568	659	414

Table H-1 (continued)

Analysis Zone [b]	Number of Establishments				
	Food Products	Pub-lishing	Machinery	Electrical Machinery	Transpor-tation Equipment
Phoenix					
1	33 [d]	51 [d]	19	7	7
2	16 [e]	17 [e]	14	5	11 [c]
3	7	5	7	1	4
4	17 [e]	11	50 [d]	10 [d]	5
5	3	8	4	1 [e]	1
6	2	1	——	——	1
7	15	14	20	13 [c]	4
8	10	26	4	7	3
9	2	1	9 [e]	3	——
10	3	4	1	1	1
11	2	12	3	5 [e]	1
12	16	20	21	9 [e]	11 [d]
13	1	4	2	——	1
14	3	4	4	2	6 [e]
Total	130	178	158	64	56

[a] Criterion for concentration is that there is twice the amount of employment or number of establishments in the zone than would have been present if the total for the SMSA as a whole were uniformly distributed across the metropolitan area.
[b] The zones are listed and described in Appendix C.
[c] Concentrated in terms of number of establishments.
[d] Concentrated in terms of number of establishments; concentrated in terms of number of employees.
[e] Concentrated in terms of number of employees.

Notes

Chapter 1
Introduction

1. See J. F. Kain, "The Journey-to-Work as a Determinant of Residential Location," *Papers of the Regional Science Association* 9 (1962): 137-60; and especially *"The NBER Urban Simulation Model: Supporting Empirical Studies,* vol. II, ed. J. F. Kain, New York, National Bureau of Economic Research, 1971 (processed), chapters 1-4.

2. This point is clearly made in H. James Brown et al., *Empirical Models of Urban Land Use: Suggestions on Research Objectives and Organization,* New York, National Bureau of Economic Research, Exploratory Report 6, 1972. See also Franklin J. James, ed., *Models of Employment and Residence Location,* New Brunswick, New Jersey, Center for Urban Policy Research, 1974.

3. For examples of attempts to employ census data for analytical purposes, see Evelyn M. Kitagawa and Donald J. Bogue, *Suburbanization of Manufacturing Activity within Standard Metropolitan Areas,* Chicago, University of Chicago Population and Training Center, 1955; and Edwin S. Mills, *Studies in the Structure of the Urban Economy,* Baltimore, Resources for the Future, 1972.

4. For examples, see Edwin S. Mills, "An Aggregative Model of Resource Allocation in a Metropolitan Area," *American Economic Review,* May 1967, pp. 197-210; Mills, *Studies in the Structure of the Urban Economy;* Edwin S. Mills, "The Value of Urban Land," in Harvey S. Perloff, ed., *The Quality of the Urban Environment,* Baltimore, Johns Hopkins Press, 1969, pp. 231-53; and Richard F. Muth, "Economic Change and Rural-Urban Land Conversion," *Econometrica,* January 1961, pp. 1-23.

5. Leon Moses and Harold Williamson, "The Location of Economic Activity in Cities," *American Economic Review,* May 1967, pp. 211-22; Harold Williamson, "An Empirical Analysis of the Movements of Manufacturing Firms in the Chicago Metropolitan Area," Ph.D. dissertation, Yale University, 1969.

6. John Kain, "The Distribution and Movement of Jobs and Industry," in James Q. Wilson, ed., *The Metropolitan Enigma,* Washington, D.C., Chamber of Commerce of the United States, 1967. John R. Meyer, John F. Kain, and Martin Wohl, *The Urban Transportation Problem,* Cambridge, Massachusetts, Harvard University Press, 1965.

7. Edgar M. Hoover and Raymond Vernon, *Anatomy of a Metropolis,* Garden City, New York, Doubleday and Co., Inc., pp. 32-40.

8. Williamson, "Movements of Manufacturing Firms," is a partial exception.

9. This so-called "cross-section bias" is more fully discussed in John F. Kain, "The Distribution and Movement of Jobs and Industry," and H. James Brown et al., *Empirical Models of Urban Land Use.*

10. For a description of the shift-share technique, see Franklin J. James and James W. Hughes, "A Test of Shift and Share Analysis as a Predictive Device," *Journal of Regional Science,* August 1973, pp. 223-31.

11. One of the best of the surveys is Eva Mueller, Arnold Wilken, and Margaret Wood, *Location Decisions and Industrial Mobility in Michigan, 1961,* Ann Arbor, University of Michigan Institute of Social Research, 1961. For a planning application of an attitudinal survey, see Michael Goldberg, "An Industrial Location Model for the San Francisco Bay Area," *The Annals of Regional Science,* vol. I, no. 1, 1967, reprinted in James, *Models of Employment and Residence Location.*

12. Moses and Williamson, "The Location of Economic Activity in Cities."

13. See Roger Schmenner, "City Taxes and Industry Location," New York, National Bureau of Economic Research (processed); and Peter Kemper, "Determinants of the Location of New Manufacturing Firms," New York, National Bureau of Economic Research (processed).

14. Robert A. Leone, "The Location of Manufacturing Activity in the New York Metropolitan Area," Ph.D. dissertation, Yale University, 1971. This study is briefly summarized in Robert A. Leone, "The Role of Data Availability in Intrametropolitan Workplace Location Studies," *Annals of Economic and Social Measurement,* April 1972, pp. 171-82.

15. Gordon C. Cameron, "Intraurban Location and the New Plant," *Papers of the Regional Science Association,* 1973, pp. 125–43.

16. Ibid., p. 142.

17. Franklin J. James and James W. Hughes, "The Process of Employment Location Change: An Empirical Analysis," *Land Economics,* November 1973, pp. 404-13, reprinted in James, *Models of Employment and Residence Location.*

18. See Leone, "The Role of Data Availability in Intrametropolitan Workplace Location Studies."

19. This discrepancy is discussed in greater detail in Leone, "The Role of Data Availability in Intrametropolitan Workplace Location Studies."

Chapter 2
Cleveland

1. For a description of the relation between the national business cycle and the performance of the Cleveland economy, see "Economic Trends

and Fluctuations in a Heavy Industrial Area—The Case of Cleveland," *Economic Review,* Federal Reserve Bank of Cleveland, August 1969.

2. See Victor Fuchs, *Changes in the Location of Manufacturing in the United States Since 1929,* New Haven, Yale University Press, 1962, pp. 38-43, for a more detailed description and examples of how the measures have been used in another context. The measures used in the paper correspond, respectively, to Fuch's measures 2, 9, and 10.

Chapter 3
Minneapolis-St. Paul

1. For a detailed study of the relation between national cycles and their effects on various areas see Phillip Neff and Annette Wiefenbuch, *Business Cycles in Selected Industrial Areas,* Berkeley, University of California Press, 1949.

Chapter 4
Boston

1. For some general evidence of trends in the location of jobs and population in central cities vis-à-vis the rest of the SMSA, in which the experience of industrially more mature cities is compared with younger ones, see J. R. Meyer, J. F. Kain, and Martin Wohl, *The Urban Transportation Problem,* Cambridge, Massachusetts, Harvard University Press, 1965, chap. 3, especially tables 5 and 6.

2. Christine Bishop, "An Analysis of the Response of Population Change to Employment Change in an Urban Area," Ph.D. dissertation, Radcliffe College, March 1968, Figure VII, p. 60.

Chapter 5
Phoenix

1. For an amplification and demonstration of this point see Leo Schnore, "The Spatial Structure of Cities in the Two Americas," in Philip Hansen and Leo Schnore, eds., *The Study of Urbanization,* New York, John Wiley and Sons, 1965.

Chapter 7
Changes in the Location of Industry
in Centralized Locations

1. Raymond Vernon, *Metropolis 1985,* Cambridge, Massachusetts, Harvard University Press, 1960; Robert Leone, *Location of Manufactur-*

ing Activity in the New York Metropolitan Area, New York, National Bureau of Economic Research, forthcoming.

Chapter 8
The Incubator Hypothesis: A Test

1. Raymond Vernon and E. M. Hoover, *Anatomy of a Metropolis,* Cambridge, Massachusetts, Harvard University Press, 1959, chap. 2; and Raymond Vernon, *Metropolis 1985,* Cambridge, Massachusetts, Harvard University Press, 1960, chap. 5.

2. Leone, *Location of Manufacturing Activity in the New York Metropolitan Area,* New York, National Bureau of Economic Research, chap. 8.

3. *Manufacturing Employment by Type of Location: An Examination of Recent Trends,* New York, National Industrial Conference Board, 1969.

Chapter 9
Manufacturing Activity in Poverty Areas

1. For examples of this in the literature see J. R. Meyer, J. F. Kain, Martin Wohl, *The Urban Transportation Problem,* Cambridge, Massachusetts, Harvard University Press, 1966, pp. 144-67; O. A. Ornati, *Transportation Needs of the Poor: A Case Study of New York City,* New York, Praeger Publishers, 1969; Advisory Commission on Intergovernmental Relations, *Urban and Rural America: Policies for Future Growth,* April 1968; John F. Kain, "Housing Segregation, Negro Employment, and Metropolitan Decentralization," *Quarterly Journal of Economics,* May 1968, pp. 175-98; Joseph D. Mooney, "Housing Segregation, Negro Employment, and Metropolitan Decentralization; An Alternative Perspective," *Quarterly Journal of Economics,* May 1969, pp. 299-311; Wilfred Lewis, Jr., "Urban Growth and Suburbanization of Employment—Some New Data," Washington, D.C., Brookings Institution, 1969 (mimeo). Bennett Harrison argues forcefully against this argument in two monographs: (1) Bennett Harrison, *Education, Training, and the Urban Ghetto,* Baltimore, The Johns Hopkins University Press, 1972; and Bennett Harrison, *Urban Economic Development: Suburbanization, Minority Opportunity and the Condition of the Central City,* Washington, D.C., The Urban Institute, 1974.

2. See Edward D. Kalachek and John M. Goering, "Transportation and Central City Unemployment," Working Paper INS 5 (processed), Institute for Urban and Regional Studies, Washington University, 1970, for a

description of the St. Louis experience. Similar findings emerge from the Los-Angeles project reported in California Business and Transportation Agency, *Transportation—Employment Project,* Sacramento, 1970. Both projects were carried out for the U.S. Department of Housing and Urban Development.

3. For a critique of this type of program, see William K. Tabb, "Government Incentives to Private Industry to Locate in Urban Poverty Areas," *Land Economics,* November 1969.

4. For one such report, see Chris Kristensen et al., *The Suburban Lock-Out Effect: Suburban Action Research Report Number 1,* New York, Suburban Action Institute, 1971.

Chapter 10
Industrial Concentrations and Changes in the Location
of Industrial Employment

1. Alfred Weber, *Theory and Location of Industry,* trans. Carl J. Friedrich, Chicago, University of Chicago Press, 1956.

2. For a critique of some of these models, see discussion in Chapter 1 and H. James Brown et al., *Models of Urban Land Use: Suggestions on Research Objectives and Organization,* New York, National Bureau of Economic Research, Exploratory Report 6, 1972.

3. See Raymond J. Struyk, "A Progress Report on a Study of Intra-metropolitan Industrial Location," Inter-University Committee on Urban Economics Research Conference Papers (processed), Brown University, 1969.

Appendix G
Regression Analysis of Incidence of Marginal
Employment in Analysis Zones

1. This hypothesis was advanced and supported by Leon Moses and Harold Williamson in "The Location of Economic Activity in Cities," *American Economic Review,* May 1967, pp. 211-22.

Index

Alao, Nurudeen, 125n
Analysis zones: criteria for delineation, 30; definitions, 30–31, 49, 65–66, 85, 165–166

Bishop, Christine, xv–xvi, 70n, 72
Bogue, Donald J., 4n
Brown, H. James, 1n, 6n, 102n, 126n
Brown, H. Walter, 3n

Cameron, Gordon C., 10–11, 39n, 111n
Central cities: summary of findings for four SMSAs, 93; summary of regression results, 173–175
Central industrial district: defined, 14n; summary findings for four SMSAs, 93
Congestion, 94–95, 125; measured for regression analysis, 135
Creamer, Daniel, 3n, 109

Dun's Market Identifiers, 18–20; branch establishments, 23; business cycle, 23n; comparability with other data sources, 21–23; geographic coding, 30; small establishments, 21; verification of, 155–157

Economies of localization, 124
Economies of urbanization, 124
Employment change, process of: description, 2, 13–14, 39–42, 56–60, 73–77, 88–90; reasons for studying, 2–3,7–8; summary for four SMSAs, 96–100
Employment decentralization: descriptive studies, 3–4; rationalization, 4–5; summary of findings for four SMSAs, 93–94, 97–99
Employment growth, regional trends, 27–29, 47–49, 63–65, 82–84
External economies, 123–125
Externality, defined, 127

Fales, Raymond L., 7n
Fuchs, Victor, 42, 43

Ganz, Alexander, 108n
Goering, John M., 115n
Goldberg, Michael, 9n, 125n
Goldstein, G. S., 4n

Hamer, Andrew M., 5n
Harrison, Bennett, 3n, 115n, 126n

Hoover, Edgar M., 5, 8n, 109, 118, 124n
Hughes, James W., 6n, 11, 39n

Incubator hypothesis, 14, 109 passim, 177
Industrial concentration, 15–16; 49–52, 66–67, 83–85; definition of, 30–32; summary for four SMSAs, 100–101
Internal economies, 125
Isard, Walter, 123

James, Franklin J., 1n, 6n, 11, 39n, 102n

Kain, John F., 1n, 3n, 5, 6n, 63n, 95n, 115n
Kalachek, Edward D., 115n
Kemper, Peter, 9n, 126n
Kenyon, James B., 7n
Kitagawa, Evelyn M., 4n
Kristonson, Chris, 119n

Leone, Robert A., 10, 19n, 21n, 39n, 99, 107, 109, 125n
Lewis, Wilfred Jr., 115n
Lösch, August, 123

Major industries: Boston, 63–65; Cleveland, 27–29; Minneapolis-St. Paul, 47–49; Phoenix, 83–85
Metropolitan areas, study definitions: Boston, 63; Cleveland, 27; Minneapolis-St. Paul, 47; Phoenix, 81
Meyer, John R., 5n, 63n, 95n, 115n
Mills, Edwin S., 4n, 126n
Models: employment location, 4, 56; land-use transportation, 1–2; regression, 137, 144, 176; residential location—work place, 1
Mooney, Joseph D., 115n
Moses, Leon N., 4n, 5, 7n, 9
Mueller, Eva, 9n
Muth, Richard F., 4n

Neff, Phillip, 47n
Nuisance industries, and poverty areas, 118

Ornati, O. A., 115n

Payroll, average of manufacturing industries, 116–117, 119–121
Physical constraint argument, 123n

189

About the Authors

Raymond J. Struyk was an undergraduate at Quincy College and he received his doctorate in economics at Washington University in 1968. He has taught economics at Rutgers University and Rice University. More recently, he has been at The Urban Institute studying economic aspects of urban housing, focusing on the homeownership decision and a comparison of owner-occupants and landlords as suppliers of housing services. Dr. Struyk has also published several articles on metropolitan industrial location and water use by manufacturers.

Franklin J. James is a research associate of The Urban Institute. He has taught at Brown University and Rutgers University in the areas of computer simulation models and economic theories of urban land use. He is the co-author of a study of computer models of urban land use entitled *Empirical Models of Urban Land Use* and the editor of *Models of Employment and Residence Location*. He has written numerous monographs and articles in the areas of urban housing abandonment, regional growth, intrametropolitan industry location, and the fiscal impact of housing growth in suburban areas. He is currently investigating relationships of tax subsidies of homeownership and urban housing markets.

DATE DUE

GAYLORD			PRINTED IN U.S.A.